Contemporary State Building

If economic elites are notorious for circumventing tax obligations, how can institutionally weak governments get the wealthy to shoulder a greater tax burden? This book studies the factors behind the adoption of elite taxes for public-safety purposes. Contrary to prominent explanations in the literature on the fiscal strengthening of the state – including the role of resource dependence and inequality – the book advances a theory of elite taxation that focuses on public-safety crises as windows of opportunity and highlights the importance of business–government linkages to overcome mistrust toward government from corruption and lack of accountability. Based on the evidence from across Latin America and rich case studies from experiences in Colombia, Costa Rica, El Salvador, and Mexico, the book provides scholars and policymakers with a blueprint for contemporary state-building efforts in the developing world.

Gustavo A. Flores-Macías is Associate Vice Provost for International Affairs and Associate Professor of Government and Public Policy at Cornell University.

Contemporary State Building

Elite Taxation and Public Safety in Latin America

GUSTAVO A. FLORES-MACÍAS
Cornell University

CAMBRIDGE
UNIVERSITY PRESS

Shaftesbury Road, Cambridge CB2 8EA, United Kingdom

One Liberty Plaza, 20th Floor, New York, NY 10006, USA

477 Williamstown Road, Port Melbourne, VIC 3207, Australia

314–321, 3rd Floor, Plot 3, Splendor Forum, Jasola District Centre, New Delhi – 110025, India

103 Penang Road, #05–06/07, Visioncrest Commercial, Singapore 238467

Cambridge University Press is part of Cambridge University Press & Assessment, a department of the University of Cambridge.

We share the University's mission to contribute to society through the pursuit of education, learning and research at the highest international levels of excellence.

www.cambridge.org
Information on this title: www.cambridge.org/9781009095983

DOI: 10.1017/9781009091992

First published 2022
First paperback edition 2023

A catalogue record for this publication is available from the British Library

ISBN   978-1-316-51512-9   Hardback
ISBN   978-1-009-09598-3   Paperback

To Sarah, Luke, and Sebastián

Contents

Figures

Tables

Acknowledgments

This book grew out of a desire to understand how taxes on the wealthiest can come about, especially the lessons we can learn from both successful and failed experiences in Latin America. By exploring this issue in the context of Latin America's public-safety crisis, the book tackles simultaneously two important and complex problems facing the region: low levels of taxation and rising violent crime. The findings in the book are meant to contribute solutions to address the region's state weakness, from a contemporary state-building perspective.

In writing the book, I accrued multiple intellectual debts. I am grateful to many scholars who commented on parts or all of the manuscripts at different stages, including David De Micheli, Jakob Frizell, Sabrina Karim, Sarah Kreps, Marcus Kurtz, Vincent Mauro, Eduardo Moncada, Tom Pepinsky, Ken Roberts, Mariano Sánchez-Talanquer, Hillel Soifer, Jimena Valdez, Nic van de Walle, Jessica Zarkin, and two anonymous reviewers. I also owe many insights reflected in the book to scholars focusing on taxation, state capacity, and business politics, including Marcelo Bergman, Tasha Fairfield, Odd-Helge Fjeldstad, Frances Hagopian, Imke Harbers, Bob Kaufman, Jim Mahon, Mick Moore, Gabriel Ondetti, Wilson Prichard, Omar Sánchez, Ryan Saylor, Aaron Schneider, Ben Ross Schneider, Mónica Unda Gutiérrez, and Mathias von Hau. A book workshop that deeply shaped the final manuscript was organized by Cornell's Latin American Studies Program, which provided funds, and its program manager, Bill Phelan, who seamlessly handled the logistics. Much of this book was written during a Democracy and Development Fellowship to spend a sabbatical in residence at Princeton University, where I especially benefited from Deborah Yashar's intellectual generosity.

    The findings reflected in the book would not have materialized with-
out the help of scores of business leaders, government officials, legislators, and members of civil society in Latin America, who kindly agreed
to share their perspectives with me. I am grateful to John Bailey, Freddie
Barrero, Ludovico Feoli, Ollie Kaplan, Angelika Rettberg, Álvaro Salas
Castro, Michael Shifter, and Richard and Maritza Williamson for making many of these interviews possible and to the International Center for
Tax and Development for supporting part of the field research. Barby
Hernández Cantú and José Benjamín Montaño were also central to the
project through their research assistance, and the Cambridge University
Press team, led by Sara Doskow, was exceptional in their shepherding of
the project, especially under the difficult circumstances of the pandemic.
    My deepest gratitude goes to my family, who supported me in count-
less ways throughout the project.

I

Introduction

Contemporary State Building in Latin America

> The revenue of the state is the state. In effect, all depends upon it, whether for support or reformation.
>
> Edmund Burke[1]

In 2002, decades into the country's civil war, the Colombian government initiated elite-financed security taxes equivalent to an additional 1 percent of the country's gross domestic product (GDP) – a major achievement in a region notorious for stagnant tax-to-GDP ratios (Everest-Phillips 2010).[2] More surprising than the sharp increase in yearly tax revenue is that the government did so by extracting it from the wealthiest taxpayers and that these taxpayers supported the tax. Charles Tilly (2009, xiii) observed that taxation "constitutes the largest intervention of governments in their subjects' private life." Colombia's government not only generated this revenue but also did so from the politically best-connected echelon of society, a group that has historically been able to resist taxation (Atria 2015; Bogliaccini and Luna 2016; Centeno 1997, 2002; Fairfield 2015; Kurtz 2009, 2013; Saylor 2014; Schneider 2012; Soifer 2009, 2015).

Costa Rica, El Salvador, and Honduras also adopted similar taxes to finance additional public-safety efforts, while in Mexico such taxes were adopted at the subnational level in some states. Yet other countries have made progress only to see negotiations collapse, as in Guatemala, and in

---

[1] From *Reflections of the Revolution in France, and on the Proceedings in Certain Societies in London Relative to That Event in a Letter Intended to Be Sent to a Gentleman in Paris* (1790).

[2] As Everest-Phillips (2010, 76) has observed, "tax levels remain surprisingly static in countries over long periods of time, despite frequent tax policy reforms."

most other countries, there was no effort to extract additional resources from elites through targeted security taxes. What explains this variation? Why have efforts to extract additional fiscal resources to provide public safety been successful in some countries but not in others? What explains successful efforts to strengthen the state more generally? How have some countries compelled economic elites to pay taxes that finance increased security efforts, while others have remained incapable of engaging them in such efforts? Insofar as economic elites in Latin America contribute a large proportion of the state's economic resources – in part due to the region's high degree of inequality (UN Economic Commission for Latin America and the Caribbean 2010) – their involvement in the process of fiscal state building not only becomes essential but also puzzling and problematic.

Latin America has historically had low levels of state building relative to other regions. Why and how some countries have overcome those historical impediments is the subject of this book. The conventional wisdom points to crises involving, for example, the economy (Bird 1992; Mahon Jr. 2004a; Saylor and Wheeler 2017), security (Porter 1994; Thies 2005), and natural disasters (Fairfield 2015, 265) as drivers of state building, since they generate a sense of urgency among elites to accept higher tax burdens than they otherwise would. While this argument has intuitive appeal, most of the Latin American cases discussed earlier have experienced severe public-safety crises in the context of fiscal duress, yet elite engagement in state building has taken place in some places but not others – which suggests that more nuance is required in explaining the different outcomes.

To explain the adoption of elite taxes for public safety,[3] I argue that the main conventional crisis-centered explanations in the literature fall short in terms of explaining this outcome. Instead, I advance a theory of state strengthening through elite taxation based on the interaction of both demand and supply factors. The demand factors include not only crises as potential windows of opportunity for state building, but also the type of public good provided in exchange and the degree to which elites can find acceptable substitutes privately.

The supply factors are related to avenues through which elites can overcome mistrust toward governments' corruption and lack of

---

[3] By elite tax I mean a government-mandated compulsory contribution whose incidence falls disproportionately on the wealthiest sectors of society, including taxes on property, personal income, and corporate income.

accountability. These include the government's ideology and mechanisms of cooperation that derive from linkages between economic elites and governments. Contrary to research that points to left-of-center governments as conducive to greater fiscal extraction (Stein and Caro 2013), I argue that right-of-center governments generate a "Nixon goes to China" effect,[4] since they can more credibly commit to protecting elites' economic interests. Design features of elite taxes, including earmarking, sunset, and oversight provisions, can further contribute to assuaging elites' concerns.

In brief, whereas economic elites are generally reluctant to shoulder a greater tax burden, public-safety crises can soften this opposition – when affecting elites directly – and open the door to negotiations with the government. However, the deterioration of public-safety conditions is not enough to elicit elite taxation. Rather, the resulting tax arrangement will depend on the strength of business–government linkages. Robust linkages, which are typically present in right-of-center governments, contribute to overcoming mistrust between business elites and the government. These linkages – in the form of formal and informal collaboration mechanisms – facilitate agreements that in turn incorporate design features to tie governments' hands – including earmarks, sunset provisions, and civil society oversight. When linkages are weak, elite taxation is likely to fail, if attempted at all. Stronger linkages will make elite taxation more likely.

I support this theory by presenting empirical evidence from Latin America. Additionally, I evaluate competing explanations for their ability to account for variation in the extent to which elites have been engaged in the state-building process. These explanations include the availability of nonfiscal resources, such as natural resource rents and foreign aid (Morrison 2009; van de Walle 2001), and the degree of inequality in society (Agosín, Machado, and Schneider 2009). In the remainder of this chapter, I examine the historical difficulty in engaging elites in the state-building enterprise and contemporary crisis of violent crime affecting the region. Further, I discuss the importance of studying contemporary state building in Latin America and situate the book's scholarly contributions. Finally, I clarify the use of key concepts employed throughout and provide an outline of the organization of the book.

---

[4] In 1972, US President Richard Nixon traveled to the People's Republic of China as a first step in the thawing of Sino-American relations. Arguably, he was able to do so because of his credentials as a staunch anticommunist who could not be accused of being soft against Communism or China.

ECONOMIC ELITES AND STATE BUILDING
IN LATIN AMERICA

Economic elites have occupied a prominent place in the literature on state building, not only because of elites' concentration of resources but also because of their expectations regarding the prerogatives that must come in exchange of financing the coercive capacities of the state (e.g., Bensel 1991; Centeno 1997, 2002; Kurtz 2013; Lopez-Alves 2000; North 1981; Rasler and Thompson 1985; Slater 2010; Soifer 2015; Spruyt 1994; Tilly 1985, 1992). In particular, the literature points to existential crises as events that prompt elites to invest in state building in order to guarantee their own subsistence (Peacock and Wiseman 1961; Slater 2010). In the context of war, for example, medieval rulers often bargained with noble-dominated Estates over access to revenue to support the monarch's battlefield campaigns (Tilly 1992, 22). In fact, the extraction of resources from elites is so central in this literature that scholars have often defined the state in terms of its ability to tax. For Douglass North (1981, 21), for instance, the state is "an organization with a comparative advantage in violence, extending over a geographic area whose boundaries are determined by its power to tax constituents." Similarly, for Hendrick Spruyt, "the successful monopolization of violence itself will correlate with the ability of central governments [...] to raise revenue" (2007, 202). In the words of Joseph Schumpeter, "an enormous influence on the fate of nations emanates from the economic bleeding which the needs of the state necessitates" (Swedberg 1991, 100).

In the Latin American context, however, scholars have documented the difficulty in engaging elites in the state-building enterprise compared with their European counterparts – even during times of existential crises such as war. Studying the responses of elites in Chile and Peru in the context of the War of the Pacific (1879–1883), for example, scholars have highlighted elites' reluctance to support the strengthening of the state's coercive apparatus (Centeno 1997, 2002; Kurtz 2009, 2013; Soifer 2009, 2015). When Chile's armies were approaching Lima in 1880, the Peruvian government attempted to levy a tax among elites to pay the troops and maintain the war effort, but the initiative was defeated in the legislature (Ugarte 1926, 165). Further, when the Peruvian government tried to borrow ten million soles from the population, it only raised one million mostly from the popular sectors because economic elites did not want to risk their wealth (Bonilla 1978, 99). On the Chilean side, the government failed on several occasions to adopt a wealth tax or an income tax (Sater 1986, 131).

This experience was far from an anomaly in the region. During the first decades of independent life, the Mexican government sought to adopt a direct tax on elites to prepare for an imminent invasion from Spain in 1829. The opposition from elites was such that the government was overthrown by an elite-sponsored coup (Tanenbaum 1986, 34). This reluctance was prevalent again during the first French intervention in 1838 – also known as the Pastry War (Guerra de los Pasteles). Similarly, as American troops closed in on Mexico City in 1847 during the Mexican–American War, the Mexican government had a very difficult time negotiating loans from domestic sources because taxation was out of the question (Centeno 1997, 1593). In Bolivia, efforts by Antonio José de Sucre to adopt a direct tax on wealth contributed to an uprising that ended his government in 1828 (Lofstrom 1970). In Brazil, landowners consistently escaped the reach of the taxman, and discussions about adopting property or income taxes were consistently blocked by elites (Leff 1982). In fact, from the early years of independence, Latin American elites resented not only the financial burden that came with taxation but also being treated the same as other sectors of society – mainly Indians – for tax purposes (Lofstrom 1970, 282).

As Centeno (1997, 1594) has noted, "elites did not see the wars as threatening their social positions and thus did not have the incentive to permit greater political penetration. That is, the relevant elite did not appear to care which state ruled them as long as it was not markedly stronger than its predecessor." Rather, elites were more concerned about internal enemies. These enemies tended to be class or race based – and sometimes ideological as well – but keeping internal order did not require investing in the state apparatus.

Although major wars have been absent in the contemporary period in the region, elites' reluctance to invest in the state-building enterprise remains. In Guatemala, for instance, the government of President Julio César Méndez Montenegro (1966–1970) had to back down after adopting progressive tax reforms in 1966 that increased property taxes and closed loopholes because of the strong opposition of business sectors. Another attempt at increasing revenue through taxes on luxury goods ran the same fate the following year, in spite of the country's dire fiscal crisis (Best 1976, 63). This reluctance has not subsided even today. As Guatemala's former Minister of Finance Juan Alberto Fuentes Knight laments about recent efforts to tax elites,

It is well known that in practice, many Guatemalan companies keep three books: what they show to the SAT [the tax authority] that reflects extremely low profits or losses in order to pay low taxes; what they show to the banks to get loans, where they increase their profits to appear very successful; and the true accounts, that are secret (2012, 22).[5]

Although this discussion highlights the difficulty in engaging elites as partners in the state-building enterprise, economic elites are a sine qua non in the construction of the state. They are key actors in strengthening or undermining the core of political authority upon which regimes rest and depend (Centeno 2002, 2). As Benedicte Bull (2014, 119) points out, their "choices affect the centralization of power in the state, the ability to extract resources from society, and the establishment of a monopoly on legitimate violence."

To be sure, at times, elites have certainly played a favorable role in the construction of the state in Latin America not only in the early period of state formation but also in the contemporary period. For example, economic elites have played a fundamental role in post-conflict periods in Colombia, El Salvador, and Guatemala. Although one might disagree with their type of state-building project, in all three countries, "the domestic private sector was important in shaping both the political environment preceding the initiation of peace talks and the development of negotiations" (Rettberg 2007, 464). In Mexico, economic elites were central to the construction of the postrevolutionary state, both partnering with the government in the maintenance of the political regime and the creation of the so-called "stabilizing development" of the 1950s and 1960s (Ortiz Mena 1998; Tello 2010).

Further, there is evidence from other contexts that negative externalities in society can reach a point that compels elites to invest in state building. For example, de Swan (1988) points to the origins of the welfare state in Western Europe as an instance in which the potential threats of rising poverty prompted elites to fund the state's effort to expand social security institutions. In particular, the risk of internal revolt, the spread of disease, and the lack of labor due to migration were potential consequences that could affect elites' interests. More recently, Rueda and Stegmueller (2016) found that fear of crime results in more pro-distributive attitudes among European elites, including paying more in taxes. As Reis (2011, 95) observes in the Brazilian context, social awareness rather than good will might lead elites to perceive the problem as creating negative

---

[5] The recent revelations of elites' widespread use of offshore accounts meant to shelter wealth from the taxman, dubbed as Panama Papers and Paradise Papers, suggest that this behavior is more the rule than an exception. For respective overviews, see Harding (2016) and Forsythe (2017).

externalities, believe that something can be done about it, and feel that it is their responsibility to address it. Thus, although elites' investments in state building have been historically difficult, they have done so in key historical moments when their interests have been threatened.

PUBLIC SAFETY AND THE CONTEMPORARY THREAT TO ELITES

Contemporary public-safety threats can be more direct for elites' interests than the limited conflicts of the nineteenth century. Whereas which state elites belonged to – whether Chile, Bolivia, or Peru – might not have been a concern for their economic interests and personal well-being then, the severe deterioration of domestic public-safety environments over the first decades of the twenty-first century directly threatened elites' wealth and lives in some countries. Latin America is today the most violent region in the world. It also holds the unenviable distinction of being the only region where homicide rates have increased in the twenty-first century (UN Office on Drugs and Crime 2014). The region averaged over 300 homicides per day, 110,000 per year, and more than 1.5 million between 2000 and 2015 (Villalobos 2015).

This public-safety situation is grim in comparative perspective. Latin America's average rate of twenty-three homicides per 100,000 people is almost four times the global average of six, about twice the rate of Africa, and more than seven times the rate of Europe. According to the UN Office on Drugs and Crime (2014), about a third of the homicides in the world take place in Latin America, but only 9 percent of the world's population lives there. Honduras is the most dangerous country in the world outside of a war zone, with 104 homicides per 100,000 people. The second most dangerous is Venezuela (58), followed by Colombia (44), El Salvador (44), and Guatemala (40). Although there is considerable variation in the region, as Figure 1.1 shows, only the countries at the bottom of the list – Argentina (6), Chile (5), and Cuba (5) – experience rates of violent crime close to the world's average.

Not surprisingly, public safety has replaced economic problems as the main public concern across Latin America. As Figure 1.2 shows, Argentines, Colombians, Costa Ricans, Ecuadorans, Salvadorans, Guatemalans, Hondurans, Mexicans, Panamanians, Peruvians, Uruguayans, and Venezuelans identify public safety as the number one problem in their country. In the rest of the countries where surveys have been conducted, it is a close second (Latinobarómetro 2013).

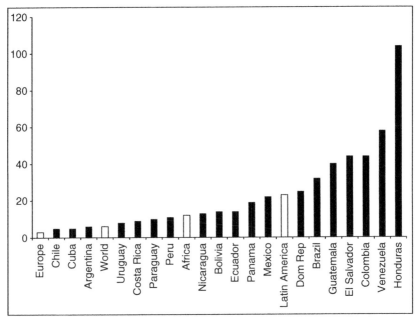

FIGURE 1.1 Homicide rates in Latin American countries and selected regions, ca. 2014.
Source: UNODC (2014).

The security threats generating such levels of concern across the region can be fairly concrete, such as the Armed Revolutionary Forces of Colombia (Fuerzas Armadas Revolucionarias de Colombia [FARC]) – a well-identified guerrilla group that would wear military uniforms and even control part of the Colombian national territory – or fairly abstract or diffuse, as is the case of the violent but loosely organized drug cartels operating as a multinational corporation under a franchising scheme, such as Mexico's Sinaloa Cartel. Either way, however, these threats translate into what Diane Davis (2010, 36) has referred to as "insecurity that permeates the most routine of daily activities, and is best seen in rising homicides, accelerating crime rates (despite a decline in reportage by victims), unprecedented levels of police corruption and impunity and an inability to move freely around with fear of armed robbery, violent attack, or extortion."

This type of violence is different from the historical patterns of civil conflict the region had experienced until the late twentieth century. Latin America had seen its fair share of internal conflict in the form of civil wars and insurgencies, such as Mexico's social revolution of 1910 and

FIGURE 1.2 Public safety as a public concern in Latin America.
Source: Latinobarómetro (2013).

the Cristero War that ensued in the late 1920s or Costa Rica's Civil War in 1948. During the Cold War, proxy wars between the United States and the Soviet Union were fought in El Salvador and Nicaragua, for example. In all of these cases, there was major mobilization among internal factions. In addition to civil conflicts, the region also witnessed a high degree of organized violence perpetrated by the state during the period of military dictatorships – mainly right wing but also left wing – in the 1960s, 1970s, and 1980s.

The region's contemporary landscape of violence has changed. In contrast to the politically motivated and often state-led violence that had prevailed in the twentieth century, patterns of violence have again become less political and more Weberian. Rather than leading violence against certain social sectors, governments find themselves unable to assert control over it.

This shift in the nature of violence poses a very different security dilemma for elites in the contemporary period. Whereas, historically, business elites tended to benefit from state-led violence in the region – by eliminating competing political and economic projects – the new form of violence affects them directly and more indiscriminately in democratic contexts.

For example, the poor public-safety environment can affect elites' wealth directly in several ways. These include the lost wealth when they become victims of theft or extortion, the foregone business because of depressed economic activity, and the increased costs associated with protection. The private security industry has boomed since the 1980s at an average annual growth rate of 10 percent, even in countries considered safe as in Chile (Ungar 2007, 20). There are almost 50 percent more private security personnel (3,811,302) than government police (2,616,753) for the region as a whole. In Brazil, Costa Rica, Honduras, Guatemala, and Panama, the ratios are greater than two private guards to one police officer (United Nations Development Program 2013, 150). The region's private security guards are the most armed in the world, estimated on the basis of rates of gun possession per employee (United Nations Development Program 2013).

According to an estimate by the Inter-American Development Bank, the region's GDP per capita would be 25 percent larger if the region had a crime rate comparable to the world's average (Prillaman 2003, 1). In some places, the costs associated with the loss of property brought about by crime are a considerable proportion of GDP, as in Honduras (8 percent) or Paraguay (6 percent) (United Nations Development Program 2013, 103).[6] At the firm level, companies spend on average about 6 percent of their budgets in security, similar to Colombia (Nelson 2000, 22). While violent crime tends to affect all sectors of society, evidence suggests that in some countries – such as Costa Rica and Honduras – the wealthiest sectors are most affected by this type of crime (United Nations Development Program 2013, 65).

---

[6] This figure does not take into account the dollar value corresponding to the loss of lives or the cost to the government associated with investigation, prosecution, and social rehabilitation.

Further, the region's transition to democracy constrained governments' ability to address violent challenges. Although repression still takes place, the protection of civil liberties and human rights more broadly has taken a more prominent place in the region. Authoritarian solutions in the form of states of emergency, torture, and extrajudicial executions are politically costly for democratically elected governments.

The implications for business elites are significant. No longer able to benefit from state-sanctioned violence, and with governments unable to guarantee the necessary security conditions, elites are confronted with state-building imperatives in the form of public-safety crises. At the same time, with wealth highly concentrated in a handful of elites in each country, they are governments' natural go-to place to find additional resources to face the crises.

This type of threat is consistent with Peacock and Wiseman's (1961, 27) notion that, due to their importance for the fate of the polity, national crises generate state-strengthening dynamics "that in quieter times would have been intolerable." If Slater (2010, 5) is correct that "violent internal contention can 'make the state' as surely as international warfare," then the contemporary public-safety threat can translate into state-building efforts given what is at stake for elites.

THE IMPORTANCE OF CONTEMPORARY STATE BUILDING IN LATIN AMERICA

Improving governments' provision of public safety has become a priority across the developing world since the third wave of democratization (Bergman and Whitehead 2009). However, the trend in terms of Latin American states' capacity to address this issue has run in the opposite direction since the 1980s. In particular, the period of dual transitions – to democracy and to a market economy – in Latin America led to the simultaneous retrenchment of the state in two ways.

The first one took place in the political arena, with the end of authoritarian regimes – most of them military in nature – and the transitions to democracy. Before the transitions, governments had been engaged in the persecution and control of different sectors of society and had developed domestic security apparatuses and intelligence agencies to do so. In Mexico's authoritarian regime, the Federal Security Directorate (Direccion Federal de Seguridad – DFS) – created for the purpose of "preserving the internal stability of Mexico against all forms of subversion and terrorist threats" – became an extensive and effective arm of the state for coercion and maintaining order. In countries with military dictators, these agencies engaged in more systematic repression, as with the Dirección de Inteligencia Nacional (DINA, Directorate of National Intelligence) in Chile, the Serviço Nacional de Informações (SNI, National Information Service) in Brazil, or the Secretaría de Inteligencia de Estado (SIDE, State Intelligence Agency) in Argentina, which spied on and persecuted groups suspected of subversion – often those that sympathized with leftist ideologies, community organizers, union leaders, and leftist politicians (Hunter 1997). In the political sphere, during this period, the state became synonymous with control over society and coercion – both of which require relatively strong state intervention and strength.

However, with the transitions to democracy came the withdrawal of the state from the political and social arenas. The coercive arms of the state were curtailed, and its budgets and personnel were reduced (Stepan 2015). Although to different degrees, and rarely to the extent that we see in advanced democracies, civil society gained considerable room to conduct activities without government intervention.

The second retrenchment took place in the economic sphere. During the 1950s, 1960s, and 1970s, Latin America enjoyed a gilded period of economic development – what has been dubbed in some countries as the period of stabilizing development – in which economic growth took place with relatively low inflation in the context of Import Substitution Industrialization (ISI), at least in the large economies where a domestic market was feasible as an engine of growth such as Argentina, Brazil, and Mexico. However, the ISI model ran into difficulties and out of steam during the late 1960s and 1970s (Hirschman 1968). Whereas governments had made important strides toward industrialization, the closed nature of the economy and the absence of competition resulted in goods and services of poor quality and high prices. Inflation and large government bureaucracies became important problems, and government intervention came to be associated with inefficiencies (Murillo 2001). Therefore, one of the main objectives of the structural reforms adopted by governments across the region during the 1980s and 1990s was to take the government out of the economy and bring in the market (Williamson 1990). To achieve this, governments privatized state-owned industries, laid off government employees, and eliminated subsidies and price controls, following the mantra that only the market would cure what the government had corrupted (Corrales 2002).

Although structural reforms did bring many benefits, including reining in inflation, reducing government inefficiencies, and improving the quality and prices of goods and services available to consumers (Baker 2009), they also brought important costs. Almost overnight, for example, it brought an increase in inequality as formally employed workers were pushed into the informal sector, relative prices increased substantially, and social security systems were decimated (Huber and Zolt 2004; Roberts 2012; UN Economic Commission for Latin America and the Caribbean 2010, 53). An important long-term consequence of these reforms was that the state became much less able to provide a social safety net for its citizens, from education and health care to pensions.

State retrenchment in both arenas has contributed to the deterioration of public order in Latin America. The vacuum left behind in terms of a safety net generated inequality and the weakening of a floor that guaranteed a minimum level of education, health, and general well-being. The legacy of the reforms included the "deregulation and contractual flexibilization, which fostered informal employment and unemployment, [...] privatized and commoditized social security, [...] and the underfunding of education and health services," all of which exacerbated inequality in the region (UN Economic Commission for Latin America and the Caribbean 2010, 190). Although there was a slight dent in the region's inequality in the 2000s (Huber and Stephens 2012; Lopez-Calva and Lustig 2010), Latin America remains the most unequal in the world. This inequality has contributed to the visibility of social disparities, whose salience can become fodder for alienated sectors of society that might seek redress through extralegal means.[7]

However, the minimalist mantra that has prevailed since the 1980s for the role of the state in economic matters has affected governments' ability to respond to the public-safety challenge. A common denominator across the region is governments' struggle to fund law enforcement agencies, prosecutors' offices, and courts systems (Bailey and Dammert 2005), without compromising prevailing levels of spending in other areas.[8] In particular, police forces tend to be underpaid and poorly equipped compared

---

[7] Research by Soares (2004) has found that there is a strong association between inequality and violent crime. Soares points to a 1 percent increase in the Gini coefficient resulting in a 1.5 percent increase in homicides. Other studies by the World Bank support the relationship between the two variables (Fajnzylber, Lederman, and Loayza, 1998, 2002). For a critique arguing the relationship is spurious, see Neumayer (2005).

[8] Existing social safety nets were generally dismantled during the period of structural reforms in the 1980s and 1990s (Pribble, Huber, and Stevens 2009, 390). This has contributed to the steady rise of crime rates – particularly violent crime – in many countries, which has undermined the quality of democracy in these places.

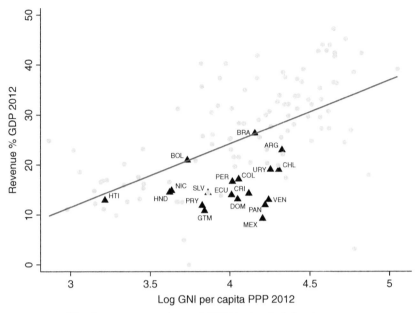

FIGURE 1.3 Fiscal revenue as a share of GDP by level of development.
Source: UN Economic Commission for Latin America and the Caribbean (2015) and Organization for Economic Cooperation and Development (2015).

to organized crime. Most policy discussions point to the need to improve police and justice systems, but governments' ability to increase extraction is largely taken for granted. This is an important oversight, given the difficulty in extracting resources from society (Migdal 1988). The elements of struggle arise because taxation represents "a permanent transfer of purchasing power by the taxpayer to the government," (Gilbert 1970, 4) a decrease in the value of their wealth as a result of taxation.

At the same time that Latin American countries are facing this public-safety challenge and citizens' demands to address it, governments have struggled to find the resources necessary to fund their security efforts. Indeed, the region has had difficulty in extracting adequate levels of fiscal resources from society, with most countries collecting in taxes between 9 and 26 percent of GDP.[9] As Figure 1.3 shows, with a handful of exceptions, Latin American countries' levels of fiscal extraction are well below the expectation for countries with comparable levels of development across the world. These low levels of taxation impair governments' ability to

---

[9] Excluding social security taxes.

invest in alleviating poverty, improving security forces, and administering justice, all of which are crucial for the provision of public safety.

CONTRIBUTIONS TO THE STUDY OF TAXATION, PUBLIC SAFETY, AND STATE BUILDING

This book combines the study of three main topics, namely taxation, public safety, and state building. It advances our understanding of different state-building arrangements between government and society, the role that economic elites play in them, and the factors that make such arrangements possible. Compared to previous studies, this book makes contributions in each of the following areas.

State Building

First, this book makes a contribution to our understanding of the state in Latin America. Much of the research on the state in the region focuses on the early period of state formation after independence from the Spanish and Portuguese crowns (e.g., Centeno 1997, 2002; Centeno and Ferraro 2014; Kurtz 2009, 2013; Lopez-Alves 2000; Saylor 2014; Soifer 2009, 2015). However, there is comparatively little research in political science on the strengthening of the state in more recent times. Instead, work on the contemporary period has focused on bureaucratic capacity (e.g., Bersch, Praça, and Taylor 2017; Bresser Pereira and Spink 1999; Geddes 1996; Grindle 2000; Schneider 1991) or methodological considerations regarding the conceptualization and measurement of state capacity (e.g., Altman and Luna 2012; Giraudi 2012; Kurtz and Schrank 2012; Luna and Toro Maureira 2014; Soifer 2012).

In contrast, this book builds on the insights from the literature on internal conflict and state building to evaluate the consequences of the prevailing situation of violence in the region. In doing so, it engages existing debates as to whether internal conflict results in state building or state-weakening dynamics, but is among the first to apply it to violent crime. Whereas some authors have made the case that there are state-building consequences of civil conflict (Holden 2004; O'Kane 2000; Rodríguez-Franco 2016; Slater 2010), the prevailing view is that it "destroys, by definition, state capacity" (Cárdenas 2010, 2; see also Barnett 1992; Centeno 2002, 141; Lopez-Alves 2001, 162; Migdal 1988, 274).

Contrary to this dominant perspective, I argue that contemporary public-safety challenges have exposed elites to threats that elicit similar state-building opportunities as scholars have identified for other types of conflicts. However, I also show that high-stake public-safety crises are not a sufficient condition for state building to take place. Rather, the crises have to affect elites and the right combination of factors on the supply side must be present to overcome mistrust between economic elites and the government.

Taxation

With notable exceptions, studies on taxation in Latin America have tended to ignore the political underpinnings of taxation. This is a significant oversight because political conflicts are at the heart of the obstacles to reforming tax systems. As Wagner Faegri and Wise (2011, 246) have noted, "Despite the central role of taxation in economic development and growth, political economists have yet to develop a program of research that fully captures the politics of tax reform in emerging-market economies. Although legislative coalitions for economic reform have emerged in even the most contentious political environments, tax reform remains one of the more contested and understudied issues in Latin America."

This book aims to contribute to addressing this oversight, by helping to understand the determinants of fiscal reforms in general and elite taxation in particular. It helps to understand the relative merits of different factors deemed central by the literature, including the role of crises (Bird 1992; Mahon Jr. 2004a), elites (Castañeda 2017; Fairfield 2015; Lieberman 2003; Schneider 2012; Weyland 1997), and the nature of the relationship between interest groups and the state (Schneider 2004, 2012).

Until recently, little attention had been paid to elite taxation as a matter of political economy.[10] Instead, the assumption has been that elites already paid taxes in systems with highly narrow tax bases. Whenever specific groups have been studied to find ways to extract additional revenue, it has tended to be the informal sector and micro and small enterprises. For example, a volume by Alm, Martinez-Vazquez, and Wallace (2004) focuses on assessing the magnitudes and implications of not taxing the informal sector – what they aptly call "the Hard to Tax." Similarly, research by Joshi, Prichard, and Heady (2014) on hard to tax sectors focuses on strategies to extract fiscal revenue from the informal economy. Only recently has elite taxation gained interest (e.g., Fairfield 2010,

---

[10] Although not strictly on taxation, Elisa Reis' (2011) work on elites' attitudes toward inequality constitutes an exception. Other recent work includes Amsden, DiCaprio, and Robinson (2015).

2013, 2015; Flores-Macías 2014; Lieberman 2003; Mahon Jr. et al. 2015; Scheve and Stasavage 2016; Schneider 2012), along with the increasing recognition that the wealthiest sectors in society do not necessarily pay the highest effective tax rates in many developing countries (e.g., Fairfield and Jorratt 2015).

In this context, this book contributes to theorizing the conditions under which governments can extract additional revenue from society to provide public goods, and elites might be willing to contribute funds for this purpose. By shedding light on both the conditions under which elites are willing to pay taxes toward public safety and the type of taxes they might support, this research seeks to provide much-needed tools with which to strengthen the state. The findings should inform taxation efforts across the developing world, where low levels of fiscal extraction, deteriorating security conditions, and mounting public-safety expenditures are common.

Public Safety

The third contribution of this book is that it reconsiders the relationship between the demand for public goods and the willingness to pay for them in the context of public safety. Thus far, most of the literature has focused on the general aspects of a theoretical fiscal contract between governments and citizens. As Margaret Levi (1988) and others (e.g., Castañeda 2017; Castañeda, Doyle, and Schwartz 2020; Mahon Jr. 2019; Moore 2004; Timmons 2005) have argued, there is an expectation that comes with handing over part of one's wealth to the government, or what Fjeldstad and Semboja (2001) have dubbed the "terms of trade" in this relationship. In other words, there is a theoretical expectation that the level of satisfaction with the provision of public goods will contribute to determining people's support for increased taxation. Individuals feeling shortchanged in the exchange will likely be less supportive of increases in the tax burden.

However, the empirical work in this regard has ignored public safety in spite of its importance in the public good hierarchy. Instead, much of the research has been conducted with respect to compliance as a function of general views toward the government (e.g., Cummings et al. 2009; Fjeldstad and Semboja 2001) or has focused on willingness to pay for public goods such as parks and recreation (e.g., Glaser and Hildreth 1996).

This research is among the first to study the relationship between public safety and fiscal extraction. On the one hand, it seeks to understand how perceptions of public safety affect elites' willingness to pay more in taxes.

It shows that, for the purposes of engaging elites in the state-building enterprise, perceptions of poor public-safety provision are different from those of deficits in other public goods such as education or healthcare. On the other hand, it analyzes the difference that extractive efforts have made in the public-safety realm. It suggests that elite taxes for public-safety purposes can make a difference in generating virtuous state-building cycles in which both fiscal extraction and public safety are strengthened.

CONCEPTUAL CLARIFICATION

Several concepts employed throughout the book require clarity in their definition, because they might have multiple connotations or might even be normatively charged.

The first one is economic elites, defined as those individuals who, due to their control over economic resources and means, "stand in a privileged position to formally or informally influence decisions and practices that have broad societal impact" (Bull 2014, 120). Or following James Robinson (2010, 3), I consider economic elites as a "distinct group within a society which enjoys privileged status and exercises decisive control over the organization of that society" because of their financial resources. In societies where wealth is concentrated in the hands of a few, economic elites are a natural sector for governments to turn to in order to gain additional resources. Unfortunately for governments, economic elites are also the sector best positioned to resist taxation (Castañeda 2017; Fairfield 2015).

The second is elite taxes, by which I mean government-mandated, compulsory contributions, including financial charges based on the value of the property, personal income, and corporate income, whose incidence falls disproportionately on the wealthiest sectors of society. While there can be other ways through which governments force economic elites to transfer wealth to public coffers, including the forced expropriation of assets, this book does not consider such extreme forms of extraction. Rather, it focuses on the formal and informal negotiations between governments and elites that can inform potential tax reforms in the future.

The third is state building. I borrow from Hillel Sofier and Matthias vom Hau (2008) in defining state building as improving the state's ability to exercise control over the territory and regulate social relations.[11] In the words of Centeno et al. (2017, 3) it is the ability to implement

---

[11] This definition is based on Mann's (1984) conceptualization of infrastructural power. See Soifer and Vom Hau (2008) for a distinction from state autonomy.

governing projects. While scholars diverge on the relevant dimensions of state capacity, two are recurrent in most prominent definitions (e.g., Mann 1984; Skocpol 1985; Soifer 2012; Tilly 1985). The first is *public safety*, or the extent to which order is maintained across the country, which follows Weber's logic of the monopoly of legitimate violence in a given territory and responds to the fact that, regardless of ideological preconceptions about the role of the state, the provision of security remains one of its fundamental functions (Weber 1965). The second dimension, *fiscal extraction*, is often considered an approximation of administrative capacity writ large because of the centrality of extraction for the state to perform the rest of its functions (North 1981, 21; Spruyt 2007, 202).

Regardless of ideological disagreements as to what constitutes the core functions of the state – that is, whether the state should be involved in providing such services as health care and education, and to what extent – there is a consensus regarding the centrality of public safety and fiscal extraction as among the main functions of the state. The focus of the book – elite taxation toward public safety – embodies these two fundamental dimensions of the state like few other issues. They combine a state's first and foremost responsibility toward its citizens – guaranteeing their personal safety – with the sine qua non to fulfil it – the extraction of fiscal resources.

Although much of the research on state capacity focuses on the period of early state formation, this definition understands state building *not* as a feature that ended with the genesis of nation-states, but as a process that continues into the contemporary period and can take place at key moments related to the establishment of the legitimate monopoly of violence and the extraction of resources to fund it (Mazzuca 2021).[12] This implies that state capacity is likely to vary, not only across states but also over time (Kurtz and Schrank 2012, 617). Although many of the forces shaping state capacity can be slow moving (Kurtz 2013, 11; Soifer 2009), historical examples suggest that changes in state capacity may also occur in a relatively short period of time, particularly in the developing world. Cases in point are the rapid deterioration of state capacity in Cuba after foreign resources dried up with the Soviet collapse (Eckstein 2004, 316), and the quick setback for Haiti's state capacity as a result of the 2011 earthquake (Messner and Knight 2011).

---

[12] As noted by Aaron Schneider (2012, 31), state building is something that can occur at different points in time.

In particular, although the literature emphasizes major crises such as war and other critical junctures (Collier and Collier 1991; Kurtz 2013; Lipset and Rokkan 1967) as key moments shaping states, they are also shaped by everyday practices. Therefore, "in order to understand why and how weak or strong institutions evolve, we must also consider how key actors relate to weak institutional contexts and how the practices they apply contribute to further weakening or strengthening" (Bull 2014, 119).

RESEARCH DESIGN AND PLAN OF THE BOOK

The main objective of the study is to contribute to our understanding of the political factors behind the adoption of elite taxes for public safety in some countries but not others. For this purpose, in the following pages, I make the case for the importance of understanding both demand and supply factors that make possible the fiscal and security strengthening of the state. I do so through small-n qualitative research.

Throughout the book, I rely on a number of primary and secondary sources to support my findings, including interviews with relevant actors such as leaders of business organizations, prominent businesspeople, government officials, legislators, party leaders, and journalists. In doing so, I incorporate views from a variety of perspectives to triangulate and corroborate accounts as much as possible. Additionally, the book draws on government reports, congressional transcripts, business organizations' documents and minutes, political party platforms, local newspaper articles, and other scholars' work.

Chapter 2 introduces the dependent variable by documenting variation in the adoption of security taxes in Latin America. It describes in detail the cases where security taxes on elites have been adopted, including in Colombia, Costa Rica, Honduras, and Mexico,[13] as well as cases where these taxes were first defeated in the legislature but subsequently approved, as in El Salvador, discussed but abandoned, as in Guatemala, or not discussed, as in the rest of the region. These countries span the potential values across the dependent variable, namely the adoption of wealth taxes on elites, adoption of a lighter tax burden on elites through more general taxes, or no adoption of elite taxes. These cases also show variation longitudinally, with Colombia, Costa Rica, and Honduras approving the taxes on more than one occasion, and El Salvador adopting the security taxes only the second time they were debated in Congress.

---

[13] In Mexico, only subnational taxes for public safety have been adopted at the state level.

In discussing the different experiences, Chapter 2 documents the types of security taxes adopted, their purpose, and impact on public-safety expenses and the government's fiscal income more generally. By identifying the different types of security taxes and their destination, this chapter contributes to our understanding of the extent to which economic elites have participated in the strengthening of the state in the contemporary period.

Chapter 3 introduces the causal logic behind a theory of elite taxation. It explains how the conventional crisis-oriented approach in the literature cannot explain variation in efforts to involve elites in the state-building enterprise. Instead, it argues that both demand and supply factors must be taken into account, and disaggregates the components of each, including whether elites can satisfy their demand for public goods in the private market, the ideology of the government, and the extent to which linkages between business elites and the government exist.

Drawing on the main explanations put forth to account for the elite's efforts to strengthen the state, Chapter 3 also evaluates alternative explanations, including the availability of nonfiscal resources such as oil rents and foreign aid (Morrison 2009; van de Walle 2001), and the degree of inequality in society (Agosín, Machado, and Schneider 2009). These explanations are less parsimonious and show a weaker ability to account for differences in state strengthening among elites across cases. The evaluation takes place in three steps. First, I introduce the relevant theoretical considerations for each explanatory factor and formulate corresponding hypotheses. Second, I operationalize each factor with empirical evidence from the region. Finally, I compare the extent to which these explanatory factors covary with the dependent variable.

The causal logic of elite taxation in the adoption of security taxes is further explored through case studies in the following four chapters. Chapter 4 studies the case of Colombia's recurrent security taxes. Beginning in 2002, the government in that country adopted a series of security taxes on the wealthy to address a deplorable public-safety situation. With a historically difficult conflict and traditional set of elites, Colombia is the least likely case in which elites would have become invested in financing the strengthening of the state. Moreover, with the approval of security taxes on the elites on multiple occasions across administrations, the Colombian case allows us to study the conditions under which this investment becomes sustained over time.

Chapter 5 studies the case of Costa Rica, an example of a diminished form of elite taxation due to weak linkages between the government and business elites. Whereas average levels of violence have remained lower in Costa Rica compared to several of its Central American neighbors, economic elites concentrated in the province and canton of San José experienced sharp increases in violent crime. In 2011, the country adopted a flat tax on corporations and earmarked its revenue for public-safety purposes. However, Costa Rica's left-of-center administrations struggled to overcome obstacles related to elites' mistrust in government, which led to a much less targeted form of taxation.

Chapter 6 focuses on the case of El Salvador, which illustrates how temporal variation in the strength of government-elite linkages played a role in explaining the difference between a failed attempt in Mauricio Funes' administration and a successful one in Salvador Sánchez Cerén's administration. Even in the context of one of the highest levels of violent crime in the region, the country's first left-of-center administration failed to adopt elite taxes in order to increase public-safety expenditures. It wasn't until the government formed a coalition with right-of-center parties and linkages with the business sectors improved, that an increased tax burden on the wealthy became possible.

Chapter 7 studies the case of Mexico. This country's security situation has deteriorated dramatically over the last decade; yet, whereas a crisis-driven explanation would predict elites' investment in strengthening the state, the federal government has not adopted – or even entertained – security taxes. Instead, this chapter shows how Mexican elites have been relatively less affected than their counterparts elsewhere in the region. This has translated into much less pressure on the government to address the public-safety situation. Consequently, elites' impetus to invest in the fiscal strengthening of the state has been subdued at the national level and has taken place instead at the state level.

I conclude the book with Chapter 8 by addressing the broader implications of the study's findings. First, I discuss the theoretical implications for the study of state building, public safety, and taxation. Next, I evaluate the security benefits that elites' investment in strengthening the state has brought about in the region. In the final section, I address the sustainability of these efforts and their potential consequences for other aspects of political and economic development.

2

Latin America's Elite Security Taxes[*]

The security tax will target the upper middle and upper classes, since they
are the ones with the capacity to pay it, and it would be unfair to levy a tax
on the general public, since not everyone is in a condition to pay.[1]

Mauricio López Bonilla, Guatemala's Minister of the Interior, upon
announcing a new elite tax initiative.

The government proposal is not only inadequate but unfeasible.

Jorge Briz, vice president of Guatemala's powerful business group CACIF,
responding to the government's announcement of a security tax.[2]

The literature on state building in Latin America tends to character-
ize elites more as a hindrance for, rather than being conducive to, state
building. For example, Benedicte Bull (2014, 117) suggests that elites are
one of the main reasons behind the region's developmental problems.
Similarly, other studies (Casaús Arzú and García Giráldez 1996; Paige
1997) blame the conservative oligarchy for preserving the status quo. In
the view of Sánchez-Ancochea and Martí i Puig (2014, 4), "the region's

---

[*] The discussion of Colombia's elite taxes in this chapter draws on Flores-Macías, Gustavo,
"Financing Security through Elite Taxation: The Case of Colombia's Democratic Security
Taxes," *Studies in Comparative International Development* 49, 4 (December): 477–500.

[1] "El impuesto estará dirigido a la clase media alta y alta, pues ellos tienen la capacidad
de pagarlo y sería injusto cobrar un impuesto a la población en general, pues no todos
están en condiciones de erogarlo." Mauricio Lopez Bonilla, Minister of the Interior (*El
Periódico de Guatemala* 2015).

[2] Jorge Briz, vicepresidente del Comité Coordinador de Asociaciones Agrícolas, Comerciales, Industriales y Financieras (CACIF), calificó como "inadecuada e improcedente"
la propuesta, y aseguró que es necesario que el actual gobierno tenga un gasto eficiente
y transparente, que acompañe con un eficaz combate a la corrupción (*El Periódico de
Guatemala* 2015).

problems ultimately have much to do with the perpetuation of an elite-dominated socio-political system that still concentrates wealth and political influence in a small number of people."

It is no coincidence that Latin American countries have historically relied for revenue on nontax mechanisms – including debt and inflation – or indirect taxes – such as taxes on trade and the value-added tax (VAT) – both of which protect elites from direct taxation. As Centeno (1997, 1585) has noted, throughout the nineteenth century, governments avoided taxing elites by resorting to debt, inflation, and taxes on trade, none of which generated the state-building effects associated with direct taxation. Rather than taxing elites' wealth or income directly, governments would borrow heavily – often internationally – or print money in order to maintain spending levels or pay for additional commitments (Flores-Macías and Kreps 2013). When governments had to tax, they largely relied on customs taxes, which could be easily collected at customs facilities concentrated in a number of ports.

With the trade liberalization of the 1980s and 1990s and the significant decline in the importance of taxes on trade, today half of Latin America's tax revenue comes from general and specific consumption taxes, compared to a more modest 31 percent in the Organisation for Economic Cooperation and Development (OECD) countries. Conversely, taxes on income and profits correspond to 27 percent in Latin America, compared to 34 percent in the OECD (Organization for Economic Cooperation and Development 2015, 26).

This reliance on consumption taxes has become prevalent in the region because the VAT is easier to collect than other types and tends to have a broad base, since all sectors of the population pay it when purchasing goods and services regardless of income level or wealth. For these reasons, and in spite of their regressive nature, indirect taxes have been proposed as a solution to the region's low levels of tax collection. International organizations such as the International Monetary Fund and the Inter-American Development Bank became champions of this course of action to address the problem of low fiscal revenue, while recommending that the money be channeled back to the poorest sectors in the form of government spending (e.g., Stotsky and WoldeMariam 2002, 38).[3]

Not surprisingly, indirect taxes have traditionally been appealing to economic elites. Because of the very high concentration of wealth across the region, economic elites are governments' usual "go to" sector

---

[3] Not surprisingly, very few survey respondents consider taxes and effective tools for redistribution. In Mexico, for example, only 16 percent do (Casar 2013).

in society to extract additional fiscal revenue. In several Latin American countries, more than 90 percent of the population does not pay income taxes (DIAN 2014; Lamuno 2014), which is only somewhat better than the 1 percent of the population that paid income taxes in the 1960s and 1970s in some countries (Best 1976). For this reason, economic elites often denounce the narrow tax base in Latin America and complain that they bear a disproportionate fiscal burden.

Moreover, economic elites tend to resent targeted efforts to get them to pay taxes. The main reasons articulated by elites include mistrust in the government's ability to spend tax revenue on the intended purpose rather than embezzling it or wasting it. This sentiment is shared by broad sectors of the population, not just the wealthy but also elites often express this as one of the main reasons why they oppose tax increases. The logic is that governments have to show results with existing resources first, in order for elites to be willing to bear a great fiscal burden (Flores-Macías 2014). As Haggard, Maxfield, and Schneider (1997, 41) have pointed out about business–government relations, credibility in delivering results is a fundamental factor for successful collaboration.

To be sure, economic elites are the sector in society with the greatest ability to resist governments' efforts to extract fiscal resources both because of their ability to take their resources elsewhere and their political influence (Haggard, Maxfield, and Schneider 1997; Fairfield 2015; Mahon Jr. 2004a, 22; Schneider 2012). In the words of Albert Hirschman (1981, 257),

exit of capital often takes place in countries intending to introduce some taxation that would curb excessive privileges of the rich or some social reforms designed to distribute the fruits of economic growth more equitably. Under these conditions, capital flight and its threat are meant to parry, fight off, and perhaps veto such reforms' whatever the outcome, they are sure to make reforms more costly and difficult.

As Tasha Fairfield (2015, 2019) has shown, business elites can exercise instrumental and structural power to advance their interests. Instrumental power refers to the political relations between the owners of capital and policymakers on which the former rely to advance their economic interests, including through conservative parties and through technocratic positions in the government bureaucracy. Structural power rests on business elites' ability to shape policymakers' anticipations of market behavior detrimental to the government's development goals. Due to this influence, the holders of capital in Latin America have been characterized as "virtual senates – places where a narrow, internationally-oriented elite of households and firms is represented and wields a veto over economic policy" (Mahon Jr. 2004b, 23).

Given this difficulty in extracting fiscal resources from economic elites, the adoption of elite taxation in contemporary Latin America is especially puzzling. We would expect attempts to fund security efforts on elites to be unsuccessful, and for taxes that affect broad sectors of the population – such as generalized consumption taxes – to be the way forward since, after all, poor public-safety provision affects all sectors of society.

Yet, there have been several instances in which taxes on elites become a successful course of action to fund and improve public-safety efforts. Such taxes have been an expedient way to raise revenue in Colombia in 2002, 2003, 2006, and 2009; in Costa Rica 2011 and 2016; and in Honduras in 2011 and 2014. In El Salvador, the legislature first debated and defeated security taxes in 2011 and then approved a revised version in 2015. In Mexico, a national elite tax was not adopted, but state-level taxes aimed at elites have been implemented. In other countries with high levels of violent crime or sudden deterioration of public safety, such as Guatemala, these taxes have not been adopted, even in the context of fiscal crises. Why were some fiscal arrangements approved in some countries but not in others? What has been the incidence in terms of the tax burden? How meaningful have these arrangements been for governments' coffers and public-safety expenditures contributing to state capacity?

In answering these questions, this chapter seeks to take stock of the extent to which elites have been engaged in the fiscal strengthening of the state across the region. With this objective in mind, the following pages discuss country-specific details of what will constitute the dependent variable of this study.

Security taxes – tax revenue earmarked for public-safety purposes – are important for state building because they are directly related to two central aspects of state strength, namely the capacity to extract fiscal resources from society and the capacity to protect citizens' personal well-being and wealth. Since the interstate war has become rare in contemporary Latin America, protection against crime in general and violent crime in particular has become governments' main focus to exercise their monopoly over the use of force. Security taxes provide the resources required for the government to perform this central task: Governments leverage the public-safety deficit to increase the tax burden in order to increase the level of expenditures in public safety. Revenue from security taxes goes to fund the entire law enforcement apparatus, including police departments, intelligence agencies, correctional facilities, and prosecutors' offices. They can be spent on capital investments, such as vehicles and telecommunications equipment, or they can be spent on personnel and salaries.

In principle, all tax revenue can be destined toward public safety, but security taxes make the nexus between taxes and security explicit. Any tax increase adopted by the government can fund increased levels of public safety, but by earmarking a specific tax, those bearing the tax burden are explicitly confronted with the state-building imperative.

In the following paragraphs, I present an overview of the security taxes adopted in several countries in the region, both at the national level (Colombia, Costa Rica, El Salvador, Honduras) and at the local level (Mexico), as well as comparable cases where elite taxes were discussed but not adopted (Guatemala) or not discussed at all (elsewhere in the region). I show that in the countries where greater tax burdens for security purposes were adopted or discussed, the security taxes were designed with the intention to target economic elites. Among the countries that adopted a tax, there is variation regarding the way in which elites were targeted. In some countries, as in Colombia and Honduras, governments adopted taxes whose incidence fell mostly on elites. In Costa Rica and El Salvador, governments adopted more diffuse, less targeted taxes, including flat taxes on corporations or taxes on telecommunication services, which less directly target elites than wealth taxes and have a greater incidence among broader sectors of the population. For each country that adopted the elite tax, I also show how the additional tax revenue was spent to strengthen the public-safety apparatus.

COLOMBIA

In Colombia, governments have adopted a series of wealth taxes on elites since 2002. In that year, President Álvaro Uribe (2002–2010) adopted a wealth tax aimed at the wealthiest taxpayers – those whose assets surpassed COP$169.5 million (US$65,000)[4] – and set for 1.2 percent over individuals' and corporations' liquid assets.[5] About 420,000 taxpayers were required to pay the tax or about 1 percent of the population. Of these, an estimated 120,000 were corporations and 300,000 were individuals. Exempt from paying the tax were foundations and nonprofit organizations, departments, municipalities, indigenous reservations (*resguardos indígenas*), unions, and parent–teacher associations, among others.

In December 2003, the Colombian legislature approved a second tax for the 2004–2006 period on assets surpassing COP$3,000 million (US$1 million). Three years later, in December 2006, Congress established a

---

[4] All dollar figures are nominal and were converted using the average yearly representative exchange rate figures from Colombia's Central Bank (Banco de la República).
[5] That is, gross assets minus debt. The calculation of wealth included real estate, vehicles, cattle, ranches, banks accounts, factories, plants, and equipment.

third security tax for 2007–2010.[6] In December 2009, as Uribe's presidency was coming to an end, Congress adopted another tax for the 2011–2014 period. These subsequent taxes targeted a narrower, wealthier base of about 33,000 Colombians with at least COP$3,000 million in liquid assets. In 2014, the wealth tax was renewed for the 2015–2018 period. However, for this iteration, the tax was no longer earmarked for public safety. Instead, it was renamed "impuesto a la riqueza," or "tax on riches," and was meant to help close a fiscal gap.[7] Table 2.1 summarizes the main features of Colombia's Democratic Security Taxes.

The Democratic Security Taxes added considerably to the government's coffers. When the tax was first adopted, it covered a gap of COP$2 billion (US$797 million) – about 5 percent of total government revenue or 1 percent of the country's GDP. Since then, the tax revenue as a share of the government's total has fluctuated between 2.5 and 5 percent (Dirección de Impuestos y Aduanas Nacionales 2011). The revenue from the security taxes was also significant for the armed forces. It represented 20 percent of the defense and security budget, including the armed forces, national police, and intelligence services.

During the first four years of Uribe's presidency, these resources funded an increase in the size and professionalization of the military (interview with Ramírez 2010; Ministerio de Defensa Nacional 2009). In addition to the procurement of fuel and food rations and maintenance of equipment, the funds allowed the armed forces personnel to grow by more than 100,000. They created 2 divisions, 18 brigades, 15 battalions, 13 urban antiterrorist units, and 598 town guard (*Soldados de mi Pueblo*) platoons, among other units (Ministerio de Defensa Nacional 2009). As a result, armed forces personnel increased by about 36 percent and combat forces by 45 percent during Uribe's first term in office (Vargas and García 2008, 46). This objective was at the core of the government's plan – dubbed Democratic Security Plan – to expand its presence across the territory. During Uribe's second term, these resources allowed the armed forces to increase capital expenditures (interview with Giha 2011). In particular, between 2007 and 2010, the tax raised COP$7.54 billion (US$3.9 billion), which contributed to the purchase of weapons, airplanes, helicopters, submarines, and frigates (Ministerio de Defensa Nacional 2009, 26).

---

[6] The calculation of wealth excluded the first COP$200 million (US$117,000) of main residence (home or apartment), as well as the net value of stock in domestic companies.

[7] Decree 1739 of December 23, 2014, established different tiers and duration of the taxes for individuals and corporations. Corporations were required to pay the tax with declining rates for three years (2015–2017), whereas individuals had to pay the tax with a constant, higher rate for four years (2015–2018).

TABLE 2.1 *Colombia's democratic security taxes*

Year approved	Tax	Duration	General objective	Public-safety expenditures
2002	1.2 percent of total liquid assets over COP$169.5 million (US$65,000) as of August 31, 2002.	1 year (2002)	Expansion of state presence across the territory.	Financed fuel, food rations, and the increase and professionalization of the armed forces personnel.
2003	0.3 percent of total liquid assets over COP$3,000 million (US$1 million) as of January 1, 2004.	3 years (2004–2006)	Continuation of the effort to expand state presence in the context of the Democratic Security Plan.	Armed forces personnel increased by 36.3 percent and soldiers increased by 45 percent between 2002 and 2006.[a]
2006	1.2 percent of total liquid assets over COP$3,000 million (US$1.3 million) as of January 1, 2007.	4 years (2007–2010)	Consolidation of Democratic Security; improving mobility, intelligence, and manpower (pie de fuerza).	Purchase of equipment including weapons, airplanes, helicopters, submarines, and frigates.
2009	2.4 percent of total liquid assets above COP$3,000 million (US$1.4 million) and 4.8 percent of total liquid assets above COP$5,000 million (US$2.3 million), as of January 1, 2011.[b]	4 years (2011–2014)	Consolidate Democratic Security; alleviate natural disasters.	Armed forces and disaster relief.

[a] For a detailed account of the expansion and modernization of the armed forces, see Schultze-Kraft (2012).

[b] Decree 4825 of December 29, 2010, created two additional tiers: 1 percent of liquid assets between COP$1,000 million and COP$2,000 million, and 1.4 percent of liquid assets between COP$2,000 million and COP$3,000 million. The decree also mandated a 25 percent surcharge for those in the two original tiers.

Source: Flores-Macías (2014, 2015).

In the absence of the security tax, the government was severely constrained in carrying out these goals. Before the tax was adopted, about 92 percent of the yearly defense budget was committed beforehand to cover ongoing operating expenses including wages, pensions, and fuel. Only 8 percent of the funds could be invested in increasing the number of troops or acquiring new equipment (Departamento Nacional de Planeación 2007). As a result of the security tax, investment expenditures more than doubled (interviews with Jiménez 2010 and Ortiz 2010).

The security tax also assisted in filling the gap left by decreasing resources received from Plan Colombia (interview with Jaramillo 2010) – the multiyear assistance plan by the United States secured by President Pastrana. By 2010, the last year of Uribe's presidency, Plan Colombia contributed COP$0.6 billion (US$316 million) to the armed forces, about a third of the funds received in 2000 (Haugaard et al. 2011, 5). In 2010, revenue from the security tax represented about four times Plan Colombia's military funds. By compensating for the loss of resources in foreign assistance, the security tax played a key role in preserving the government's room for maneuver (interview with Giha 2011).

COSTA RICA

Although Costa Rica's public-safety situation is different from that of the rest of Central America in that its levels of violent crime are comparatively lower, the deterioration of public safety among elites opened the window for the adoption of security taxes. Given how important this issue has become for Costa Ricans, recent administrations have been concerned that the trend might result in the loss of the country's reputation for being a peaceful and prosperous place. In the words of President Laura Chinchilla (2010–2014), of the National Liberation Party (Partido de Liberación Nacional PLN), "The public safety challenges we face jeopardize everything Costa Ricans have fought for" (*Revista Diálogo* 2011). In 2011, the country – which abolished its military in 1948 – only had 300 police vehicles, 1 helicopter, and 6 airplanes. The coast guard only had 26 vessels to guard 1,290 km of coasts along both the Atlantic and Pacific oceans (*Revista Diálogo* 2011). At the same time, Central American countries, including Costa Rica, have become an important transit country of narcotics from South America to North America and to Europe.

In response to these public-safety shortcomings, Costa Rica adopted taxes earmarked for public safety on two occasions. The first tax was adopted in 2011 but was struck down in 2015 by the Constitutional Court for procedural irregularities. The second was adopted in 2016 in an effort to reestablish the original tax.

For the first tax, in August 2011, President Chinchilla presented to the legislature a security tax on corporations, colloquially known as the "Tax Incorporated" (Impuesto S.A.).[8] Based on an estimated 485,000 companies required to pay the tax, the government's initiative was approved on December 22, 2011.[9] The tax rate was set at 50 percent of a base monthly salary – the unit employed by the government for standardization – for active corporations and 25 percent of a base monthly salary for inactive corporations. In 2015, the base monthly salary was set for $403,400 colones (about US$754), so the tax amounted to US$378 for active corporations and $188 for inactive ones. Micro and small enterprises officially registered as such – about 4,934 enterprises, according to Rodríguez (2013) – were exempt from paying the tax. In 2014, 542,600 corporations were required to pay the tax (Arias 2015).[10] Penalty for not complying was set for ten to fifteen times the amount due. Not paying the tax three years in a row resulted in the dissolution of the corporation.

In the 2012–2013 period (the first year of the tax, from when it became effective in April 2012 to December 2013), the government collected $60 billion colones (about US$112.1 million) (Herrera 2014). In 2014, the government collected $40 billion colones (about US$75 million). The yearly revenue amounted to about 1 percent of the government's revenue or 0.2 percent of GDP (Ministerio de Hacienda de Costa Rica 2015).

The tax revenue was earmarked as follows: 95 percent for public-safety expenditures and 5 percent for the prison system. In particular, the tax would finance equipment, vehicles, and training for law enforcement personnel. The law required the Ministry of Public Safety to present a report to the legislature every six months regarding how the tax revenue has been spent.

On January 28, 2015, however, Costa Rica's Constitutional Review Court declared the tax unconstitutional because the amount to be paid was changed in the final version – from US$300 in the original to 50 percent of the base monthly salary for active corporations and 25 percent for inactive corporations – without following the proper legislative process. The Court declared the tax to be due as scheduled through 2015, but that

---

[8] S. A. stands for Sociedad Anónima, the legal structure for corporations.
[9] The tax was published as Law 9024 in the Official Gazette 249 on December 27, 2011.
[10] Rodríguez (2014) estimated 545,000 corporations, a slightly larger number.

it could not be collected in 2016 (Oreamuno 2015). As a result of the ruling, 2015 was the last year for which revenue was collected.

In 2017, the legislature approved Law 9428, which established a new security tax on corporations. After the original tax was declared unconstitutional, President Luis Guillermo Solís (2014–2018) began efforts in April 2015 to reissue the previous law verbatim in order to preserve the tax revenue for public safety and maintain expenditures for that purpose. In the preamble of the tax bill, the government justified the law as necessary given that:

> The fiscal context described in the initiative of the Law 16306 introduced in July 2006 has not only not improved, but more than 8 years later, the country's fiscal crisis has deteriorated and the fiscal deficit reaches levels that require drastic and urgent measures. The conditions of scarcity of resources for public safety programs and the Bureau of Social Readaptation continue.

Almost two years later, the legislature adopted the security tax in March 2017, whose collection would start in September of that year. In an effort to get the bill approved, Minister of Public Safety, Gustavo Mata, asked legislators to approve the tax on corporations in order to channel additional resources to fighting organized crime.

The new measure was more progressive than the first, with several tiers based on revenue. The measure would tax inactive corporations ₡63,930 colones (US$112) and active corporations with revenue under ₡51.4 million colones (US$90,914) would pay ₡106,550 colones (US$187). Corporations with revenue between ₡51.4 million and ₡119 million colones (US$210,481) would pay ₡127,860 colones (US$225). Those with revenue over ₡119 million would pay ₡213,100 colones (US$374). Micro and small enterprises were exempt from paying the tax. The government estimates collecting ₡42 billion colones or close to US$74 million in revenue from the security tax each year (*La Nación* 2017a).

As with the previous tax, the revenue was earmarked for public safety. In this case, 90 percent of total revenue was assigned to the Ministry of Public Safety to invest in infrastructure, acquisitions and maintenance of equipment, and other capital expenditures. Five percent of total revenue was assigned to the Ministry of Justice and Peace to support its Bureau of Social Readaptation (Dirección General de Adaptación Social), which runs the country's prisons. The remaining 5 percent was assigned to the Judiciary, in particular, toward prosecuting organized crime. In the three cases, the funds could not be used toward salaries, overtime, transportation, or per diem. The exception was a one-time creation of 1,000 police positions that could be financed from the security tax revenue as long as they exist (Gaceta Oficial de Costa Rica 2017). Table 2.2 summarizes this discussion.

TABLE 2.2 *Costa Rica's security taxes*

Year approved	Tier	Tax	Duration	General objective	Public-safety expenditures
2011	Inactive corporations	25 percent of base salary or ₡100,850 (US$188)	Indefinite in law, but lasted 3.8 years	95 percent for police	Vehicles, equipment, weapons
	Active corporations	50 percent of base salary ₡201,700 (US$378)		5 percent for prisons	
2017	Inactive corporations	15 percent of base salary or ₡63,930 (US$112)	Indefinite	90 percent for police	One-time hiring of 1,000 additional personnel, infrastructure, equipment
	Active corporations with revenue < ₡51.4 million (US$90,914)	25 percent of base salary or ₡106,550 (US$187)		5 percent for the judiciary	
	Active corporations – revenue between ₡51 million (US$90,914) and ₡119 million (US$210,481)	30 percent of base salary or ₡127,860 (US$225)		5 percent for prisons	
	Active corporations – revenue over ₡119 million (US$210,481)	50 percent of base salary or ₡213,100 (US$374)			

33

HONDURAS

Citing "the disproportionate economic resources between organized crime and the agencies of the state in charge of the provision of public safety and justice" as well as the need "to urgently increase the funds available to the institutions in charge of fighting and preventing crime," Honduras adopted the "Tasón de Seguridad" or security tax as part of the Law for Public Safety approved on July 8, 2011 (Decreto 105, Ley de Seguridad Poblacional, *Gaceta Oficial de Honduras* 2011).

Although the government's original proposal was to adopt a tax on large corporations, the final bill reflected a combination of taxes targeting both corporations and goods and services typically used by the upper-middle and upper-income sectors. These include a tax of 0.3 percent tax on banking transactions, a 1 percent tax on the income of cell phone service providers, a 5 percent tax on mining activity calculated on the free-on-board value of the minerals extracted, a 1 percent tax on income from casinos and slot machines, a 0.5 percent tax on the commercialization of food and beverages by multinational franchises, and a 3.5 percent tax on the profits of cooperatives.

The revenue of the tax increased gradually over time. In 2012, revenue from the tax amounted to 834.4 million lempiras. In 2013, revenue increased to 1,097.7 million lempiras. In 2014, the government collected 1,914 million lempiras or about US$87 million. This is equivalent to about 4 percent of the government's total revenue and 0.5 percent of GDP.[11]

These taxes were originally adopted as a temporary tax for a five-year period, that is, until 2016, given "the national emergency regarding public safety, which requires fighting crime to reclaim security among the population and bring greater investment to the country" (Decreto 105, *Gaceta Oficial de Honduras* 2011). In January 2014, however, the legislature modified the duration of the tax to last ten additional years. Other important modifications along the way included the reduction in the rate of the tax on financial transactions from 3 to 2 × 1,000 lempiras – exempting remittances from abroad and accounts averaging less than 120,000 lempiras (US$5,467) – as well as the reduction in the mining tax from 5 to 2 percent (*El Heraldo de Honduras* 2015a).

---

[11] Based on calculations from data on overall collection given by Based on calculations from data on overall collection given by *El Heraldo de Honduras* (2015b).

TABLE 2.3 *Rates and relative shares of Honduras'*
security taxes

Type of tax	Tax rate (%)	Share of total security tax revenue (%)
Financial transactions	0.2	88
Mining	2	6
Food distribution	0.5	4
Cell phone services	1	1
Cooperatives	3.5	0.9
Casinos	1	0.1

The bulk of the revenue from the tax originated from the levy on financial transactions, which was estimated to target the wealthiest 2 percent of the population (*La Prensa de Honduras* 2013b). This tax excluded the Catholic Church and other religious organizations, remittances from abroad, and bank transactions below $10,000 lempiras (about US$457). The law stated that the Banking Commission (Comisión Nacional de Banca y Seguros) was obligated to ensure that the financial transactions tax was not passed along to consumers. The penalty for not complying was twice the value of the violation.

Table 2.3 shows the rates and breakdown of the sources of revenue from the security tax. The tax on financial transactions contributed 88 percent of the total – whose incidence affects the wealthiest sectors of society[12] – followed by the tax on mining corporations, which contributed 6 percent. The tax on fast food yielded 4 percent. The tax on cell phone communications brought in 1 percent. Finally, the combination of the taxes on cooperatives and on casinos and slot machines contributed about 1 percent altogether.

Article 32 of the law established that the funds could be used by the Judiciary, the Attorney General's Office, the Public Safety Ministry, the Defense Ministry, the Firefighters' Brigades, and other institutions in

[12] Financial transaction taxes have been shown to affect the wealthiest sectors of society. In a study on the US case, for example, Baker and Woo (2015) show that the top decile, which holds more than 65 percent of financial assets, would bear the bulk of the burden. In more unequal societies, as in Latin America, this is likely to be higher.

charge of preventing and controlling crime.[13] The Ministries of Public Safety and Defense are the agencies that have benefited most from the funds. Of the total revenue since 2011, the Ministry of Public Safety has received 35 percent of the funds, while the Ministry of Defense has received 37 percent. The intelligence service has received 18 percent, whereas preventive efforts have received the remaining 10 percent (*La Prensa de Honduras* 2013a).

The tax revenue has been spent on the purchase of bulletproof vests, airplanes, motorcycles, police cars, and communications equipment. It was also employed in the creation of two battalions of the country's recently created Military Police. Some of the funds were also destined for preventive measures, such as the rehabilitation of public spaces (*El Heraldo de Honduras* 2015a, 2019).

Article 3 of the Law 105 of 2011 established a Technical Committee for the Oversight of the Security Tax (Comité Técnico de la Tasa de Seguridad) formed by members of the government, the private sector, and civil society. It is the responsibility of the committee to inform every three months about revenue and disbursements. The committee is formed by three directors. A director of the committee is appointed by the president and has veto power. Another is appointed by the Honduran Council for Public Enterprise (Consejo Hondureño de la Empresa Privada – COHEP). A third is appointed by the Forum for National Convergence (Foro Nacional de Convergencia – FONAC), an organization representing civil society and in charge of evaluating the government's progress toward achieving the objectives set forth in the National Development Plan (Plan Nacional de Desarrollo).[14]

Decree 322 of 2013 (*Official Gazette*, January 31, 2014) allowed the Technical Committee to incur debt and use the projected revenue stream as collateral. As a result, the committee borrowed 1,318 million lempiras

---

[13] One of the main changes of the Decreto 166 of 2011 was that the earmarking provision was eliminated, and a reminder that it was unconstitutional to earmark. However, the specifics of the fund were left untouched, earmarking the tax revenue for practical purposes.

[14] The government representative was Reinaldo Sánchez – who was President Lobo's chief of staff – the COHEP representative was its president, Eduardo Facusse, and FONAC's representative is Juan Ferrera. In September 2013, Juan Ferrara was removed from the FONAC and the Technical Committee, allegedly because of his opposition to lax oversight of expenditures and to the spending on stadiums and other infrastructure projects less strictly related with public safety (*El Heraldo de Honduras* 2013).

(about US$60.2 million) to buy radars and airplanes to fight drug traf-
ficking (*El Heraldo de Honduras* 2015c).

EL SALVADOR

In El Salvador, a first effort to adopt a security tax failed, but a second
one was successful. The first proposal sought to levy a tax on taxpayers
with liquid assets over US$500,000, but it was defeated by Congress
in 2011.[15] The government's proposal was to adopt a wealth tax on
economic elites that would have targeted an estimated 2,300 taxpayers. As Table 2.4 shows, the government intended to make the wealth
tax progressive, with a tiered system for marginal rates given different
levels of wealth. Wealth up to half a million dollars would be exempt
from paying the tax. Wealth exceeding that threshold and up to US$1
million would pay 0.5 percent in tax. For the highest two tiers (up to
US$5 million and greater than US$5 million), the marginal rate would
be 1 and 1.5 percent, in addition to a flat fee of $2,500 and $42,500,
respectively.

The government hoped to collect $120 million annually (about
3.3 percent of total government revenue and 0.5 percent of GDP) to
finance a projected $360 million for additional public-safety expen-
ditures during a three-year period – the intended duration of the tax.
Among the government's goals was to hire 4,000 additional police. It
also intended to buy aircraft and speedboats to fight drug traffickers. In the words of President Mauricio Funes (2009–2014), of the

TABLE 2.4 *Proposed security tax on wealth in El Salvador*

From	To	Marginal rate	In addition to
0.01	$500,000	Exempt	–
0.5 million	1 million	0.5	$0
1 million	5 million	1.0	$2,500
5 million	–	1.5	$42,500

Source: Draft of the president's initiative for the security tax for public
safety. Figures in US$.

[15] The US dollar is the legal tender in El Salvador.

left-of-center Farabundo Martí National Liberation Front (FMLN) Party, "the air force doesn't even have fuel for the training of its pilots. We don't have frigates to chase narco-boats. At the same time, criminals move about feely with all the technology" (*La Prensa Gráfica* 2011b).

Facing strong opposition among the business sectors, the Funes administration was unable to adopt the security tax. However, his successor, President Salvador Sánchez Cerén (2014–2019), adopted a modified version of the originally proposed security tax. The tax revenue would be earmarked to pay for the public-safety program "Safe El Salvador" (El Salvador Seguro), in particular, to strengthen the National Civilian Police (Polícia Nacional Civil) (*La Prensa Gráfica* 2015).

On October 30, 2015, the legislature approved a security tax – Decree 161, Ley de contribución especial para los grandes contribuyentes para el plan de seguridad ciudadana – El Salvador's second attempt. Rather than the wealth tax proposed by Funes, the measure included a 5 percent tax on telecommunications services and a 5 percent tax on corporate income over US$500,000.[16] The tax was adopted for a period of five years, and the government estimated to collect $140 million from the country's 9 million cell phone lines – most of them prepaid plans – and 3 million landlines.[17] The increase in revenue from the taxes on telecom services and large corporations has amounted to 0.5 percent of GDP (Ministerio de Hacienda de El Salvador 2019, 5).

The bill earmarked the revenue exclusively for public safety and required the government to generate quarterly reports for the Consejo Nacional de Seguridad Ciudadana y Convivencia about the use of the tax revenue. Although the revenue was earmarked for public safety in general, the bill did not specify percentages for different agencies. Instead, the distribution of resources would be decided each year. Since the adoption of the tax, revenue has allowed for the recruitment, training, and retention of police, soldiers, and prison wardens, the purchase and maintenance of equipment and vehicles, the funding of prevention programs

---

[16] The government's original proposal included a 10 percent tax on telecommunications, but there was not enough support in the legislature. See the draft of the Ley de Contribución Especial para la Seguridad Ciudadana y Convivencia presentada por el Ejecutivo a la Asamblea Legislativa introduced on October 18, 2015.

[17] The tax also included cable TV but excluded international call centers (Velásquez 2015b).

among youth, and the monitoring of human rights violations (Policía Nacional Civil 2017).

GUATEMALA

In Guatemala, the government began in 2011 negotiations to adopt a security tax during the administration of President Álvaro Colom (2008–2012). The proposal gained increased visibility and traction but was ultimately derailed by the ouster of President Otto Pérez Molina (2012–2015). In March 2015, Mauricio Lopez Bonilla, President Molina's Minister of the Interior, announced that the tax would target the wealthiest sectors of society because the average Guatemalan could not afford to pay any more taxes. The government intended to earmark the tax for the National Police (Policía Nacional Civil – PNC), the Prison System (Sistema Penitenciario – SP), the Intelligence Service (Dirección General de Inteligencia Civil – Digici), and the Criminal Investigations Bureau (Digicri).[18] In particular, the funds aimed at increasing investment in infrastructure, as well as equipment, and salaries for new specialized units along the different agencies in charge of addressing violence and drug trafficking (*El Periódico de Guatemala* 2015).

Although the government did not make known the rate structure it envisioned, it planned to levy the security tax on taxpayers whose wealth exceeded US$1 million (Font 2015). A report by Guatemala's Banking Bureau estimated the existence of about 672 bank accounts in foreign currency surpassing this amount (Noticias de Guatemala 2010).[19] The government expected to collect about $4 billion quetzals (about US$521.5 million), corresponding to about 10 percent of all government revenue or about 1 percent of GDP (Alonzo 2015).[20]

---

[18] At the time of writing, President Molina had just replaced Minister Lopez Bonilla due to corruption allegations related to the tax collection agency. The government arrested the head of the Tax Collection Agency, Omar Franco, as well as his predecessor, Carlos Muñoz. As a result, the government's plan to introduce the measure in Congress is on hold.

[19] Additionally, the report estimated 304 bank accounts with 1 million quetzales or more (i.e., US$130,000 or more).

[20] The relative figures were calculated based on the annual figures published online by the Guatemalan Tax Collection Agency (Superintendencia de Administración Tributaria 2015).

In spite of the influence of Colombian initiatives to address the drastic deterioration of public safety in Mexico, the federal government has not adopted security taxes as a potential avenue to address the country's fiscal and security deficits. Whereas President Enrique Peña Nieto (2012–2018) appeared eager to adopt reforms that seemed to have contributed to the improvement of public safety in Colombia – such as the unification of the police under a single chain of command and the formation of a "gendarmerie-style" paramilitary force – and even hired retired Colombian General Óscar Naranjo as an adviser to the president on security measures, neither security-related taxes nor taxes on the wealthy have been part of the federal government's reform agenda.

Instead, Mexico's latest fiscal reform – approved by the legislature on October 30, 2013 – was mainly based on general consumption taxes, including excise taxes (Impuesto Especial Sobre la Producción y Servicios – IESPS) on sugary drinks aimed at curbing the consumption of products contributing to the country's obesity epidemic, environmental taxes on fuels and pesticides, and the elimination of special VAT rate considerations for border areas. Although the reform made changes to the personal income tax – adding three new brackets to make a 35 percent rate the highest bracket for income above $3 million pesos (about US$191,000) – and introduced a 10 percent tax on dividends, these changes were offset by the elimination on the tax on bank deposits (Impuesto a Depósitos en Efectivo – IDE) and the flat tax on business income (Impuesto Empresarial Tasa Única – IETU) (Pricewaterhouse Coopers 2013; Unda Gutiérrez 2015).

Rather than adopting an elite tax for public safety at the national level, a version of such taxes was adopted in several Mexican states. In the states of Chihuahua, Nuevo León, and Tamaulipas, for example, the government adopted one of the only modes of taxation available to state governments in the country, namely payroll taxes. These taxes are less ambitious than the wealth taxes adopted in Colombia but are the most ambitious tax available to Mexico's state governments in terms of revenue.

In the rest of the countries in the region, no security taxes were adopted. As with Mexico at the national level, governments did not introduce any security tax initiatives. Table 2.5 summarizes the state of security taxes in the cases discussed above.

TABLE 2.5 *Summary of national-level security taxes in Latin America*

	Colombia	Honduras	El Salvador	El Salvador	Costa Rica	Guatemala	Rest of Latin America
Object	Wealth	Financial transactions and mining	Wealth	Telecom and corporate income	Corporations	Wealth	–
Year adopted	2002, 2003, 2006, 2009, 2012	2011, 2014	2011 (defeated)	2015	2011, 2017	2015 (debated)	none
Threshold (US$)	1.4 million and 2.3 million	Accounts with average balance over US$5,467	$0.5 million, $1 million, and $5 million	All telecom services and income over $0.5 million	All corporations, except for micro and small businesses	$1 million	–
Rate or amount	2.4 percent and 4.8 percent	0.2 percent of transaction. 2 percent of mining	0.5 percent, 1 percent + $2,500, and 1.5 percent + $42,500	5 percent of telecom services and 5 percent of income over threshold	$378 (50 percent of base monthly salary)	Not defined	–
Incidence	33,000 taxpayers	161,960 (2 percent of population)	2,300 taxpayers (0.4 percent of population)	9 million cell phone lines and 3 million landlines; main corporations	542,600 corporations	1,000 taxpayers (estimate)	–

(continued)

TABLE 2.5 (*continued*)

	Colombia	Honduras	El Salvador	El Salvador	Costa Rica	Guatemala	Rest of Latin America
Duration	4 years	5 years and extended 10 more	3 years	5 years	3.8 years, then struck down by court. Permanent since 2017	Temporary, but duration not defined	—
Share of govt. revenue	5 percent	4 percent	3.3 percent	1.5 percent	1 percent	10 percent (projected)	—
Share of GDP	1 percent	0.5 percent	0.5 percent	0.25 percent	0.2 percent	1 percent (projected)	—
Destination	Airplanes, helicopters, submarines, frigates, recruitment of police and soldiers.	Airplanes, motorcycles, police cars, Military Police battalions.	Intended for increasing police personnel and acquiring equipment and vehicles	Helicopters, police vehicles, equipment, recruitment of police, soldiers, and prison wardens.	Public-safety infrastructure, equipment, one-time recruitment of police.	Intended for increasing police personnel and acquiring equipment and vehicles	
Outcome	Targeted Elite Taxation	Targeted Elite Taxation	Targeted Elite Taxation (Defeated)	Diffuse Taxation	Diffuse Taxation	Targeted Elite Taxation (Aborted)	Not Discussed

Note: Mexico did not adopt a national-level elite tax for public safety, but several state governments adopted comparable taxes given constraints within the Mexican fiscal federalism. For a discussion, see Chapter 7.

CONCLUSION

As discussed in this chapter, there is variation across cases regarding the types of taxes adopted and whether they affected economic elites exclusively or broader sectors of the population. The cases of Colombia and Honduras are cases of successfully adopted and highly targeted taxes on elites. Costa Rica and El Salvador are examples of successfully adopted, but more diffuse taxes with a lower tax burden. Guatemala is a case of unsuccessful adoption of a wealth tax, in part due to the sudden ouster of President Otto Pérez Molina for corruption charges, and in Mexico, subnational taxes for public safety have been adopted. Finally, no attempt has been made to adopt security taxes in the rest of the region.

Bearing in mind how difficult it has been for Latin American countries to increase their fiscal revenue relative to total output over time, these increases are significant. Whereas Colombia added 1 percentage point of GDP as a result of wealth taxes on elites, Mexico, which has not adopted a similar tax at the national level, has seen its current fiscal burden of 11 percentage points of GDP remain unchanged since the 1960s.[21] In Honduras, where the security tax represented half a percentage point, the tax to GDP ratio has increased only 2 percentage points over the last quarter century.

Further, there is also variation within cases across time. In Colombia and Honduras, the taxes were originally adopted as provisional, but they have been renewed over time. In Costa Rica, security taxes have been adopted with no expiration date. In El Salvador, a first attempt to tax elite's wealth failed, but a second more diffused attempt succeeded and its renewal is currently being debated in the legislature. These experiences suggest that the revenue from these taxes may not be as temporary as governments and business elites originally envisioned; instead, they are becoming a consistent supply of funds to state coffers.

If the historical record is any guide, even temporary taxes tend to be fairly sticky, and once tax-to-GDP ratios increase, they tend to experience a ratchet effect and remain at the new levels (Viswanathan 2007). This has been the case for both extreme examples, as when the Sandinistas in Nicaragua almost doubled the tax-to-GDP ratio and the new levels were maintained after they were voted out of office (Bird,

---

[21] A report by British economist Nicolas Kaldor commissioned by the Mexican Government in the 1960s already pointed to the country's GDP ratio as being inadequate to fulfill the government's most basic responsibilities and one of the lowest in the world (Tello and Hernández 2010, 39).

Martinez-Vazquez, and Torgler 2008), as well as for the more moderate increases in Guatemala or El Salvador since their respective civil wars.

The additional resources from the security taxes are of great significance for the law enforcement and military agencies to which the new funds are assigned. Even in Costa Rica and El Salvador, where the relative contribution to government coffers is smallest, the additional fiscal revenue has provided security agencies important room for maneuver, allowing for increases in capital expenditures and salaries that would not have otherwise been possible. In Colombia, revenue from the wealth tax on elites was fundamental to replace the dwindling assistance from the United States through Plan Colombia.

This is not to say that these taxes have not been controversial or their management has always been transparent. In the Colombian and Honduran cases, where oversight committees are required to generate reports regarding the collection, management, and use of the funds, the documents are not available to the general public but only to a small group beyond the parties involved in the committee. Additionally, they are often criticized by opposition parties because of this lack of transparency and the seemingly discretionary nature of expenditures.

In spite of these shortcomings, however, governments have credited these taxes with making possible important improvements in state capacity. With the additional tax revenue, governments have increased and improved on resources dedicated to addressing public safety, including personnel, equipment, and technology. From the purchase of helicopters, to the installation of surveillance equipment, to the recruiting and training of additional police, security taxes on elites have expanded the state's territorial reach, reaction time, and intelligence apparatus, to name a few examples.

In short, experiences with fiscal arrangements for public safety in the region have varied from the adoption of highly targeted, and repeatedly adopted taxes on elites – as in Colombia – to the adoption of subnational taxes for public safety – as in Mexico – to complete absence of such fiscal arrangements – as in most countries in the region. What accounts for these differences? In the following chapter, I advance an account based on demand and supply factors in the state-building enterprise and evaluate alternative explanations including resource dependence and inequality.

3

A Theory of Elite Taxation and the Determinants of Security Taxes

The art of taxation consists in so plucking the goose as to get the most feathers with the least hissing.

Jean-Baptiste Colbert, Louis XIV's Finance Minister[1]

Most of the literature on state building in general (Bensel 1991; Herbst 1990, 2000; Porter 1994; Tilly 1985, 1992; Hui 2005) and in Latin America in particular has focused on the incentives for state building generated by crises such as war (e.g., Centeno 1997, 2002; Lopez-Alves 2000; Rodríguez-Franco 2016; Rouquie 1987; Thies 2004, 2005, 2006).[2] The logic behind this view is that only severe threats compel economic elites to accept higher taxes because they believe "someone else can be forced to bear the burden" in the absence of the crisis (Drazen and Grilli 1993, 598). As Dan Slater (2010, 13) has pointed out in the Southeast Asian context, "Given their propensity for parochialism, elites will not deemphasize their narrow factional interests on behalf of broader class interests except under extreme duress."

The literature on fiscal extraction has followed a similar tack (Bird 1992; Fairfield 2015; Mahon Jr. 2004a; Sanchez 2006, 2011; Weyland 1996). It argues that, whenever society perceives the situation to be untenable, it becomes willing to "swallow the bitter pill" and accept policies previously considered unacceptable (Weyland 1996). As Richard

---

[1] As attributed by *The Economist* (2014).
[2] Less common is research focusing on domestic social and political configurations. See Harbers (2014), Kurtz (2009, 2013), Saylor (2014), and Soifer (2015) for Latin American examples and Mares and Queralt (2013) for an example beyond.

Bird (1992, 22) has suggested, "When the choice is as stark as 'adapt or cease to exist,' the fundamental societal instinct for survival might force almost any country to adopt reforms necessary to avoid extinction."

Latin America is no exception to this pattern. Governments' ability to carry out revenue-increasing tax reforms in the face of elite opposition has been associated with crises – from drastic economic conditions, to conflict, to natural disasters. In the words of Margaret Levi (1988, 46), this is because "Individual, self-interested actors are united in the face of threats to their individual and common property rights. The threat can be internal, external, or both." In line with this logic, in seminal articles on the determinants of tax reform in Latin America, Richard Bird (1992, 10) points to economic down-turns and James Mahon Jr. (2004a) to high levels of inflation as key determinants of reforms. Miguel Angel Centeno (2002) suggests that conflict forces otherwise unwilling elites to contribute resources to governments' coffers. More recently, Tasha Fairfield (2015) has shown how the 2010 earthquake in Chile played a major role behind the adoption of extraordinary taxes by the business-friendly government of Sebastián Piñera.

However, one difficulty in following a crisis-based explanation is the question of how to identify ex-ante a crisis that is severe enough to trigger the state-building impetus. As Javier Corrales (1997–98, 617–18) has noted, the role of crises is hard to predict, and it is unclear what constitutes "'the real' crisis. [...] Wars, invasions, natural disasters, crass human mistakes, economic collapse, and political disasters are all likely candidates." Responding to this issue, Slater (2010, 14) proposes a benchmark based on the type of crisis. Those perceived as endemic or unmanageable are likely to elicit elite collective action whereas those perceived as contained or temporary are not. Slater's benchmark provides a useful first step in identifying the type of shock that may prompt elites to accept higher levels of taxation, although the line between existential and contained crises remains difficult to pin down.

As discussed in Chapter 1, however, there are plenty of instances in which crises have contributed to enhancing elites' parochialism rather than superseding divisions and galvanizing their support behind state-building efforts. Indeed, it is not at all clear that crises alone are a sufficient condition for this outcome (Kurtz 2009). In the context of the public-safety crisis in Latin America, for example, high levels of violent crime do not fully account for elites' investment in the fiscal strengthening of the state. We would expect this to be the case in the countries with the highest average rates of violent crime, such as Honduras – where violent crime skyrocketed to reach 104 homicides per 100,000 people – El

Salvador (44), and Colombia (44) (UNODC 2014). Similarly, we would not expect to see the adoption of security taxes in Costa Rica, where the average rate of violent crime (9 per 100,000) is the lowest in Central America and among the lowest in Latin America.

The adoption of security taxes in Costa Rica exemplifies the difficulties involved in crises-based explanations. Given the comparatively low levels of average violent crime rates, it suggests that in some cases, the sense of crisis can emerge from the sudden or sustained deterioration of public safety over time. Whereas Costa Rica has levels of violent crime closer to those of the much safer countries in the Southern Cone, such as Argentina, Chile, and Uruguay, its homicide rate per 100,000 people escalated from 6.3 in 2000 to 11.4 in 2009, almost doubling in a matter of nine years (UNODC 2014). More importantly, the average violent crime rates mask variation in the extent to which elites experience this phenomenon.

However, this sudden deterioration of public safety affecting elites was not exclusive of Costa Rica; it also took place in countries where security taxes on elites were first defeated and subsequently adopted, as in El Salvador, or only adopted in a limited fashion at the local level, as in Mexico. In El Salvador, for example, homicide rates increased from 39 to 70 per 100,000 people between 2000 and 2011, before the security tax was defeated in Congress the first time it was considered. Similarly, Mexico's rate during this period went from 10 to 23 homicides per 100,000 people, with no adoption of such a tax at the national level. These cases experienced similarly increasing trends in which rates of violent crime almost doubled or doubled (UNODC 2014); yet, the adoption of the security tax was very different.

This discussion suggests that, although some form of security emergency – whether a sudden deterioration in public safety or intolerable levels of insecurity – is necessary for governments to pursue the greater extraction of fiscal resources for security purposes, crises will not explain variation in the adoption of security taxes on elites. Even in a context of rampant violent crime, security taxes on elites may not be adopted, or they may result in diffuse taxation rather than that targeting elites.

Instead, in order to account for the variation in security taxes, the following section offers a theory of elite taxation based on both supply and demand factors affecting this outcome in democratic contexts. On the demand side, society's needs tend to prompt reelection-minded governments in democratic contexts to acquire more resources to satisfy those needs. Such needs can take the form of infrastructure, health services, education, or public safety, to name a few examples. Deficits in the provision of these public goods can lead society to pressure governments to address these needs. In the case of public safety – a public good that elites are less able to substitute privately compared to education or healthcare – the worsening of violent crime can generate a window of opportunity for governments to extract additional fiscal resource deterioration.

However, whereas these public-safety crises open windows of opportunity – akin to Soifer's view of state building as a means of accessing opportunities in Latin America's early state formation period (2015, 18) – governments must also overcome challenges on the supply side. At the core of these challenges is overcoming society's unwillingness to pay, since citizens may demand the provision of a public good without wanting to pay more for it themselves. Among the main obstacles are government corruption, lack of accountability, and changing priorities (Bird, Martinez-Vazquez, and Torgler 2008).

These considerations become even more important for economic elites, who tend to bear the bulk of the fiscal burden in the region.[3] Although pressure on governments to address public-safety crises in democratic contexts might come from different sectors of society, elites' willingness to shoulder a higher tax burden will be greater if violent crime affects them directly. Otherwise, elites will be less willing to contribute additional resources even if other sectors of society are severely affected.

Therefore, governments must then overcome elites' mistrust toward them in order to engage them in the state-building effort. Although contributing additional fiscal resources might appear a reasonable course of action from a collective perspective, from the perspective of individual elites, there is much less incentive to contribute because the costs are concentrated and the benefits are not only diffuse but especially uncertain (Olson 1971, 100). Governments across the region have been notorious for engaging in corruption and waste, which becomes an important impediment for fiscal extraction (Bergman 2019; Bird, Martinez-Vazquez, and Torgler 2008; Torgler 2007, 202). In some Latin American countries, only 24 percent of the population considers that the government manages well the tax revenue collected (Casar 2013).[4] Beyond the uncertainty that

---

[3] In Mexico, for example, fewer than 2,000 companies contribute about 65 percent of all income tax revenue, while salaried workers contribute about 10 percent (Centro de Investigacion y Docencia Economicas 2012, 8).

[4] It is both rational and consistent for elites to engage in forms of corruption that benefit them and oppose forms of corruption that negatively affect them. Elites worry about

governments will waste or embezzle additional resources, elites are also concerned about governments' changing priorities, which may shift away from the public goods that motivated the tax increase. In other words, the calculation taxpayers make – and especially economic elites comprising a significant segment of the tax base – is one of immediate losses in exchange for collective benefits that may never materialize (Scholz and Lubell 1998).

A key factor helping to overcome this mistrust is the establishment of linkages between business elites and governments, such as consultation forums, collaboration mechanisms, and the incorporation of business elites or their representatives into government positions (Flores-Macías 2014). These linkages are conducive to clarifying the needs and perspectives of each side and finding common ground on potential solutions before legislation is drafted. Although some collaboration forums and mechanisms can be fairly institutionalized and serve to connect governments and business elites across administrations, governments enjoy considerable agency in the extent to which they proactively rely on these mechanisms – whether existing or new ones – or instead maintain formal participation but, in reality, keep them as shells without meaningfully interacting with the business sectors.

While governments have agency over the establishment of these linkages regardless of the government's ideology, linkages are more likely to emerge under the auspices of right-of-center governments. Although the conventional wisdom expects left-of-center governments to extract more in taxes (e.g., Stein and Caro 2013), they have increased fiscal extraction mostly by relying on regressive taxes such as the VAT, rather than through taxes that might directly contribute to wealth redistribution.[5] Instead, right-of-center governments tend to make it easier for business elites to directly influence the decision-making process, both through formal and informal consultation and even key positions in government. Right-of-center governments are more likely to exchange information with business sectors and enjoy greater credibility among them than left-of-center administrations. Additionally, business elites tend to be less wary of government intervention – from the expansion of government bureaucracies to tax increases – when right-of-center leaders are in office.

---

corruption insofar as it affects the diversion of resources away from goals that are important to them. In the case of security taxes, elites will want the security imperative to be fulfilled, regardless of whether they engage in bribes and other forms of corruption themselves.

[5] VAT taxes might still indirectly contribute to revenue redistribution via transfers and through the provision of public services.

For these reasons, right-of-center governments are more conducive to credibly assuaging mistrust concerns and committing to using the tax revenue in ways that benefit those elites (Fairfield 2015; Gibson 1996; Hart 2010; Timmons 2010). In short, right-of-center governments are more likely to establish these mechanisms, which bring them credibility in the eyes of economic elites when arguing that tax increases are imperative and that the elite's interests are being protected – akin to a Nixon goes to China dynamic.

Although the strength of business–government linkages is central to overcoming mistrust, economic elites will tend to incorporate mechanisms of restraint into the design of the security taxes they agree to pay, such as earmarks, sunsets, and civil society oversight provisions. For example, elites will be more inclined to pay taxes when governments can make credible commitments that tax revenue will be spent on public goods of their liking. Which public goods elites prefer will vary depending on the country, but there is one that constantly appears as a top priority in Latin America, and that is the provision of public safety (Latinobarómetro 2013). This is because elites tend to be able to procure most government services privately. If the public school system is deficient, they might send their children to private school. If the public healthcare system is poor, they can receive quality medical care at a private hospital or in the United States.

However, this substitution of public services for private ones is much less straightforward in the realm of public safety. Although economic elites in the region might live within gated communities, drive armored vehicles, and hire bodyguards for their protection (Álvarez and Rettberg 2008; Ungar 2007), a poor public-safety environment affects them in ways they cannot circumvent: First, they live in constant stress or fear of becoming victims of crime, and second, it negatively affects their businesses. These are two considerations elites cannot entirely address privately, and right-of-center governments will be more likely to sympathize with the "tough-on-crime" approaches demanded by the elites.[6]

Whether governments' hands are actually tied in practice will depend on the country's laws, but earmarking tax revenue serves both a crucial public policy objective and an important political purpose. In terms of policy, earmarking contributes to make possible the influx of additional

---

[6] For research on tough-on-crime approaches in Latin America, see Cruz (2011), Flores-Macías and Zarkin (2019), Flores-Macías and Zarkin (2022), Rosen and Cutrona (2020), and Ungar (2007).

resources to fill a gap in one of the state's most fundamental tasks: the provision of public safety. In this sense, the additional tax revenue allows the government to cover a higher level of expenditures in a policy area of concern for economic elites. Politically, earmarking can help convince elites that politicians will give priority to elites' concerns, regardless of the government's ideology or changing concerns over time. It can also help the approval of the tax in Congress by making the direct connection between the adoption of a highly progressive tax and addressing a generalized concern among the population at large.

Provisions related to sunset clauses and civil society oversight also contribute to making elite taxation politically palatable. Sunset provisions can help to make possible the adoption of the initial tax because they allow for the automatic interruption of the tax in a relatively short time horizon if conditions change. Sunset clauses also help facilitate subsequent adoptions of the tax by generating a sense that elites and their representatives in Congress remain in control and can pull the plug on the tax in the near future. In turn, incorporating civil society oversight into the tax arrangement can help assuage concerns that the additional resources will be embezzled or wasted, making elite taxes more acceptable on average. In light of the potential for abuse that comes with strengthening the security apparatus, civil society oversight can also help elites establish some control over the way the additional tax resources are spent.

In short, security crises present an opportunity when they directly affect economic elites, but security taxes on elites will have a greater chance of success in the presence of features that overcome mistrust between business elites and the government. These include robust business–government linkages, which are typically present with right-of-center administrations. These linkages will facilitate agreements that in turn incorporate formal design features to tie governments' hands – including earmarks, sunset provisions, and civil society oversight. These dynamics are illustrated in Figure 3.1.

These theoretical considerations generate the following expectations. Public-safety crises affecting elites can generate windows of opportunity for governments to increase the tax burden on that sector, both because increases in violent crime affecting elites are likely to result in their pressuring the government to address the public-safety deficit and because the public-safety threat makes elites more willing to shoulder a greater tax burden than they otherwise would. I therefore expect security taxes to be adopted in countries with sharp increases in rates of violent crime affecting elites. I also expect public safety to become a lot more acceptable

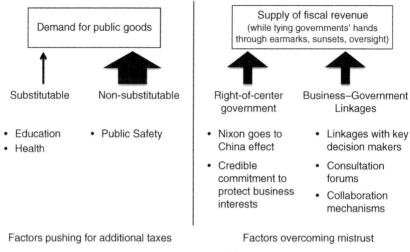

FIGURE 3.1 Theory of elite taxation.

for elites as a reason for a greater tax burden than other types of public goods they can acquire in the private marketplace, such as education and healthcare.

By themselves, public-safety crises will not result in efforts to adopt security taxes. Some windows of opportunity derived from such crises will open and close without prompting elite taxation. However, certain factors can increase their likelihood, For example, large fiscal deficits or looming fiscal crises will encourage governments to incur the political costs involved in adopting a greater tax burden. Whenever governments are facing fiscal pressure, the public-safety imperative can become a reasonable justification to generate resources to cover additional expenditures toward providing public safety. Additionally, the general public will be unlikely to oppose having the wealthy pay for public safety, making the taxes politically palatable.

In the developing world, however, rarely are governments in a comfortable fiscal position that would make them prefer redirecting funds away from social programs rather than finding additional sources of revenue. In the Latin American context, for example, governments typically struggle to collect in taxes their expected levels based on their level of development, with the important exception of Brazil – the country in the region with the largest tax revenue as a share of GDP. Moreover, in the aftermath of the

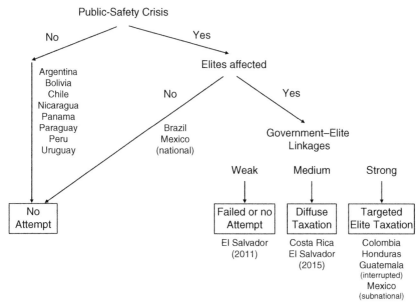

FIGURE 3.2 Theoretical expectations for the adoption of security taxes.

2008 and 2009 crisis, the entire region's fiscal positions deteriorated. For natural resource-exporting countries, the end of the commodity boom in 2014 further worsened fiscal balances (Flores-Macías 2019).

Further, the nature of business–government relations will determine the type of tax adopted. The stronger the linkages between business elites and the government, the more elites will be willing to shoulder a tax burden, and, in turn, the more significant the security tax will be for public coffers. Strong linkages combining right-of-center presidents, consultation forums, collaboration mechanisms that give business elites a voice in government, and a revolving door between business and government personnel at the highest levels will tend to result in targeted elite taxation and high revenue. Whenever weak business–government linkages exist – that is, presidents have a left-of-center ideology and business elites are not incorporated into the decision-making process – security taxes on elites are bound to fail. Finally, when medium linkages are created – for example, a left-of-center administration that incorporates business elites in the decision-making process to some extent – weaker and more diffuse forms of taxation (those eliciting a lower tax burden and affecting broader sectors of the population beyond elites) are likely to follow. These expectations are illustrated in Figure 3.2.

As Figure 3.2 shows, the empirical evidence supports these theoretical considerations. First, in places where rates of violent crime remained generally low and stable, as in Argentina, Bolivia, Chile, Ecuador, Nicaragua, Panama, Paraguay, Peru, and Uruguay, no security taxes were pursued. Among countries facing relatively higher levels of average violent crime rates, Brazil and Mexico did not adopt security taxes at the national level because Brazilian elites in Rio de Janeiro and São Paulo and Mexican elites in Mexico City were less affected by violent crime than the rest of the country.

Among those countries facing sharp increases in violent crime affecting economic elites directly, the type of business–government linkages determined the type of tax adopted. First, governments with weak linkages failed in their attempt to adopt security taxes. This was the case of President Mauricio Funes' 2011 attempt in El Salvador, where a left-of-center president with few linkages with the business sectors failed to negotiate a security tax on business elites.

Second, governments with moderate linkages were successful in adopting security taxes, but the tax burden was diffuse rather than targeting economic elites exclusively. Examples are Costa Rica's flat tax on corporations and Sánchez Cerén's 2015 tax on telecommunications and corporate income in El Salvador. In both cases, left-of-center administrations with more established ties to the business sectors adopted security taxes whose incidence is partly transferred to consumers and less directly targeting elites.

Third, governments with strong linkages were successful in adopting more ambitious security taxes that directly targeted elites. This was the case of Colombia and Honduras, where conservative presidents with a number of institutionalized collaboration mechanisms with the business sectors assuaged elites' concerns about the use of resources to secure their buy-in. It was also the path followed by Guatemala, where these conditions existed but negotiations were suddenly interrupted because of the dismissal of President Pérez Molina.

The Colombian experience is the one that most clearly illustrates how the theoretical expectations play out in the adoption of a security tax targeting elites and meaningfully contributing to public coffers. Following President Andrés Pastrana's (1998–2002) failed attempts at negotiating a peace process in El Caguán with the guerrilla groups, the demand for public safety was at a historical high. During the 1990s, an already dire public-safety environment had steadily deteriorated (Romero 2002). Armed groups constantly targeted the country's infrastructure, and traveling by road between cities became dangerous for the average Colombian (Restrepo 2006). Because of this precarious security situation, discontent among the wealthiest taxpayers became generalized. According to a Gallup survey conducted among 498 private-sector executives from the largest 5,000 companies in the country, more than two-thirds of respondents supported a Fujimori-style, authoritarian government if the peace talks collapsed altogether (*El Tiempo* 1999). Álvaro Uribe's campaign based on a tough-on-crime message won him the presidency in 2002 by capitalizing on this discontent.

From the beginning of Uribe's presidency, the new government and business sectors established a close relationship. In particular, strong linkages between business elites and the executive branch prevailed throughout Uribe's administration. First, in line with his right-of-center orientation, Uribe appointed prominent members of the business community to key cabinet positions, from the Minister of Finance to the Minister of Defense. This resulted in a cabinet formed by a majority of members with close ties to the business community throughout his administration.

Second, consultation mechanisms were established. These mechanisms facilitated a series of meetings between the government and the representatives of Colombia's peak business organizations at the presidential palace and Club El Nogal – an exclusive social club in Bogotá – to discuss elites' concerns regarding public safety and the government's needs to address it. As a result, these business people first, and later the heads of Colombia's National Business Association (ANDI) and other business groups, gave their support to the president's initiative and committed to lobbying their affiliates on behalf of the proposal.[7]

Third, ongoing cooperation mechanisms were instrumental in the adoption of design features to ameliorate economic elites' concerns. Although businesses acknowledged the need to provide additional resources to the state, they requested strict oversight of expenditures to ensure that resources be spent effectively (interview with Junguito 2012). Consequently, the government created a joint oversight committee – dubbed Ethics and Transparency Commission – to monitor security expenditures (interview with Pinzón 2011). These linkages between government and economic elites resulted in the adoption of a meaningful wealth tax that would translate into 1 percent of GDP in additional revenue.

---

[7] On business' influence in Congress see *Revista Dinero* (2011b).

A similar sequence of events took place in Honduras. Following the steady deterioration of public safety to the point where the country became the most violent in the world outside a war zone, Porfirio Lobo (2010–2014) reached the presidency with the right-of-center National Party. Lobo had built his political career advocating tough-on-crime policies and pushing for the reintroduction of the death penalty. He also made a point to incorporate prominent business leaders in the cabinet, including the ministry of foreign affairs – Mario Canahuati – and to establish regular consultation meetings with the leaders of the country's peak business association, the Honduran Council for Private Enterprise (COHEP), to discuss the state of the national budget (Gobierno de la República de Honduras 2013). As a result of these meetings, the government accepted the creation of an oversight committee with the representation of the business sectors to monitor how the government would spend the security tax revenue (*La Prensa de Honduras* 2011). Following these meetings, the highly cohesive business elites – through COHEP and the Honduran Association of Banking Institutions (Asociación Hondureña de Instituciones Bancarias) – convinced the bulk of the business sectors that the tax was worth supporting, given the economic elites' monitoring prerogatives.

In Costa Rica, more diffuse security taxes were adopted twice by the left-of-center governments of Laura Chinchilla and Luis Guillermo Solís. Although the country's programmatic spectrum is narrow, and both of the main historical parties – the National Liberation Party (Partido de Liberación Nacional – PLN) and the Social Christian Unity Party (Partido de la Unidad Social Cristiana – PUSC) – had similar proposals on most issues, the leftist governments struggled to convince economic elites that their taxes would not be wasted. In particular, both the Chinchilla and Solís administrations struggled to convince economic elites that additional taxes were required to address the large fiscal deficit that resulted from the expansionary policies of left-of-center President Óscar Arias' second presidency (2010–2014). For the 2011 tax, even though Chinchilla came from the leftist PLN, her platform pledged to be tough on crime, pro-free trade, and even socially conservative – many of the marks of a right-of-center ideology – which helped to some extent to ameliorate the business sectors' mistrust toward the government. Further, the President's Competitiveness Council incorporated representatives from the country's main peak business association and served as a formal mechanism to negotiate the security tax, but other types of linkages between the government and business sectors – such as incorporating a number of business people into the cabinet – were lacking, especially during the Solís administration. In the end, the earmarking of the security tax contributed to assuaging elites' concerns that the tax revenue would be put to a different use, but only reluctantly because elites valued public safety more than the alternatives (interviews with Muñoz 2016; Mesalles 2016; González 2016). Because the government and business elites did not agree on the need to reduce government spending in exchange for the tax, business elites did not trust the government not to channel tax revenue toward current expenditures in other areas, such as salaries for public employees in education and healthcare.

Once the government and the UCCAEP agreed on an acceptable tax – a modest flat tax on corporations, which is ultimately passed along to consumers and collects 0.25 percent of GDP in revenue – the well-organized (Sánchez-Ancochea 2005, 697–704) Costa Rican Union of Chambers and Associations of Private Enterprise (Unión Costarricense de Cámaras y Asociaciones de la Empresa Privada – UCCAEP) helped convince the business community to support the tax. As discussed in detail in Chapter 5, this tax arrangement reflects the government's inability to adopt a more ambitious tax targeting elites' wealth more directly, as in Colombia and Honduras.

In El Salvador, presidents' left-of-center ideology also became an impediment to the establishment of linkages between the government and business sectors, which ultimately further contributed to elites' concerns about voice and accountability. The first leftist president in the country in decades, Mauricio Funes (2009–2014), became president under the Party of the Farabundo Martí National Liberation Front (Partido del Frente Farabundo Martí de Liberación Nacional) – the political heir of the leftist guerrilla in El Salvador's Civil War.

President Funes and business leaders had a series of meetings in June and July 2011 to discuss the government's plans.[8] Business elites made clear two main concerns at the meetings: They asked to see a public-safety plan outlining a strategy to address insecurity and they asked for transparency in the government's spending of any additional fiscal revenue (*La Prensa Gráfica* 2012). Ultimately, in the absence of meaningful linkages – such as consultation forums – to promote collaboration and understanding, elites' mistrust in the government's ability to protect

---

[8] The meeting included Jorge Daboub, leader of the National Association of Private Enterprises (Asociación Nacional de la Empresa Privada – ANEP), Luis Cardenal, president of the Chamber of Commerce and Industry (Cámara de Comercio e Industria), Javier Simán, president of the Salvadoran Industrial Association (Asociación Salvadoreña de Industriales – ASI), Agustín Martínez, president of Camagro, Francisco De Sola president of FUSADES, and Elena de Alfaro and Armando Arias, representing Abansa (*La Prensa Gráfica* 2011a).

their interests became an insurmountable obstacle to the adoption of a wealth tax, even in the midst of a public-safety crisis.

The government's initiative to introduce the wealth tax elicited strong opposition from business sectors and elites more generally, pointing to the risk of capital flight and economic contraction as a result of the taxes. Further, business elites lamented the government's inability to generate a concrete strategy for public safety and denounced instead a wish list from individual cabinet members regarding the needs of each agency. As the National Association of Private Enterprises (Asociación Nacional de la Empresa Privada – ANEP) put it, "rather than a strategic plan to solve crime, the meeting was about a fiscal problem. The additional funds the government is seeking (about US$500 million), correspond in part to expenditures that are already underway or committed, instead of financing new actions that might generate positive expectations" (Asociación Nacional de la Empresa Privada 2011). As is further discussed in Chapter 6, for the ANEP, it was essential to "first improve trust in the institutions in charge of monitoring the execution of the plans and their respective budgets" (ANEP 2011).

Funes' successor, Salvador Sánchez Cerén (2014–2019), also proposed the adoption of a security tax on elites. This course of action gained urgency after the Constitutional Tribunal (Sala de lo Constitucional de la Corte Suprema de Justicia) blocked the government's efforts to raise $900 million for public-safety expenditures through bonds, which had been the preferred policy course of business elites and their representatives in Congress (Avelar 2015).

The country's main business association remained skeptical of the left-of-center government's commitment to spend the proposed tax revenue, but improved linkages between business elites and the Sánchez Cerén administration allowed for a compromise. Although representing the leftist FMLN, Sánchez Cerén relied on an alliance with an important segment of right-of-center parties to adopt a more diffuse security tax focusing on telecommunications and corporate income. In particular, President Sánchez Cerén relied on the right-of-center Gran Alianza por la Unidad Nacional (GANA), which was created in 2012 by former members of the rightist ARENA.

In Guatemala, the left-of-center government of Álvaro Colom (2008–2012) was unable to overcome mistrust barriers between the economic elites and his administration. The first left-of-center president since Jacobo Árbenz was overthrown in a coup in 1954 – over half a century ago – Colom was seen as a threat to business interests and was never able to establish the cooperation mechanisms necessary to assuage elites' concerns that their interests would be ultimately protected. In particular, the country's main business association, the Coordinating Committee for Agricultural, Commercial, Industrial, and Financial Associations (Comité Coordinador de Asociaciones Agrícolas, Comerciales, Industriales y Financieras – CACIF), was instrumental in stopping the government's attempt to introduce legislation calling for a tax on wealth over US$1 million (*El Periódico de Guatemala* 2015).

Conversely, when right-of-center candidate and retired general Otto Pérez Molina became president in 2012, his administration was well on its way with negotiations for the adoption of the security tax with the country's economic elites. Unlike his predecessor, Pérez Molina was a staunch conservative who had embraced a tough-on-crime approach in Guatemala and could appease elites' concerns about an increased tax burden.

The wealth tax that the government intended to adopt was earmarked for public safety and would be temporary – two important mechanisms to ameliorate elites' concerns – and would collect an estimated 1 percent of GDP. At the time, Guatemala was facing a fiscal deficit of −3.1 percent of GDP in 2009 and −3.3 percent of GDP in 2010 – its largest deficit since 1990 and well above the government's 2 percent target.

Although the adoption of wealth taxes on elites would have been consistent with the argument advanced in this chapter – a public-safety crisis directly affecting the country's main business elites and a fiscally constrained government, combined with a right-of-center administration and strong business–government linkages – Pérez Molina's presidency was interrupted by his resignation in 2015 due to corruption allegations and the tax negotiations have stalled.

Mexico has experienced a considerable increase in violent crime rates but has not adopted a security tax at the national level. Public safety deteriorated dramatically beginning in 2006, when the homicide rate was 9 per 100,000 people. Since, the rate has tripled, reaching 22 in 2014 and 27 in 2018. Although the homicide rate is not as high as those of El Salvador or Honduras, such a sharp increase in a short period of time follows the Costa Rican pattern and has led most observers to declare a public-safety crisis in the country.

Two highly pro-business presidents were in power during the escalation of violence between 2006 and 2018.[9] Both the right-of-center government

---

[9] In 2018, Andrés Manuel López Obrador became president with the left-of-center candidate party MORENA.

of Felipe Calderón (2006–2012) and the more centrist administration of
Enrique Peña Nieto (2012–2018) enjoyed close ties to generally cohesive
business groups.[10] While neither reached the presidency based on tough-
on-crime campaigns, Felipe Calderón militarized antidrug efforts and
Enrique Peña Nieto vowed to rein in drug trafficking organizations.

Whereas this configuration would predict the adoption of security
taxes in Mexico, there are several factors that make the Mexican case
exceptional, as is further discussed in Chapter 7. An important factor
is the degree to which economic elites have been directly affected by the
violence. Because of the regional concentration of drug-related violence
in a few states and because Mexico City has remained relatively unaf-
fected by this violence compared to other parts of the country, important
parts of the business elite have not been directly affected by it.[11] Further,
in the border states where violence is concentrated, Mexican economic
elites enjoy a greater "exit" option compared to elites elsewhere because
of their proximity to the United States. Elites from the areas most affected
by drug-related violence along the border states have the opportunity to
move their families across the border to the United States, from where
they can supervise their business operations in Mexico. One estimate
puts drug violence-related migration from Mexico into the United States
at about 115,000 people between 2006 and 2010 (Internal Displacement
Monitoring Center 2010).

Whereas no security tax has been established at the national level,
several states adopted taxes earmarked for public safety. In the states of
Chihuahua, Nuevo León, and Tamaulipas, for example, governments facing a combination of a drastic increase in violence, fiscal duress, and meaningful linkages with economic elites increased payroll taxes. Conversely,
states with high levels of violence but governed by left-of-center governments and weak business–government linkages, such as Guerrero and
Michoacán, did not adopt security taxes. Although the true incidence of
payroll taxes is a matter of debate, they are one of the few taxes Mexican
states can adopt by law, and their adoption followed a logic of taxing
elites through their corporations rather than the general public.

Similar to Mexico, Brazil is another country where crime rates are
relatively high compared to Argentina or Chile, but where no elite taxes

---

[10] Although recent clashes between the Slim and Azcarraga clans over telecommunications
concessions have somewhat undermined the historical unity.
[11] The rate of kidnappings has increased considerably since 2010. This might become a
relevant factor potentially compelling elites to put pressure on the government.

for security have been adopted. This is due to two main reasons. First, although violent crime has experienced a gradual rise in Brazil since democratization, violent crime has experienced a downward trend in the country's two wealthiest cities, São Paulo and Rio de Janeiro, since the late 1990s. During this period, elites in the country's two wealthiest cities have seen public-safety conditions improve over time, even if violent crime has behaved differently in other parts of the country. In the city of São Paulo, for example, the homicide rate declined from above 50 per 100,000 in the 1990s to single digits by 2014 (Muggah and Szabó de Carvallo 2018). Second, Brazil is the country in Latin America that collects most in taxes (Ondetti 2019; Schneider 2019), which has also reduced some of the fiscal pressures facing other countries.

Several countries with low and relatively stable levels of violent crime have not adopted elite taxation for public safety. In the absence of violent crime as a major concern for elites, governments in Argentina, Bolivia, Chile, Ecuador, Nicaragua, Panama, Paraguay, Peru, and Uruguay have not experienced the pressure coming from the wealthy sectors that their counterparts in other countries have. To illustrate, I briefly discuss the cases of Nicaragua and Panama. Both countries are located in the middle of the main drug trafficking routes that run through Central America, but levels of violent crime are low and no security tax has been adopted.

With an average homicide rate of 11 homicides per 100,000 people between 2000 and 2016 and a decreasing trend since, in Nicaragua, there has been little social pressure that could open a window of opportunity to generate additional tax revenue in this fashion. In particular, the country's economic elites do not consider crime as an important obstacle to do business. According to a survey of business executives in that country conducted in 2016, crime ranked 16 out of 16 possible concerns respondents were asked about, with no respondent including it as one of the top five problems facing business (World Economic Forum 2016).

Consequently, the president of the Consejo Superior de la Empresa Privada (Cosep), Nicaragua's main peak business organization, José Adán Aguerri, stated that since the country's police were already keeping levels of crime in check, there was no support among the business sectors behind any attempt by Daniel Ortega's government (2007–present) to increase the tax burden for this purpose, especially since they are already financing public safety through existing taxes (Navas 2011).

Like Nicaragua, Panama is another country where moderate violent crime has kept society's pressures contained. In 2017, the country's homicide rate fell to 10 homicides per 100,000 people – a thirteen-year low (Sweigart 2018). In the absence of strong pressures among elites to address public safety, there have been no attempts to negotiate with the private sector over the adoption of a security tax.

Finally, I do not consider the high violent crime case of Venezuela in the analysis because democratic electoral dynamics have been absent and the degree of government intervention in the economy far exceeds the avenues of extraction reserved for taxation. While the leftist administrations of Hugo Chávez (1999–2013) and Nicolás Maduro (2013–present) have nominally shied away from adopting security taxes targeting elites – consistent with expectations – despite the dire deterioration of public safety, the government's generalized reliance on price and exchange rate controls, land expropriations, and nationalization of private industries as extraction mechanisms does not allow for an evaluation of elite taxation in that country.

As this evidence from Latin America suggests, the drastic or sudden deterioration of public safety to critical levels is not a sufficient condition to engage in the fiscal strengthening of the state through elite taxation. Political considerations are at the center of the process pushing governments and business elites to agree on a form of security taxes. In the absence of a government that can credibly commit to looking after business elites' interests, and lacking mechanisms of accountability and voice for elites, the government's extraction of fiscal resources to address public-safety concerns is much less likely to take place.

ALTERNATIVE EXPLANATIONS

The literature on the determinants of the fiscal strengthening of states offers alternative explanations, including those related to nonfiscal revenue, inequality, and populism. Although they may play a role in specific cases, these explanations show a weaker ability to account for differences in patterns of elite taxation across cases. The evaluation of these explanations takes place in three steps. First, I introduce the relevant theoretical considerations for each explanatory factor and formulate corresponding hypotheses. Second, I operationalize each factor with empirical evidence from the region. Finally, I compare the extent to which these explanatory factors are correlated and covary with the dependent variable.

Nonfiscal Revenue

One of the most prominent explanations behind state building from a fiscal perspective focuses on the availability of nontax revenue (Kurtz 2009, 480) – including resource rents but also foreign aid or debt. The logic behind this perspective is that governments that depend on nontax revenue for a sizable share of their total revenue enjoy less accountability than when taxes are involved (Brautigam and Knack 2004; Flores-Macías and Kreps 2017; Karl 1997; Morrison 2009; van de Walle 2001). This lack of accountability results in corruption and poor government service provision, which in turn undermines people's willingness to pay for those services. In the case of natural resource dependence, rents "discredit the neoliberal insistence on constraints [and] suggest the availability of great opportunities. [...] The abundance in the ground and the resulting windfall gains make the neoliberal quest for wealth creation through productivity, efficiency, and competitiveness look unnecessary" (Weyland 2009, 146 and 151). In the Latin American context, for example, Fernando Coronil (1997) suggests that oil has generated an illusion of wealth that leads the population to believe that any fiscal discipline is unnecessary. Oil, he argues, has generated the impression that "the state is a magnanimous sorcerer endowed with the power to replace reality with fabulous fictions propped up by oil wealth" (1997, 2). Several authors (Elizondo Mayer-Serra 2014; Instituto Mexicano para la Competitividad 2013; Romero 2015) have pointed to similar consequences in the Mexican context – where oil is responsible for a third of government revenue. Oil is thought to allow the government both to shield special interest groups from taxation, which distorts the system's progressivity (Romero 2015, 176), and to postpone tough decisions about taxation (Instituto Mexicano de la Competitividad 2013, 11).

Scholars have attributed similar effects to other forms of nontax revenue. Research by Kevin Morrison (2009), for example, points to institutional decay as a consequence of rents from foreign aid. According to this research, foreign aid works in the same way as natural resources in that it does not come from citizens who tend to be reluctant to turn over their wealth and demand accountability in return (Collier 2006, 1483). As Morrison (2009) notes, these foreign aid rents contribute to the preservation of the status quo and have the same stabilizing consequences attributed to oil.

For our purposes, the expectation that follows is that the availability of nonfiscal revenue should help preserve the status quo – whether by weakening the government's incentives to tax its population, by undermining citizens' willingness to pay taxes due to the availability of external sources of funding, or both. Countries with high levels of dependence on nonfiscal revenue, such as Colombia, would be expected not to adopt elite taxation for public safety. Conversely, countries without alternative sources of nontax revenue, such as El Salvador, would be candidates for adopting such taxes.

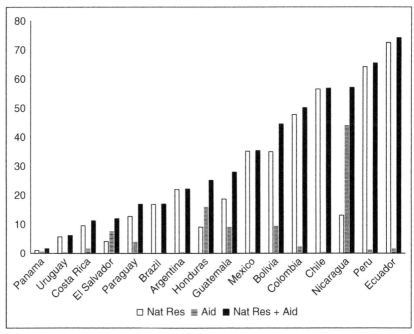

FIGURE 3.3 Natural resources and foreign aid as a share of total revenue.
Source: World Bank (2020). Bars reflect five-year averages between 2007 and 2011.

Figure 3.3 shows countries' reliance on both natural resource rents and foreign aid as a share of total revenue based on data from the World Bank (2020). White bars represent natural resource rents, striped bars represent foreign aid, and black bars represent the sum of the two. It suggests that the degree to which governments rely on nonfiscal resources is not correlated with the adoption of public-safety taxes on the wealthy. Such taxes were adopted in Costa Rica, where the share of nonfiscal resources is low, as well as in Honduras where it is comparatively higher. Further, although Colombia and Mexico have experienced similar reliance on nonfiscal income, the Andean country has adopted the elite taxes on numerous occasions, whereas they have been absent in Mexico at the national level and adopted only in certain states.

Inequality
Another major explanation in the literature on fiscal extraction concerns inequality. The logic behind this view is that willingness to pay taxes

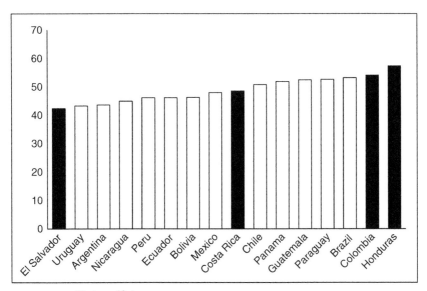

FIGURE 3.4 Gini coefficient, ca. 2011.
Source: World Bank (2020). The Gini coefficient ranges between 0 and 1. Higher values indicate greater inequality. Coefficients for Mexico and Nicaragua correspond to the 2010 and 2009, respectively, because of data availability. Coefficient for Colombia is for 2011 and its coefficient for 2002, when the first security tax was adopted would be even higher, at 58. Black bars reflect countries that adopted security taxes at the national level.

decreases as the level of inequality increases (Agosín, Machado, and Schneider 2009). This is because of discontent at both the higher and lower levels of wealth in society. The wealthier sectors resent becoming overburdened by taxes that continuously target them as the holders of resources, while sparing a large part of society that does not pay. At the same time, paradoxically, the lower socioeconomic echelons resent the wealthy for not contributing more, since their wealth is much greater than that of the median taxpayer.

This view would expect the countries with the highest levels of inequality, such as Honduras and Colombia, to have the most difficult time adopting taxes on elites. It would also anticipate taxes on elites in El Salvador and Nicaragua, where the gap between rich and poor is smaller. As Figure 3.4 shows, however, this relationship does not hold.

Security taxes were adopted in two of the most unequal countries in the region: Colombia and Honduras. In Colombia (54), ambitious security taxes in the region were adopted several times.[12] In Costa Rica (49) and El Salvador (42), countries with lower levels of inequality in comparative perspective, security taxes were also adopted. Mexico (48), where no security tax was adopted at the national level, is in the middle of the group. In most of these cases, however, the differences in inequality across countries are fairly small and slow moving over time and do not account for differences in the adoption of security taxes.

Populism and Ideology
A third explanation has to do with the type of leadership and its ideology. Some scholars have argued that the prevalence of populist leaders has resulted in low levels of taxation among the poorest sectors of society to gain and maintain the support of the masses (Profeta and Scabroseti 2010). Similarly, others have claimed that leaders with a leftist ideology will tend to tax at higher levels and adopt more progressive taxes (Santos de Souza 2013). This view would expect greater propensity to tax elites among leftist and/or populist leaders, since the left has historically embraced redistribution as one of its main demands (Stein and Caro 2013).

However, the empirical evidence does not support this view. The most ambitious taxes targeting elites were adopted by right-of-center presidents, whereas taxes with more diffuse incidence were adopted by leftist presidents. Whereas the most ambitious tax was adopted in Colombia's conservative government of Álvaro Uribe (2002–2010), Felipe Calderón's (2006–2012) ideologically similar administration in Mexico did not resort to any measures that would place an additional fiscal burden on economic elites. Similarly, while an elite tax was adopted in Costa Rica during the left-of-center presidency of Laura Chinchilla (2010–2014), another was defeated in El Salvador during the government of President Mauricio Funes (2009–2014), also with a left-of-center orientation. As Table 3.1 suggests, in the absence of other factors discussed in the theory previously, the government's ideology *alone* cannot explain variation in the adoption of elite taxes. Instead, the empirical evidence runs opposite to the expectation of higher elite taxation emerging from left-of-center governments.

Although the extent to which a president is a populist – that is, a leader who circumvents representative institutions by establishing a direct relation with the people through top–down mobilization in order

---

[12] Colombia's Gini coefficient for 2002, when the first security tax was adopted, was 58 – even higher than the 2011 coefficient of 54.

TABLE 3.1 *Presidents' ideology and security taxes on elites*

Country	President	Party	Ideology	Outcome
Colombia	Uribe (2002–2010)	Partido de la U	Right	Targeted elite taxation
Colombia	Santos (2010–2018)	Partido de la U	Right	Targeted elite taxation
Honduras	Porfirio Lobo (2010–2014)	Partido Nacional	Right	Targeted elite taxation
Honduras	Juan Orlando Hernández (2014–present)	Partido Nacional	Right	Targeted elite taxation
Costa Rica	Laura Chinchilla (2010–2014)	Partido Liberal	Left	Diffuse taxation
Costa Rica	Luis Guillermo Solís (2014–2018)	Partido Acción Ciudadana	Left	Diffuse taxation
El Salvador	Mauricio Funes (2009–2014)	FMLN	Left	Defeated
El Salvador	Salvador Sánchez Cerén (2014–present)	FMLN	Left	Diffuse taxation
Guatemala	Álvaro Colom (2008–2012)	Unidad Nacional de la Esperanza	Left	Discussed
Guatemala	Otto Pérez Molina (2012–2015)	Partido Patriota	Right	Interrupted
Mexico	Felipe Calderón (2006–2012)	PAN	Right	No discussion national level
Mexico	Enrique Peña Nieto (2012–2018)	PRI	Center	No discussion national level
Argentina	Néstor Kirchner (2003–2007)	PJ	Left	No discussion
Argentina	Cristina Fernández (2007–2015)	PJ	Left	No discussion
Brazil	Lula da Silva (2002–2010)	PT	Left	No discussion
Brazil	Dilma Rousseff (2011–2016)	PT	Left	No discussion

(continued)

TABLE 3.1 *(continued)*

Country	President	Party	Ideology	Outcome
Bolivia	Evo Morales (2006–2019)	MAS	Left	No discussion
Ecuador	Rafael Correa (2007–2017)	Alianza País	Left	No discussion
Nicaragua	Daniel Ortega (2007–present)	FSLN	Left	No discussion
Panama	Ricardo Martinelli (2009–2014)	Cambio Democrático	Right	No discussion
Panama	Juan Carlos Varela (2014–2019)	Panameñista	Right	No discussion
Paraguay	Nicanor Duarte (2003–2008)	Asociación Nacional Republicana	Right	No discussion
Paraguay	Fernando Lugo (2008–2012)	Partido Demócrata Cristiano/ Frente Guasú	Left	No discussion
Peru	Alan García (2006–2011)	APRA	Center	No discussion
Peru	Ollanta Humala (2011–2016)	Partido Nacionalista Peruano	Left	No discussion
Uruguay	Jorge Battle (2000–2005)	Colorado	Right	No discussion
Uruguay	Tabaré Vázquez	Frente Amplio	Left	No discussion

Source: Generated by the author. Countries that adopted elite taxes for public safety are in bold.

to challenge elites (Roberts 2007, 5) – is difficult to ascertain, several examples that are relatively easy to classify are helpful to evaluate this view. At one extreme, Nicaragua's Daniel Ortega is considered a populist by most accounts (Weyland 2013). However, none of these leaders moved to adopt security taxes on elites. Among those who adopted elite taxes, only Colombia's Álvaro Uribe is classified as a populist (e.g., Doyle 2011, 1456).

The theory of elite taxation advanced here is further evaluated in detail in the context of four case studies. Chapter 4 studies the case of Colombia, where the government adopted a series of security taxes on the wealthy to address a dire public-safety situation. Chapter 5 discusses the case of Costa Rica, an example of a diffuse form of taxation because of the inability to fully overcome obstacles related to mistrust in left-of-center governments. Chapter 6 examines the case of El Salvador, where, in spite of skyrocketing violence, governments from the leftist FMLN proved unable to adopt a wealth tax on elites due to weak business–government linkages, but succeeded in adopting a less targeted tax following the strengthening of those linkages. Chapter 7 studies the case of Mexico, where the security situation deteriorated considerably, but national security taxes were not adopted. Instead, a handful of states adopted subnational taxes whenever strong government–elite linkages were present. In Chapter 8, I address the security benefits of elites' investment in strengthening the state, as well as the broader implications of the study's findings.

4

Colombia's Targeted Security Taxes[*]

> We struck a gentlemen's pact with business leaders guaranteeing that, in exchange for the funds, the tax would be temporary and the extraordinary tax revenue would only be used towards security expenditures.
>
> Member of President Álvaro Uribe's cabinet[1]

As the following case study will show, both demand and supply factors play a differentiated role in explaining the adoption of Colombia's highly targeted security taxes. Colombian elites' inability to travel safely from one city to another generated the demand for the improvement of public safety, and the advent of a fiscal crisis contributed to generate the impetus for elite taxation. Further, both the strong government–elite linkages and cohesion among business sectors played a key role in reaching an agreement to implement the security tax and convincing the private sector to support it. In the following paragraphs, I first illustrate the theory at work in the Colombian case and then evaluate the extent to which alternative explanations played a role in accounting for the adoption of security taxes.

CRISIS AS IMPETUS FOR TAXATION

A crisis perceived as pervasive and beyond the government's control in 2002 opened a window of opportunity for the adoption of the wealth taxes on elites, which became known in Colombia as Democratic Security

---

[*] This chapter draws on Flores-Macías, Gustavo (2014). "Financing Security through Elite Taxation: The Case of Colombia's 'Democratic Security Taxes,'" *Studies in Comparative International Development* 49, 4: 477–500.
[1] Author's interview, June 2011.

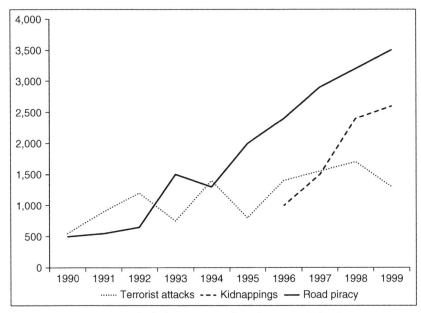

FIGURE 4.1 Terrorist attacks, kidnappings, and road piracy in Colombia, 1990–1999. *Source:* Ministerio de Defensa Nacional (2009, 28). For kidnappings, no data are provided before 1996.

Taxes (*Impuesto de la Seguridad Democrática*). This crisis was both security-related and fiscal. It did not initially prompt elites to ameliorate their opposition to the adoption of the tax, but it did force the government to take extraordinary measures to secure resources, including declaring a state of emergency. These measures were effective in circumventing opposition and raising much-needed funds in a short period of time.

Álvaro Uribe (2002–2010) was inaugurated president of Colombia on August 7, 2002, amid a precarious security situation, dismal economic conditions, and discontent among the wealthiest taxpayers bearing the burden of mandatory security bonds. During the 1990s, an already bleak public-safety environment steadily worsened (Romero 2002). Armed groups constantly targeted the country's infrastructure, and traveling by road between cities became dangerous for the average Colombian (Restrepo 2006). Piracy and hijacking became common problems (Figure 4.1).

Between 1998 and 2002, the duration of Andrés Pastrana's presidency, this situation further deteriorated. The number of homicides increased by 18 percent and the number of kidnappings by 15 percent (Departamento Nacional de Planeación 2003). According to one estimate, about 15 percent of the more than 2,500 kidnappings per year during this period involved the business community (Rettberg 2004, 5). Additionally, the line between drug traffickers, guerrillas, and paramilitaries became increasingly blurred as they cooperated to strengthen financially and operationally. Extortion and racketeering by these groups became pervasive. In large parts of the country, business owners and landowners were forced to pay to avoid attacks on their assets.[2]

In an attempt to respond to these challenges, Colombia more than doubled its security expenditures as a share of GDP between 1990 and 2002, from 1.5 to 3.3 percent (Ministerio de Defensa Nacional 2008). In spite of this trend, "the government always seemed one step behind in its efforts to keep up with the equipment and weapons employed by guerrillas, paramilitaries and drug traffickers because of lack of resources" (interview with Barco 2010).

In search of a solution to the armed conflict, the business sectors initially embraced and participated in *El Caguán* Peace Process (1999–2002) – the negotiations held in a demilitarized zone between Pastrana's administration and the Revolutionary Armed Forces of Colombia (FARC). However, Pastrana's attempts to negotiate with the guerilla groups were widely considered a failure (Rettberg 2007, 489). Broad sectors of society were disenchanted by the perception that the FARC had stood up to the government at the negotiating table. By November 2000, a Gallup poll showed that only 11 percent of respondents supported the continuation of the peace process, while 60 percent supported stepping up the armed confrontation (*The Economist* 1999).

Upon the breakdown of the talks, business elites' disenchantment turned into vigorous support for Uribe's "strong hand" candidacy (interview with Llorente 2010). In a Gallup survey conducted among 498 private-sector executives from the largest 5,000 companies in the country, more than two-thirds of respondents supported a Fujimori-style, authoritarian government if the peace talks collapsed altogether (*El Tiempo* 1999). Thus, an overwhelming majority of respondents had reached a point in which they would willingly trade Colombia's long-standing democracy in exchange for public safety.

However, a fiscal crisis prevented Uribe from capitalizing on this support and delivering on one of his main campaign promises: increasing security spending. During the 1990s, in an attempt to finance mounting security costs, governments mandated the purchase of bonds in

---

[2] A famous example was the FARC's Law 002 (Rettberg 2002).

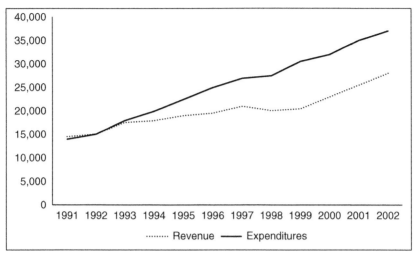

FIGURE 4.2 Revenues and expenditures 1991–2002, National Central Government (billions of 2002 COP$).
Source: Gaceta del Congreso de Colombia (2003, 11).

exchange for modest returns (Ministerio de Defensa Nacional 2009, 25). In 1992, President César Gaviria (1990–1994) created the Bonds for Social Development and Internal Security.[3] Ernesto Samper (1994–1998) issued the Peace Bonds in 1996 and the Security Bonds in 1997. In a similar effort, Andrés Pastrana (1998–2002) created the Bonds in Solidarity for Peace.

Along with mounting security expenditures, the bonds contributed to the government's increasing gap between revenue and spending. Between 1995 and 2002, expenditures increased by 65 percent, while revenue grew only by 46 percent in real terms (Figure 4.2). This discrepancy resulted in a ballooning public debt. In 1996, the net debt of the nonfinancial public sector represented 21.3 percent of GDP (Figure 4.3). By 2002, this debt had grown to 53 percent of GDP. In a matter of six years, Colombia's public debt had more than doubled.

Moreover, the Asian crisis of 1997 and the Argentine crisis of 2001–2002 made it very difficult for Colombia to continue financing deficits through debt, since these crises made borrowing very costly for emerging markets across the world. As Uribe's Finance Minister put it, "we were desperate for resources and entirely shut out of the credit markets at the time" (interview with Junguito 2012). Reining in the drastic escalation of the debt became a priority for the government.

---

[3] The Supreme Court ruled the bonds to be retroactive and therefore unconstitutional.

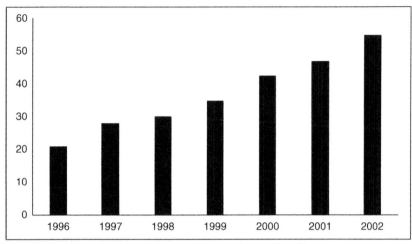

FIGURE 4.3 Net public debt 1996–2002, nonfinancial public sector (percentage of GDP).
Source: Gaceta del Congreso de Colombia (2003, 11).

To make matters worse, the economy was facing strong headwinds, making the prospect of a revenue-increasing recovery very unlikely. Pastrana presided over one of the worst four-year periods in decades: The economy contracted by 4.2 percent in 1999 and averaged 0.6 percent growth between 1998 and 2002. By the time Uribe took office in August 2002, unemployment had reached 15 percent and the Colombian peso had depreciated by almost 20 percent in the previous three months. Without securing extraordinary resources, Uribe's administration would be unable to avoid bankruptcy, let alone follow through on his campaign promise to strengthen the government's security effort.

In this context, the new administration evaluated increases to the value-added tax (VAT) and income tax rates. From the government's perspective, these taxes were more favorable than bonds, since the latter had to be paid back and contributed to expanding the government's fiscal burden (interview with Junguito 2012). This, in turn, affected the government's future ability to finance the security effort. In contrast, a tax did not mortgage the security effort since there was no obligation to pay interest on debt, and subsequent budgets would not be further constrained as a result.

However, raising the VAT and income tax rates was also problematic. Additional revenue from these taxes would trickle into the government's coffers – because of how gradually they are collected – and the government could not afford to wait. Moreover, these taxes would be paid by large sectors of the population, and the political cost was deemed to be high (*El Tiempo* 2002b). In this context, maintaining – let alone expanding – current levels of security expenditures became unsustainable.

In spite of the crisis, business sectors' opposition to any taxation efforts remained vigorous and public. The switch from bonds to taxes meant economic elites would forego both the principal and interest returned to them previously. Additionally, they pointed to the lack of results of previous administrations, the need to broaden the tax base, and the economic downturn as reasons why they opposed any extractive measure (*El Tiempo* 2002a).

For example, the Colombian Business Council (*Consejo Gremial*) – a semiformal union of the country's most important business associations (Rettberg 2005) – and the Association of Micro-, Small-, and Medium Enterprises (ACOPI) denounced that previous governments had lost credibility because taxpayers' money had been squandered. As the vice president of the Colombian Business Council put it, "We had no idea whether the government used those funds as intended" (interview with Mejía 2011). Similarly, the Federation of Colombian Insurers (FASECOLDA) expressed concern that additional extraction would hinder economic growth even further, at a time "when the country could not afford to lose investment and stop generating much needed jobs" (*El Tiempo* 2002b). Additionally, the Automakers Association (ASOPARTES) and Confederation of Chambers of Commerce (CONFECAMARAS) demanded that the government broaden the tax base instead. Between Uribe's election and his inauguration, business actively and publicly opposed any potential extraction efforts.

Although the fiscal and security conditions did not prompt business elites to change their views, they did prompt the government to take extraordinary measures. On August 11, 2002 – four days after taking office – Uribe assessed the security and fiscal situation to be so precarious that he resorted to extraordinary decree powers to achieve this goal. That day he decreed a State of Internal Commotion (*Estado de Conmoción Interior*) for three months, stating as the main reasons that "the entire Nation is submitted to a regime of terror in which democratic authority is capsizing and productive activities have become increasingly difficult to perform" (*Diario Oficial* 2002). "Moreover," the decree continued, "armed groups have successfully threatened the legitimate representatives of democracy, spreading anarchy and generating a sentiment of helplessness in wide sectors of the country."

In addition to referring to the country's precarious security situation, the decree also cited the government's fiscal troubles: "given the country's grave fiscal situation, the Nation does not have the necessary resources to finance the security forces and other state institutions in charge of addressing the issue; therefore, it is necessary to adopt new fiscal obligations." The same day, Uribe issued another decree mandating the creation of "a special tax toward financing the expenditures in the government's general budget necessary to preserve Democratic Security" (*Diario Oficial* 2002).

This course of action had two immediate consequences. First, in the fiscal realm, this measure addressed the problems of timing and collection. By mandating that the tax be collected in two installments, the government could extract extraordinary resources in a short period of time and make the tax relatively easy to pay. Additionally, a tax on liquid assets represented a relatively simple tax to collect because of the relatively small number of taxpayers.[4] Second, in the political realm, it circumvented the conventional legislative process typical of peacetime conditions. Rather than facing opposition from the business sectors and their potential allies in the legislature, the measure left dissatisfied actors in the courts as the only recourse. Indeed, both the state of emergency and the tax were contested before the Constitutional Court. In the end, the government prevailed and began receiving the extemporaneous revenue shortly thereafter.

THE LIMITS OF CRISIS AS AN EXPLANATION

The combination of the security and fiscal crises generated a major window of opportunity for the adoption of a tax on the wealthy. President Uribe circumvented the legislative process by issuing the Democratic Security tax by decree,[5] but the State of Internal Commotion could not last indefinitely and neither could the taxes adopted during this period of exception. In order to face the security and fiscal crises, the Uribe administration had to go through the regular legislative process.

Whereas crises generated the window of opportunity, less contingent factors are necessary to explain security taxes adopted in 2003, 2006, and 2009. In particular, two key factors were the linkages between the right-of-center government and economic elites and the design features

---

[4] For a discussion of the prevalence of tax evasion in Latin America, see Bergman (2009, 2019).

[5] The name of the tax is ironic given that it was adopted by decree rather than through the legislature.

of the tax, both of which were critical to overcome elites' mistrust in the governments' ability to spend the tax revenue in effective and accountable ways.

Although Álvaro Uribe began his political career with the left-of-center Partido Liberal – becoming the mayor of Medellín, governor and twice senator for Antioquia, before he abandoned the party – his conservative credentials were well established during his presidential run. For his presidential campaign in 2002, he ran as an independent under the auspice of Primero Colombia – an electoral vehicle that supported his candidacy – on a conservative platform and followed pro-business, tough-on-crime government policies.[6]

The president's right-of-center orientation facilitated the establishment of business–government linkages – such as consultation forums and collaboration mechanisms – which helped the government garner support for the adoption of security taxes in several ways. First, Uribe appointed prominent members of the business community to key cabinet positions from the beginning of his presidency. This resulted in a cabinet formed by a majority of ministers with strong ties to the business community throughout his administration. In particular, the Ministry of Defense was led by Martha Lucía Ramírez, Jorge Alberto Uribe Echavarría, Juan Manuel Santos, and Gabriel Silva Luján; the Ministry of Finance was headed by Roberto Junguito Bonnet and Óscar Iván Zuluaga; the Ministry of Interior and Justice was led by Sabas Pretelt, the former head of the Colombian Business Council, to name a few examples. Naturally, not every minister in the cabinet was a member of the business community, but business leaders occupied numerous and prominent positions related to security and public finance.

Second, the affinity that resulted from the interweaving of business leaders and government contributed to meaningful consultation between the two. These linkages facilitated a series of meetings between the government and Colombia's most influential business people at the presidential palace and Club El Nogal – an exclusive social club in Bogotá.[7]

---

[6] Contrary to many Latin American presidents who govern with diametrically different policies from the ones they pledged to adopt during their campaign (Stokes 2001), Uribe governed consistent with this conservative platform throughout his two terms.

[7] Business organizations in Colombia strengthened in great part due to government actions. Beginning in the 1920s, governments actively supported business associations in coffee, industry, and other sectors with the objective of gathering information, exchanging support for specific policies, or depoliticizing policymaking. In the 1990s, an economy-wide organization was created after the government asked business groups to form one (Schneider 2004, 16).

At these meetings, Uribe himself laid out both the need to renew the tax and his plans to allocate the funds to the security effort (interviews with two anonymous cabinet members 2011). This was one of the business elites' main demands since the yearly economic costs of the conflict were deemed to be 2 percent of GDP (Castro et al. 1999) in addition to another 2 percent in private security expenditures (Álvarez and Rettberg 2008).

Because of this close association, the government understood and was sympathetic to the concerns of economic elites. The government publicly echoed business' opposition to add to the tax burden through more comprehensive tax reforms. President Uribe argued that doing so would jeopardize economic growth and promised the business sectors – both in consultation meetings and publicly – not to follow that route (*El Tiempo* 2003a). Instead, the government pursued other ways to stretch the budget, including higher VATs and freezes for public-sector wages and pensions (*El Tiempo* 2003b). In explaining the spirit of the reforms, the government suggested that "*all sectors* of Colombian society needed to make comparable sacrifices and contributions" (*Gaceta del Congreso de Colombia* 2003, 10).

The government sent an initiative to Congress to increase the VAT, and a referendum was held for the proposal to cut expenditures. The legislature approved the adoption of a VAT of 2 percent on basic consumption goods, such as milk, fruit, vegetables, and public transportation, but the Constitutional Court struck down the tax (*El Tiempo* 2003c) in September 2003. In October of that year, the proposal to cut expenditures was defeated in the referendum. This left the government looking again for alternatives.

The government and economic elites participated again in a series of meetings to negotiate the tax reform. The main proposals on the table were a new wealth tax with a lower rate (0.4 percent) and higher threshold (COP$3000 million or US$1 million), an increase to the tax on financial transactions from COP$3 to COP$4 per COP$1,000, an increase in the VAT rate from 16 to 17 percent, and a tax on pensions. With the aim of stimulating economic activity, Uribe also proposed lowering the maximum marginal income tax rate from 35 to 15 percent for corporations reinvesting their profits (*El Tiempo* 2003d).

At the meetings, as a cabinet member put it, the government's linkages with business leaders allowed President Uribe to strike "a gentlemen's pact guaranteeing that, in exchange for the funds, the tax would be temporary and the extraordinary tax revenue would only be used towards security expenditures" (interview with anonymous cabinet member 2011). As a result, these business people first, and later the heads of

Colombia's National Business Association (ANDI) and other business groups, gave their support to the president's initiative and committed to lobbying their affiliates on behalf of the proposal.[8]

Third, the design features of the tax helped to address economic elites' concerns. Although economic elites acknowledged the need to provide additional resources to the state, they requested strict oversight of expenditures to ensure that resources be spent effectively (interview with Junguito 2012). Consequently, the government created a joint oversight committee – dubbed Ethics and Transparency Commission – to monitor security expenditures (interview with Pinzón 2011). Representatives of business, university presidents, the attorney general, and the comptroller general formed the Commission, which held several meetings during the year and generated annual reports of the government's procurement – a by-product of the managerial background of the Defense Minister (interviews with Buendía 2010 and García 2010). Meetings were held in different locations to verify equipment acquisitions and monitor progress (interview with Giha 2011).

The ability to monitor the government's compliance with its own objectives addressed one of the business sectors' main concerns: That their contributions were reaching their intended purpose (interview with Vargas 2010). As a business leader who attended several of the Commission's meetings confided, "the meetings were important to us. We were able to visually corroborate the acquisition of equipment and to talk to defense personnel on the ground, sometimes the commander of a region, sometimes the officer in charge of an outpost, to evaluate progress" (interview with Mejía 2011).

In the end, Congress adopted a modified version of the government's proposal on December 29, 2003.[9] The new measure included a new temporary security tax between 2004 and 2006 at a lower rate (0.3 percent), a temporary increase in the income tax rate from 35 to 38.5 percent for the same period, and an increase in the tax on financial transactions (*Diario Oficial* 2003). No consensus was formed regarding other measures. The VAT increase and taxes on pensions were deemed to be too costly politically (interview with Castro 2010), and the government decided not to include them in the discussion of the joint chambers to avoid any potential delays in the approval of the reform, which was running out of time to come into effect in 2004 (*El Tiempo* 2003d).

---

[8] On business' influence in Congress, see *Revista Dinero* (2011b).

[9] The approval was controversial because the president convened an extraordinary session of Congress while many legislators were away for winter holiday recess.

The reform secured resources to maintain the government's security effort, but it also protected the interests of business. It expanded the tax base, earmarked the funds for a public good of importance to elites, allowed them to oversee how the government spent the tax revenue, and established sunset provisions. Immediately after the initiative was approved, Interior Minister and prominent business leader Sabas Pretelt took the tribune to thank legislators "for their courage and service to the nation" (*El Tiempo* 2003e).

The right-of-center orientation of the president and the linkages with economic elites were instrumental in showing elites that the government ultimately had their interests in mind. This was not just due to signaling. The government shielded elites down the road from alternatives once the fiscal concerns were not as pressing. In 2004, shortly after the 2003 tax was approved, the government promoted a concession to business elites: An exception for the wealthiest taxpayers in the form of Juridical Stability Contracts (*Contratos de Estabilidad Jurídica*). Approved by Congress as the Law of Confidence for Investors in July 2005, the con-tracts were an agreement between major investors and the Colombian government in which the government guaranteed the preservation of the legal framework in place at the time a substantial investment was made. The spirit of the contracts was to attract investment by providing legal certainty. In exchange for stable rules of the game, the investor would pay the government 1 percent of investments over 7,500 minimum wages or about COP$3,000 million (US$1.2 million) (*Diario Oficial* 2005).

The contracts provided tax relief to some of the wealthiest taxpay-ers that the security tax had originally targeted. Liberal Party deputy Simón Gaviria (interview 2011) summarized the contracts' effect as, "making the security tax a discretionary tax, one that is not paid by everyone who is supposed to pay it." However, whenever this concern was raised by the opposition in Congress – mainly the few legislators from Polo Democrático Alternativo (interview with Borja 2011) – the pro-government majority (Conservative, Liberal, and Social National Unity parties) would close ranks to support the measure. They argued that much-needed investment and jobs would be forgone and economic development would be compromised in the absence of the contracts. As a Conservative Party, Senator Óscar Darío Pérez noted, "if we have inves-tors buy insurance, we have to make that commitment valid and insur-ance effective" (*Colprensa* 2009).

Toward the end of Uribe's presidency, sixty-seven companies had signed such contracts with the Ministry of Trade, Industry, and Tourism.

One estimate puts the amount foregone by the government since 2005 at about 10 percent of the annual security tax revenue (*Revista Dinero* 2011a). However, Jorge Humberto Botero (2005), who played a key role in the initiative's approval as Minister of Commerce and has headed a number of prominent business associations, justified the contracts by stating that "the legal system is full of differentiated treatments whose validity is indisputable. Not all homicides receive the same sentence. There are laws that discriminate in favor of minorities. Likewise, it is indisputable that discriminating in favor of investment is praiseworthy." The ability to circumvent the security tax through these contracts remained in place until Uribe's successor eliminated them in December 2010.[10]

In short, strong business–government linkages contributed, first, to garner support behind the wealth tax among business elites and, second, to protect them from less palatable and more comprehensive fiscal reforms down the road. On the one hand, the linkages provided confidence to wealthy taxpayers that the government had their interests in mind. Incorporating prominent members of the business community into cabinet positions facilitated the interaction and communication between the key actors in government and business sectors to enhance transparency and improve accountability regarding how the money was spent (interview with Vélez 2011). Akin to a "Nixon goes to China effect," a president ideologically sympathetic to business interests had better chances of convincing business leaders that the wealth tax would be provisional, oversight over spending would be shared, and that their interests would be protected. The incorporation of earmarking, sunset, and oversight mechanisms into the tax further contributed to allay elites' concerns that their resources would be wasted or spent elsewhere. These factors contributed to convincing the business sectors to accept paying the security tax.

On the other hand, these linkages also contributed to the government's shielding of elites from alternatives that were even less palatable to their interests. Members of the business community in Uribe's cabinet adopted pro-business positions and played a key role in interacting with business leaders through consultation forums and cooperation mechanisms. Even though the government needed to generate additional revenue, it strived to protect economic elites as much as possible given the revenue needs. Although the government could not afford not to tax elites in

---

[10] Decree 4825 of December 29, 2010. The Constitutional Court upheld the measure on April 4, 2011.

2003 following the decision of the Constitutional Court on the VAT, it protected them from subsequent reforms with tax exceptions – through juridical stability contracts – once the urgency for revenue had subsided and security conditions had improved.

Alternative Explanations

Although the nature of business–government linkages offers a strong explanation for the adoption of security taxes in Colombia, alternative explanations should be considered. The following sections examine the role of natural resources, income inequality, and ideology as potential alternatives that do not ultimately hold up to close scrutiny.

Natural Resources

Oil has played an important role for Colombia – the fourth main exporter of oil in Latin America after Venezuela, Mexico, and Brazil. Colombia exports 1.2 percent of the world's total, slightly less than Brazil's 1.5 percent (CIA World Factbook). Colombia first became an oil exporter in the 1980s and then consolidated this position with changes to the oil industry in 2003. The main changes included the adoption of concessions instead of production sharing contracts and the separation of spheres of competence for the state-owned Ecopetrol – which became an autonomous operator with enhanced ability to compete – and the National Hydrocarbons Agency – which became a regulator. In 2007, Ecopetrol also began a public stock offering to attract capital, increase accountability, and become more competitive. The country exports about half of its production, mainly to the United States. Ecopetrol is the fourth largest company in Latin America and among the top fifty oil and gas companies in the world. Since the 1990s, oil has represented between 20 and 30 percent of all exports and has contributed important revenue to the state's coffers (Steiner and Vallejo 2010).

The arrival of Álvaro Uribe to the presidency marked the beginning of a large oil windfall for Colombia (see Figure 4.4). Although the adoption of the first security taxes in 2002 and 2003 preceded the commodity boom that benefited Latin America's commodity exporters, the 2006 and 2009 security taxes were adopted in the middle of Colombia's oil bonanza.

Since 2003, the importance of Colombia's oil revenue grew and foreign direct investment poured into oil and mining. As a result, the currency appreciated considerably during this period by about 60 percent, a typical consequence of countries experiencing large revenue windfalls

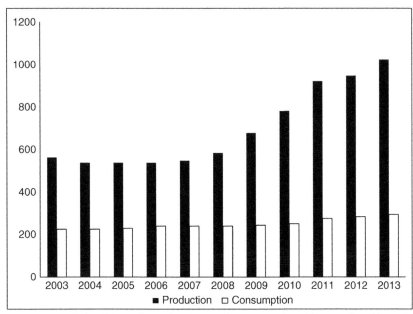

FIGURE 4.4 Colombian oil production and consumption (thousands of barrels per day).
Source: PWC (2014, 7). The Y axis corresponds to thousands of barrels per day.

(often referred to as Dutch disease) (Organization for Economic Cooperation and Development 2015, 9). Until about 2015, the region's state coffers benefited from the natural resource boom, and Colombia was no exception. In 2013, oil revenue amounted to 3.2 percent of GDP (about 23 billion pesos) (Caracol Radio Online 2016) and the government's total revenue corresponded to 16.9 percent of GDP (Organization for Economic Cooperation and Development 2015, 17). This amounts to 19 percent of total government revenue coming from hydrocarbons.

Given the importance of oil for Colombia's economy, this view would expect oil dependence to make it difficult for the Colombian government to adopt wealth taxes on the rich. It would point to oil windfalls as making economic elites less sympathetic to appeals to increase the tax burden.

In a sense, oil did play a role in the adoption of security taxes because fewer resources were available for the government to operate. The decline in oil revenue before Uribe reached office contributed to the fiscal crisis that worsened in 2002. However, although elites were aware of the gravity of the fiscal troubles facing the government, oil played an uneven role in the adoption of the security taxes. The 2002 and 2003 taxes were adopted before oil production and oil prices began to increase, but the taxes in 2006 and 2009 were adopted in the middle of the global commodity boom. It wasn't until after the peak of the hydrocarbons boom in 2013, that the decline in oil revenue left the government with fiscal pressure to balance a growing public deficit. The government responded with the extension of wealth taxes in the 2014 and 2016 tax reforms, but these taxes were no longer earmarked for public safety. In short, the decline in oil revenue played a role in generating the fiscal pressure for the government to look for revenue elsewhere, but the adoption of wealth taxes in 2006 and 2009 during the commodity boom in the region went against expectations derived from resource curse arguments.

Income Inequality

Colombia remains one of the most unequal countries in Latin America and the world. After Honduras, Colombia is the most unequal of the countries considered in this book. To be sure, economic elites in Colombia made equity appeals to influence the debate surrounding the security taxes. These appeals focused mainly on the fact that large sectors of the population were not required to pay taxes and that the business sectors tend to be captive taxpayers. The appeals also focused on the need to expand the base of the security tax, such that even sectors that were not part of the economic elite would contribute their share toward addressing the issue of public safety. Toward this end, business elites pushed for progressivity in the rate structure but with lower thresholds in order to include nonelite sectors.

Although these concerns shaped the debate to some extent (especially in allowing business elites to gain certain prerogatives regarding oversight of the revenue and expenditures) and contributed to making the rates somewhat progressive over time, they did not prevent the government from adopting a fairly ambitious wealth tax. In other words, the government adopted the tax because of the security and fiscal crises it was facing, regardless of business elites' strong appeals toward equitable burden-sharing in Colombia's highly unequal society. If anything, the high inequality in Colombia made it politically very feasible to adopt a tax on the wealthiest citizens – indeed, the measure faced little political opposition among the public compared to attempts to increase the VAT rate or introduce a tax on pensions.

The President's Ideology

The adoption of wealth taxes among elites runs counter to the view that leftist governments will adopt greater and more progressive tax burdens, whereas right-of-center governments will eschew taxation (Stein and Caro 2013). As the Colombian case study has shown, it was precisely the right-of-center orientation of the president that allowed Uribe to establish solid and credible linkages with economic elites. These linkages in turn gave the government the necessary credibility for elites to accept the wealth taxes for security purposes.

This does not mean that taxing elites was the right-of-center governments' preferred course of action. The Uribe government sought to protect economic elites from taxation from the beginning and sided with them in their arguments about the lack of fairness resulting from taxing a narrow tax base. However, given that "law and order" was a priority for the right of center government and that the government needed resources fast to face the fiscal crisis, it was better able to convince elites that it would look after their interests in exchange for accepting the tax. This is something that a left-of-center president would have had a much more difficult time accomplishing, as experiences in Costa Rica and El Salvador suggest.

CONCLUSION

As Colombia's historical difficulty in taxing elites suggests, the government's ability to extract extraordinary resources to finance the security effort was not guaranteed. Instead, a combination of a crisis-based window of opportunity, the president's right-of-center ideology, and strong linkages between the government and economic elites contributed to the adoption of taxes on the wealthy to fund the security effort.

Colombia's different security taxes should be understood as a process rather than discreet intervals independent of each other. The first event setting the process in motion was the combination of dire security conditions with a fiscal crisis that prompted the government to declare a state of internal commotion. Although the crisis did not end business elites' opposition to the government's extractive efforts, it did compel the government to adopt drastic measures leaving elites little choice but to comply. This allowed the government to circumvent potential opposition to the tax in the legislature and overcome the slow pace of alternative revenue-generating measures.

However, the crisis appears as a necessary but not sufficient condition for elite taxation. Without the close ties between business elites and the

Uribe administration, the taxation effort was likely to fail beyond the initial, one-time emergency measure. Subsequent taxes required congressional approval, and opposition among the business groups could have presented a serious obstacle to the government's plan. Indeed, business elites have presented governability problems in the past, as was the case with the acrimonious relationship between Ernesto Samper (1994–1998) and the business community (Schneider 2004).[11] Thus, the nature of business–government relations proved instrumental in extending the measure beyond an emergency palliative, allowing the government to help finance multiyear increases in security spending and the business community to preempt less favorable tax arrangements.

A key feature of the compromise hinged on elites' ability to steer funds toward their spending priorities. Investing in security is a priority for elites over other government services (interview with Mejía 2011). This is because they may rely on private education or healthcare, but they cannot entirely rely on private security since high levels of violence in society directly affect their businesses. Thus, the tax arrangement resulted in a "substitution effect": Elites agree to pay a tax earmarked for security, but receive partial concessions on taxes for the general fund.

---

[11] This contrast is also appreciated in El Salvador where business was unwilling to cooperate with President José Napoleón Duarte's peace efforts (1984–1989) but threw its support behind President Alfredo Cristiani (1989–1994) (Rettberg 2007).

5

Costa Rica's "Soft" Security Taxes

What you don't want to pay in taxes today, you'll have to pay down the road in bodyguards.

Costa Rica's President Óscar Arias[1]

Costa Rica illustrates the case of a diffuse security tax whose incidence spares elites from an onerous burden. The adoption of a security tax in this country is puzzling because the level of violence did not reach levels comparable to other countries in the region with a security crisis, let alone those of its troubled Central American neighbors, El Salvador, Guatemala, and Honduras. Instead, Costa Rica's public-safety deterioration was more sudden than dramatic, in that the homicide rate almost doubled in a handful of years but was comparatively low by regional standards. The homicide rate increased from a relatively low base of 6.4 per 100,000 people in 2000 to 11.3 in 2010 (World Bank 2020). The following year, in 2011, Laura Chinchilla's administration (2010–2014) successfully passed the security tax through Congress. However, in 2015, the Constitutional Tribunal struck it down because it found irregularities in the legislative process that approved it (see Chapter 2). After a brief dip, the rate reached 11.8 in 2016, the year in which the Solís administration attempted to revive the security tax. The rate continued to increase and reached twelve in 2017 when the second tax was adopted. Further, Costa Rica's elites faced higher rates of violent crime than what the average national rates suggest.

---

[1] President Arias words to the leadership of Costa Rica's business associations, as recalled by Roberto Gallardo, former Minister for the Economy and Planning (interview 2016).

COSTA RICA'S SUDDEN DETERIORATION OF PUBLIC SAFETY

Although Costa Rica's national homicide rate might be comparatively low, it masks the more direct exposure of the country's economic elites to violent crime. As Figure 5.1 shows, levels of violent crime in San José, Costa Rica's political capital and economic center, are higher than the national average (Instituto Nacional de Estadistica y Censos [INEC] 1993–2015). In some parts of the capital, homicide rates doubled almost overnight to reach levels more in line with those of other Latin American countries experiencing considerable violent crime.

San José Province, which includes the metropolitan area of the capital city of San José, has a homicide rate above the national rate, with an average of 2.7 homicides per 100,000 people above the rate for the whole country since 2000. Further, certain cantons (municipalities) within the Province of San José have an even greater homicide rate. Two, in particular, San José and Tibás, are among the six most violent cantons in the country (Loria 2014, 12). Although the time series in Figure 5.1 is incomplete for the full period, in Tibás the homicide rate reached 37 per 100,000 in 2010, more than twice the national rate. In the San José Canton, the rate reached twenty-seven in 2008.

Additionally, levels of violent crime also increased sharply in some parts of the capital. In the metropolitan cantons of San José, Alajuela, and Desamparados, the number of homicides went from twenty-seven to forty-three in San José canton, fourteen to twenty-seven in Alajuela, and twenty-two to forty-three in Desamparados between 2013 and 2014. This represents an increase in homicide rates from nine to fifteen in San Jose, from six to eleven in Alajuela, and eleven to twenty-one in Desamparados – the three most populous cantons of the country comprising about a fifth of the total population.[2]

As a result of this geographic concentration, the country's economic elites have not escaped the consequences of the increase in violent crime. Instead, they have experienced the cost of violence directly in San José. According to a study by the World Bank (2011, 4), violent crime has affected the wealthiest sectors more than other groups in society. This is the case in Central America in general and in Costa Rica in particular, regardless of the type of crime. In Costa Rica, a person in the top quintile of income distribution is almost twice as likely to become a victim of violent crime, according to this study.

---

[2] Homicide rates were calculated by the author with population data from the 2011 census published by Instituto Nacional de Estadistica y Censos (INEC), X Censo de Poblacion y

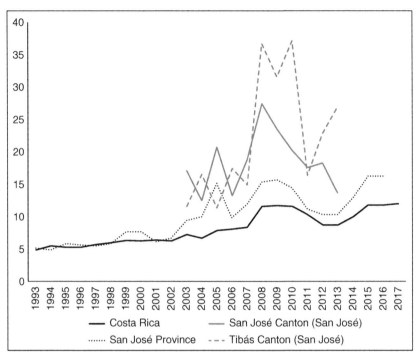

FIGURE 5.1 Homicide rate per 100,000 people.
Source: For Costa Rica, see World Bank's *World Development Indicators* Online, 2020. For San José Province, see Instituto Nacional de Estadistica y Censos (INEC) various years. For data for San José Canton and Tiba Canton, see Loría (2014).

The doubling of violent crime rates between 2006 and 2010 took place while Laura Chinchilla was Minister of Public Safety and Minister of Peace and Justice in the second administration of President Óscar Arias (2006–2010), who promised to hire 1,000 additional police each year of his administration. Worried about public safety as an issue in the looming presidential campaign, she proposed the security tax to address the public-safety crisis of 2008–2009 (interviews with Gallardo 2016 and Zúñiga 2016).[3]

VI de Vivienda 2011, Cuadro 1: Costa Rica: Población total por sexo, total de viviendas por ocupación y promedio de ocupantes según provincia, cantón y distrito (Instituto Nacional de Estadística y Censos [INEC] 2012). Homicide data from www.bbc.com/mundo/noticias/2015/10/151027_costa_rica_violencia_narcotrafico_homicidios_suiza_centroamerica_paraiso_seguridad_lv

[3] Chinchilla had promised not to raise taxes during her campaign, but reversed course once in office.

The sudden deterioration in public safety in Costa Rica came about in the context of a difficult fiscal situation for the country. As in the Colombian case, Costa Rica faced serious fiscal challenges at the time that the security taxes were first being discussed in 2011. In Costa Rica, for example, the government had been seeking to plug a large fiscal deficit since Arias's second presidency (2006–2010). In spite of the urgency of finding a way to improve the country's fiscal health, the reforms have languished in Congress for years.

Costa Rica has struggled with large fiscal deficits since 2009. The deficits are mainly a result of countercyclical policies adopted to counter the consequences of the global financial crisis in 2008–2009 (interview with Zúñiga 2016). As a response to the crisis, the government increased current spending, including wages and transfers. Since 2009, government spending has increased from 17.4 to 21 percent of GDP (Moody's 2017).

The persistent fiscal deficits have had important consequences for Costa Ricans. The government has been forced to make cuts in infrastructure and education. In particular, cuts in education are significant because of the constitutional mandate to spend at least 8 percent of GDP for that purpose.[4] In 2017, the government spent 7.6 percent, and in 2018, it cut education expenditures further to 7.4 percent of GDP. About 32 percent of government revenue goes to service the debt (*La Nación* 2017b). Due to the sustained fiscal deficits, Costa Rica's debt has quickly increased since 2008. In that year, gross general government debt amounted to 20 percent of GDP. By 2016, government debt had doubled to 41 percent (*Reuters* 2017).

As shown in Figure 5.2, the country's central government deficit grew to reach 5.3 percent of GDP in 2015. Although the government managed to reduce the deficit by 0.6 percent of GDP in 2016 by adopting measures aimed at reducing government waste, the deficit for 2017 exceeded 6 percent of GDP. In the absence of meaningful tax and spending reforms, the fiscal deficit is expected to continue to increase over the next several years due to the burden of servicing the debt and spending constraints (*Reuters* 2017).

---

[4] Costa Rica modified its Constitution (Art. 78) in 1997 to incorporate mandatory spending in education of 6 percent of GDP, and it reached this goal in 2009. In 2010, it raised mandatory share of GDP 8 percent (Leitón 2013).

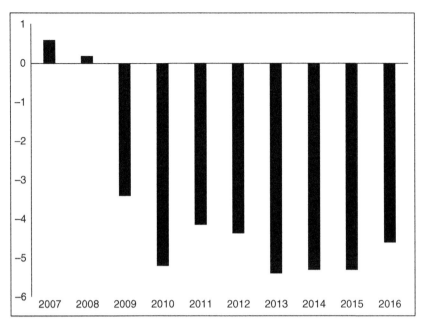

FIGURE 5.2 Costa Rica's central government fiscal balance.
Source: Costa Rica's Central Bank.

In January 2017, for example, the credit rating agency Fitch Ratings downgraded Costa Rica's long-term currency bonds to "BB" from "BB+," citing "Costa Rica's deteriorating debt dynamics driven by large fiscal deficits and continued institutional gridlock preventing progress on reforms to correct fiscal imbalances" (*Reuters* 2017). The following month, Moody's, another credit rating agency also downgraded Costa Rica's government bond rating from Ba1 to Ba2 and maintained a negative outlook on the rating. Moody's included in its rationale that the country's foreign currency debt now amounts to 37 percent of all government debt, up from less than 30 percent in 2011 (Moody's 2017).

ELITES' RELUCTANCE TO ACCEPT A GREATER TAX BURDEN

As in Colombia and elsewhere in Latin America, economic elites in Costa Rica were opposed to shouldering a greater tax burden and were very public in their opposition to both the 2011 and the 2017 taxes. Both the Union of Costa Rican Chambers and Associations of the Private Sector (Unión Costarricense de Cámaras y Asociaciones del Sector Empresarial Privado, UCCAEP), Costa Rica's peak business association, and its affiliates expressed their opposition to any negotiation with the government regarding increasing taxes. Instead, they expressed the need to reduce government spending as a necessary condition to discuss additional taxes.

For example, Juan Rafael Lizano, president of the National Chamber of Agriculture (Cámara Nacional de Agricultura y Agroindustria), stated that they would "not allow additional taxes until the government approves administrative and legal measures that show a decrease in government spending, which it has not done at all" (Gutiérrez 2016). Similarly, Francisco Llobet, president of the Costa Rican Chamber of Commerce (Cámara de Comercio de Costa Rica), stated that "new taxes cannot be approved before the government takes decisive steps toward the reduction and rationalization of public spending, which is responsible for the public finance crisis the country is in the middle of" (*CentralAmericaData.com* 2016). Further, the Costa Rican Chamber of Industries (Cámara de Industrias de Costa Rica) stated that "the solution to the fiscal deficit must be comprehensive, taking into account both expenditures and revenue" (*CentralAmericaData .com* 2016).

The UCCAEP president, Ronald Jiménez, urged the government to go after informality and expand the tax base before adding more taxes to the companies that are in the formal sector, already pay taxes, and generate jobs. He also criticized the different government's salary raises to government employees (*CentralAmericaData.com* 2014). According to Luis Mesalles, director of the egg-producing company La Yema Dorada, as well as UCCAEP's vice president and representative before the President's Council for Competitiveness and Innovation, the private sector was very concerned about the role that the tax on corporations would play in encouraging informality, which he characterized as a major problem in Costa Rica (interview with Mesalles 2016).

At the same time that economic elites expressed their opposition to a greater tax burden, they recognized the need for improved public safety. According to Pedro Morales, chief economic advisor of the Costa Rican Chamber of Industry, there was generalized concern about public safety in 2008–2010, right before the 2011 security tax was approved (interview with Morales 2016). The Chamber of Industry's position was to reduce spending before raising taxes, including measures that set a limit to government salaries. Morales also suggested that even though informality was a big issue for them that was left out of the equation when the government proposed adopting the security tax, the importance that the Chamber of Industry placed on public safety was the reason why they were willing to enter negotiations with the government (interview with Morales 2016).[5]

In short, the business sectors were well aware of the government's fiscal difficulties but were unsympathetic to the causes of the government deficit. They pointed to the largesse of the Arias administration before the financial crisis that took form as an explosion of personal expenses and salaries in the public sector (interview with Mesalles 2016).

THE MISTRUST OF COSTA RICA'S LEFTIST ADMINISTRATIONS

There was considerable mistrust in the relations between economic elites and the governments of Laura Chinchilla and Luis Guillermo Solís, both of whom had leftist reputations to overcome in the eyes of economic elites. Chinchilla represented the social-democratic Partido Liberación Nacional (PLN) and served as Minister of Public Safety and as Minister of Peace and Justice in Óscar Arias' second administration (2006–2010). However, because of the countercyclical policies adopted by Arias in response to the 2008 global financial crisis, her government was seen as providing continuity to the rampant expansion of government spending.

Solís was a member of the Partido Acción Ciudadana (PAC), a center-left party that stands for citizen participation, transparency, anticorruption, and equality of opportunity. Neither of these administrations adopted a law-and-order, tough-on-crime approach combined with fiscal austerity – the preferred course of action of economic elites – comparable to right-of-center leaders in the region.

The government's coalition partners contributed to fuel this mistrust. For example, the Solís administration mostly relied on leftist parties such as the Frente Amplio to govern. Frente Amplio was created in 2004 and incorporated members of the old communist party. Running on an anti-neoliberal platform, it became the third largest faction in Congress in the 2014 elections, mainly representing the popular sectors.[6]

The Frente Amplio's program was diametrically opposed to the interests of business elites. For example, José Ramírez, Frente Amplio congressman and member of the finance committee in the Legislative Assembly,

---

[5] In those negotiations, they pushed for the exemption of micro and small enterprises from paying the security tax.

[6] Its electoral strength comes mainly from the provinces of Guanacaste, Puntarenas, and Limón.

expressed strong skepticism of the business sectors' motives. He blamed them for the trend toward privatizing everything in Costa Rica and the accompanying strategy of not investing in government services. In his words, "This is clearly visible in public safety, which they are hoping to privatize as well" (interview with Ramírez 2016).

In Ramírez's view, public safety was an important problem, but the major fiscal deficit had become much more pressing. The Frente Amplio was in favor of the tax on corporations because it was a way to bring corporations in line: Of the 700,000 registered corporations, 400,000 are inactive. He said that the private sector's goal, especially the Chamber of Industry, wants to "turn Costa Rica into an off-shore fiscal paradise such as Panama" (interview with Ramírez 2016).

Rather than cutting government services and pensions, as the business sectors propose, the Frente Amplio advocated cracking down on tax evasion. According to Ramírez's estimates, fiscal fraud amounts to about 8 percent of GDP, and "addressing tax evasion would be more than enough to cover the fiscal deficit of 6% of GDP and even invest the remainder in education or infrastructure." The Frente Amplio agrees that pensions should be cut, but these should be "luxury pensions" or those of white-collar executives, rather than those of the average worker. "The reality is that even cutting pensions one cannot close the fiscal gap, so raising taxes is really the only way" (interview with Ramírez 2016).

The Frente Amplio representative accused the right-wing parties, the PUSC and Movimiento Libertario, of wanting to reach a breaking point, hoping to strain tax and other negotiations with the government to the point of failure. This would leave Costa Rica no option but to resort to the International Monetary Fund after a major fiscal crisis, which would lead to the deep cuts in government programs they have been seeking.

OVERCOMING MISTRUST THROUGH LINKAGES

Sharp ideological differences are not unusual in Latin America, but linkages between the government and elites contribute to bridging political divides. In Costa Rica's left-of-center governments, these linkages only partially existed. In particular, there was one main forum for interaction: the President's Council for Competitiveness and Innovation, in which representatives of UCCAEP met monthly with government officials. There were three secondary forums, respectively, chaired by the ministers of finance, social policy, and labor: the Competitiveness Council, the Council for Innovation and Human Talent, and the Alliance for Employment (interview with Mesalles 2016).[7]

However, other linkages that contribute to overcome mistrust toward the left-of-center administrations were lacking. For example, neither the Chinchilla nor the Solís administration was prone to involving business people in decision-making processes, let alone formally as part of the administration.[8] This was an important consideration for the business sectors because they felt that the government was favoring other groups instead.

The business sectors also lamented that the government was not receptive to involving them in the oversight of the security tax. The government required instead that reports be generated by the ministry of public safety and turned over to an auditing office of the legislature every six months. However, since economic elites were not involved in the oversight of the resources, they were skeptical that the reports would constrain government behavior.[9]

For its part, the government dismissed the business sector's arguments as disingenuous and uncooperative. As a member of President Solís' cabinet put it, "the business sectors in Costa Rica are always reluctant to pay taxes. Their main argument is that they are captive taxpayers and that they already pay more than they should. Even if they come around to accepting a tax reform, they always find a reason why they should get preferential treatment, regardless of the sector of the economy they are in. Their solution is to cut spending and they are deploying an army of opinion leaders to sway the public against any reform" (interview with cabinet member 2016).

Due to the lack of strong linkages that would allow for a closer understanding of divergent positions and contribute to finding common ground, the relationship between the government and the business sectors instead became confrontational. In the absence of a presence of business elites inside the administration and of champions that the business

---

[7] As in most countries, some businesspeople have direct line to government ministers and even the president.

[8] The Vice President Ana Helena Chacón is the only member with moderate ties to business in the Solís administration, since she was involved in the negotiations of the Central American Free Trade Agreement with the United States (interview with Constantino Urcuyo, former PUSC legislator and presidential adviser, 2016).

[9] In an interview, a PAC legislator expressed skepticism that the report would do much for accountability, pointing out that the Ministry of Public Safety can always find ways to switch expenditures around and report what is convenient because it all goes to the Ministry's general tax fund.

sectors could informally lobby to advance their interests, the formal forums often became an arena for acrimony.

The leadership of UCCAEP was very critical of the way the governments – especially the Solís administration – handled the tax negotiations with the business sectors. For example, business leaders criticized the administration of President Solís for trying to revive tax measures from the Chinchilla administration, such as the security tax, toward the second half of his four-year presidential term. "It took him two years to resuscitate the tax measure that had been struck down by the Sala IV of the Tribunal. Since they have wasted so much time, now they are trying to rush everything through Congress before the end of the term, and the reforms are mostly recycled. The government even brings technocrats from the IMF to put pressure on legislatures, but that is not how things should work. Overall, the President has shown very little disposition to negotiate with the private sector" (interview with Mesalles 2016).

This lack of trust also affected the effectiveness of the design features of the tax that were meant to assuage elites' concerns about how the government would use those resources, such as earmarking for public safety. The vice president of UCCAEP, Luis Mesalles, called it a fiction that the revenue from the security taxes would end up increasing expenditures in public safety because the tax revenue is fungible. He pointed out that in reality, the government chooses where it wants to spend the money depending on the priorities of the day: "For example, the 8% that the constitution says it should spend on education, whenever it's convenient for the government, it says that nobody is required to do something impossible, and it does not fulfil its obligation, even if the earmark is mandated by the constitution" (interview with Mesalles 2016).

Given the leftist governments' positions, the business sectors required more than monthly meetings to overcome their mistrust. As Edna Camacho, former vice minister of finance and a researcher at the think tank Academia Centroamericana, put it, "Few businesspeople oppose spending more in public safety, but the security tax is really about a bigger discussion of whether the government should cut spending before raising taxes. The unions are very much opposed to cutting pensions. The government has been reluctant to cut spending, so the business sectors see the government as favoring the unions even in times of fiscal crisis" (interview with Camacho 2016). The government has been reluctant to reduce spending because doing so would be impopular, but also because it would mostly affect government bureaucrats, an important source of support for the left.

With leftist governments more attuned to the demands of other interests groups and without mechanisms to overcome mistrust other than formal meetings, economic elites turned to other strategies to influence policy, including public opinion campaigns and nurturing a right-wing libertarian party, the Movimiento Libertario, as a champion of small government and low taxes (interviews with Gallardo 2016 and Rodríguez 2016).[10]

As Fernando Rodríguez, Vice Minister for Revenue in the Ministry of Finance, points out, business elites have relied on the Movimiento Libertario as a lightning rod against any attempt to tax the wealthy. The Movimiento Libertario is perhaps the only libertarian party with representation in Congress in Latin America. Although its level of support is low, with only a handful of representatives in the legislature,[11] Costa Rica's parliamentary rules give the party the ability to block reforms through filibustering (interview with Rodríguez 2016).

Representative Otto Guevara Guth, the leader of the Movimiento Libertario and several times its presidential candidate, has become a major defender of the business sectors by opposing the tax on corporations. He has made a name for himself defending them from what he calls the "voracious tax authority." Although his party does not have large representation in Congress, legislative rules allow for filibustering. Guevara has mastered the art of introducing hundreds of motions to delay votes (Solano 2016). Indeed, his strategy has been to derail tax initiatives by holding them up in order to force the government to reach political agreements.[12] His goal is to allow for a fast-track discussion of tax bills, in exchange of concessions from the government (interview with Guevara Guth 2016).

Guevara Guth justified this strategy as a consequence of the government's intransigence and unwillingness to try to reconcile "important ideological differences regarding the role of the state, how to fund it, and its civil liberties." He added that, "The government has its priorities upside down. It doesn't need more resources. It must redirect funds from

---

[10] In the words of Edna Camacho, former Vice Minister of Finance, "When the PLN and the PUSC were Costa Rica's two main parties, their platforms on the center-left and center-right became almost indistinguishable over time. This opened up room in the political spectrum for a right-of-center party, which became Movimiento Libertario."

[11] Movimiento Libertario won nine seats in the 2010 elections and three in the 2014 elections.

[12] According to Frente Amplio Representative José Ramírez, Otto Guevara is known for engaging in long monologues about the Beetles in order to endlessly delay the vote (interview with Ramírez 2016).

the public universities toward public safety and allow the private sector to run higher education" (interview with Guevara Guth 2016).

Ultimately, the Movimiento Libertario allowed for the approval of the security tax because of its tough-on-crime, law-and-order position. It considered public safety a priority worth investing in – unlike public education – but advocated the reorganization of the police under a single chain of command for the entire country and arming the police appropriately since only 12,000 police have to protect all of Costa Rica, according to Guevara. The Movimiento Libertario favors the legalization of recreational drugs as part of the solution to the public-safety problem. Guevara also suggested that the nonarmed forces tradition in Costa Rica has prevented the proper equipping of police.

Because of this support for law-and-order policies, the Movimiento Libertario allowed the 2011 tax to pass, even though it considered that the tax affected micro and small enterprises. Since the public was so concerned about public safety, Guevara did not further block the measure in the legislature. However, the 2011 security tax would live a short life. In the end, "a concerned citizen" – as Guevara put it – took the measure to court, and the tribunal ruled that proper legislative procedure had not been followed. In Guevara's words, "the court struck it down, which is only natural given the government's intransigence" (interview with Guevara 2016).

THE CONSEQUENCES OF THE LACK OF STRONG LINKAGES

This arms-length relationship between the government and economic elites had consequences for the type of taxes that were adopted. For the 2011 security tax, the best that the Chinchilla government could do was to adopt a flat tax on corporations that would end up serving more as a "control measure" than a real revenue-generating mechanism. In the words of Vice Minister of Finance Rodríguez, "the tax is useful because it helps us rein in the inactive corporations – about 57% of those registered – which are only a front for tax evasion. But the revenue, while helpful, only represents about 0.3% of GDP" (interview with Rodríguez 2016).

Further, the collection of the 2011 tax was assigned to the Ministry of Justice, which held the registry of corporations. Guillermo Zúñiga, Minister of Finance in Óscar Arias' administration, pointed out that it had been a mistake, from a revenue collection perspective, to assign the collection of the 2011 tax to the Ministry of Justice (interview with Zúñiga 2016). The problem is that the Ministry of Justice does not have the ability to oversee and audit fiscal issues. This contributed to the tax on corporations not having any major consequences for economic elites and for revenue collection. In the words of former Minister Zúñiga, "The corporations that did not pay the tax do not face any real consequences unless they need to register with the government a transaction involving their assets, and all they need to do is to pay whatever is due. This was a mistake" (interview with Zúñiga 2016).

The Solís administration was unable to make the security tax any more palatable to elites after the court ruled it could no longer be collected in 2016, especially after violent crime rates declined somewhat between 2011 and 2015 (interview with Mesalles 2016).[13] However, given the size of the fiscal deficit, the difficulty to reach alternative agreements to address it, and the appeal of earmarking the tax revenue for a public good that few social sectors would oppose, the government pushed for its renewal, almost verbatim. Except that this time around attention would be paid to the following proper legislative procedure.

For the Ministry of Public Safety, the foregone tax revenue was considerable. As the Vice Minister for Public Safety, Bernardita Marín, stated: "the tax on corporations collects about $40 billion colones, more or less. This represents about 18 percent of the ministry's budget. When the tax was eliminated due to the Court's ruling, the ministry was significantly affected. Currently, without the tax revenue, and with the fiscal deficit of 6 percent of GDP, the ministry's budget is at the same level it was in 2014. Because of the elimination of the tax and the dire fiscal situation, the ministry has had to freeze police hires since" (interview with Marín 2016).

However, opposition to the renewal of the tax did not recede. Excluded from the oversight process in the law for the 2011 tax, business elites remained concerned about the destination of the funds. Rather than providing a detailed account of how the tax revenue had been spent, the Ministry of Public Safety very generally reported a subset of expenditures that exceeded the agency's yearly budget. In particular, the police

---

[13] As a business executive confided, "The perception of public safety among the public improved after the first few years of the tax, but it has deteriorated again since. Myself and many in the business community have changed our ways in response to crime. If I'm in a different part of the country for the day, I spend the night there rather than driving back to San José at night. The private protection of security is now booming here. In Puerto Limón on the Atlantic coast, the country's most important port, violence has really deteriorated because of drug trafficking activity" (interview with business executive, 2016).

generally reported a few specifics, whereas the Ministry of Justice did not assign any specific subaccount for the revenue and could not point out how exactly the funds were spent.

For example, the police reported that in 2012, the first year the tax was collected, the ¢17,758 million in revenue was spent buying a lot and building the regional offices of the anti-narcotics police (Policía de Control de Drogas, PCD) in Alajuela, uniforms, and spare parts for police cars (Rodríguez 2017a). In 2013, the ¢30,362 million in revenue were used toward the purchase of thirty-two cars and eighty-five SUVs, as well as to cover the deficit due to excess spending (Rodríguez 2017a). In 2014, the ¢34,380 million are vaguely reported to have gone toward materials, operational expenditures, and durable goods (Rodríguez 2017a). In 2015, the ¢37,506 million went toward paying rent for sixty-two delegations and prevention programs for citizen security, covering insurance for police, police uniforms, and durable goods (weapons, boat motors, among others). The attorney general said that the funds went into the general pool and in this sense were used to pay for everything (Rodríguez 2017a).

This lack of specificity and transparency in the expenditures gave some business sectors and their representatives in Congress ammunition for opposing the renewal of the tax. They again conditioned their support to the government's commitment to reining in public spending, such as in public pensions. In the words of Armando González, Editorial Director at Grupo La Nación – a media conglomerate that owns the newspaper by the same name – "we obviously support public safety, but teachers' pensions are out of control. They earn 100 percent of the last year of employment and on top of that they get raises every year. Every time workers receive a raise, pension recipients also get a raise. Additionally, 8 percent of GDP has to go directly to education, as mandated by the Constitution. Then another chunk of revenue goes to servicing the debt. These are burdens that once adopted never go away in Costa Rica and we are left with about 8% of revenue for discretionary spending" (interview with González 2016).[14]

---

[14] González illustrated the problem with an example: "A friend of mine retired at 55 as a university professor with a very generous pension. He was then hired by *La Nación* newspaper, from where he retired again. I joke with him that he's the most expensive Costa Rican in the country, a luxury good, if you will. But the reality is that there are many people like that and that costs a lot to the social security system" (interview with González 2016).

This does not mean that business elites were dismissive of the role of public education.[15] When asked about what explained the differences between the levels of violent crime in Costa Rica compared to its Central American neighbors, different members of the economic elite consistently included the education system, the welfare state, and the good job the police were doing. However, they still considered that the government's spending was unsustainable at current levels.

These concerns were shared by the main right-of-center party, the Party of the Social-Christian Union (Partido de la Unidad Social Cristiana, PUSC). As Pedro Muñoz, President of the PUSC and founding partner of the Central America-regional law firm Arias y Muñoz,[16] put it, "the government has its priorities backwards. The first step has to be to rein in public expenditures, which are out of control. Second, governments have to show results. You can't keep asking for money without showing you are effective at governing. In order to show results, governments have to generate growth and improve public safety, for example. After you've fulfilled these two conditions then you can ask for more money through taxes" (interview with Muñoz 2016).

However, economic elites' opposition to renewing the tax was ameliorated because it was earmarked for public safety. As González put it, "The tax for public safety is different. Gupo La Nación supports the tax on corporations because the revenue is earmarked for public safety. In other words, the earmarking for public safety puts it in a different category for us, one which we can support" (interview with González 2016).

For the adoption of the 2017 tax, a deterioration of public safety contributed to reduce opposition. The Minister of Public Safety made repeated calls for Congress to provide additional funds toward fighting organized crime. In October 2016, for example, Minister Gustavo Mota promised to resign within a month if the legislature failed to bring additional resources. He estimated that the country needed at least 18,000 police (3,000 more) to achieve the desired ratio of 300 per 100,000 people. Mota lobbied for including an additional 1,000 police as part of the tax bill because otherwise the proposal only allowed for capital expenses (*La Nación* 2016).

---

[15] Except for the Movimiento Libertario, which did advocate for allowing the private sector to take over education.

[16] The firm Arias y Muñoz, which had offices across Central America, split in November 2016, and the office in Costa Rica partnered with the global firm Dentons to form Dentons and Muñoz. Pedro Muñoz remained a founding partner in the new firm.

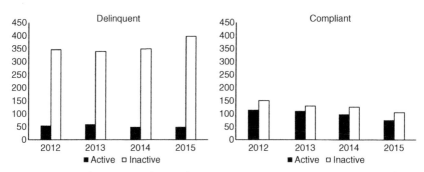

FIGURE 5.3 Delinquent and compliant corporations, 2011 Security Tax (thousands of corporations).
Note: Y axis indicates thousands of corporations.
Source: Cerdas and Sequeira (2016).

The right-of-center parties remained opposed to the tax in spite of these considerations. The PUSC first attempted to make changes to forgive any outstanding unpaid taxes to delinquent corporation. Following the government's opposition to the change, PUSC eventually opposed the tax, arguing that it was poorly designed because the number of delinquent corporations was high.[17] As Figure 5.3 shows, there were close to 450,000 corporations that owed part or all of the tax by 2015. Of those that owed the tax, more than 80 percent corresponded to inactive corporations.

Representative Gerardo Vargas, leader of PUSC in Congress, said that since inactive firms have to pay the tax, it was "unjust and not progressive at all" (Sequeira 2017). Representative Fabricio Alvarado, from Restauración Nacional, stated that the tax was a mistake because the government cannot guarantee that the funds "be used responsibly to address public safety" (Sequeira 2017).

The Costa Rican legislature approved the security tax on January 9, 2017. The tax was adopted with a vote of forty legislators in favor and ten against (most of the PUSC legislators and all of Movimiento Libertario) (Arrieta 2017).[18] According to Roberto Gallardo, former Minister

[17] This motion would have meant that the government would forgo the revenue owed by 55 percent of corporations (both active and inactive) required to pay the tax between 2012 and 2015. According to the Ministry of Finance, active corporations owed ¢41,697 million and inactive corporations owed ¢138,644 million, which combined amounts to half a percent of GDP (Cerdas and Sequeira 2016).

[18] Representatives from the evangelical parties (Restauración Nacional, Alianza Demócrata Cristiana, Accesibilidad sin Exclusión) also voted against.

for the Economy and Planning in Laura Chinchilla's Administration, the security tax on corporations is seen by Costa Ricans as affecting only the wealthy, which is why it enjoys broad acceptance (interview with Gallardo 2016). As Maureen Clarke, the leader of the PLN in Congress, emphasized after the 2017 tax was adopted, "the tax is a major achievement for the country, because the wealthy will finance programs to address insecurity that Costa Ricans experience every day" (Sequeira 2017).

Alternative Explanations

Alternative explanations are less helpful in accounting for the adoption of the security taxes in Costa Rica. That country's nonfiscal revenue is low in comparative perspective, so this was not a relevant factor toward the adoption of elite taxes. Contrary to other Latin American countries where governments rely heavily on hydrocarbons for revenue, Costa Rica is not an oil-producing country and relies mostly on renewable energy. Instead, in 2011, President Chinchilla adopted a moratorium on petroleum exploration and extraction until 2014, citing the constitutional right to a healthy environment and the risks associated with disasters such as BP's oil spill in the Gulf of Mexico in 2010 (*Gaceta Oficial de Costa Rica* 2011). In 2014, President Solís extended the ban until 2021. Without oil production in its territory, Costa Rica does not have the pressures associated with the "curse" of resource-dependent countries and the reluctance to pay taxes because of the country's natural wealth or foreign aid (e.g., Brautigam et al. 2008; Morrison 2009; Ross 2012).

Similarly, although Costa Rica ranks in the middle of the region in terms of income inequality, it remains a highly unequal society: Its Gini coefficient is 49. In this sense, it is not very different from the rest of Latin American countries, whether they adopted security taxes or not. As in other countries, Costa Rican economic elites have made it a point to highlight the unfairness of narrow tax bases, but the government adopted a security tax in spite of these considerations.

President's Ideology

This perspective's expectation is that left-of-center governments will tend to adopt greater tax burdens and more progressive taxes, compared to their right-of-center counterparts. In the Costa Rican case, the leftist ideology of presidents Chinchilla and Solís contributed to pursue tax increases as the solution to the country's fiscal woes, as opposed to making major cuts to government spending. In this sense, the behavior of the Costa Rican presidents conforms with expectations for the left in government.

Finally, although presidents Chinchilla and Solís are not considered populist, the left-of-center ideology became an impediment to achieve the presidents' goals. In both cases, the adoption of limited taxes was a result of the governments' inability to overcome mistrust among the business sectors. Stronger linkages between the government and elites would have contributed to overcome mistrust, but the presidents' ideology, constituencies, and government coalitions were important sources of concern for economic elites.

CONCLUSION

The security taxes in Costa Rica were adopted due to a combination of a sudden increase in the levels of violent crime and a severe fiscal gap. Although the average levels of violent crime in Costa Rica were much lower than those in other Central American countries, the geographic concentration of violence in San José resulted in economic elites' greater exposure than the national average suggested.

In the absence of a right-of-center president or strong government–elite linkages, the tax adopted was more a control mechanism to avoid evasion than a real burden on economic elites. The earmarking of the funds for security purposes helped ameliorate business sectors' concerns about increases in taxes, but it was nowhere close to making a real difference in closing the government deficit of 6 percent of GDP. Because of the mistrust of the private sector that the left-of-center governments would be a good steward with the tax revenue and the concerns that government spending was out of control, reaching an agreement between the government and business elites remained elusive.

Although Costa Rica's political spectrum remains fairly narrow, the leftist governments were seen as partial to the interests of unions and unwilling to meet the business sectors partway in finding an acceptable solution to the deficit. The business sectors were generally well-organized and effective in generating a public relations campaign to influence the public, as well as a narrative that different representatives echoed in an orchestrated fashion.

The business sectors' concern for public safety compared to other goods was a central aspect convincing them not to block the tax on corporations. Elites made the distinction between public safety as something that needed to be reinforced, with some sectors calling for tougher approaches on crime, and other public goods, such as education or healthcare, where they thought the government needed to make more room for the private sector. In the end, however, the tax was not a particularly onerous burden for them to pay.

6

El Salvador's Failed and Diffuse Security Taxes

It's a contribution in which all Salvadoreans will participate. I know that it will affect the majority of the population, telephone users. I wish I had a magic wand not to affect anybody. Police and soldiers are dying and sacrificing for the population and it is fair that everybody contribute against crime.

El Salvador's President Salvador Sánchez Cerén[1]

While the Costa Rican case is helpful to illustrate the challenges facing left-of-center governments without strong linkages to business elites, it does not provide analytical leverage to distinguish between the role of a relatively low-violence security environment and the medium-strength linkages between elites. Toward this end, the following pages discuss elite taxes for public safety in El Salvador, a context with much higher levels of violence than Costa Rica but similar types of linkages between elites.

The Salvadorian case is also analytically helpful because it experienced variation over time regarding the linkages between the government and economic elites. Whereas a left-of-center FMLN government first pursued the adoption of a security tax in 2011 and failed because of an acrimonious relationship with the business sectors, a broader governing coalition of parties anchored by the leftist FMLN was successful in adopting a security tax in 2015. Thus, similar to Costa Rica, El Salvador is another case of the adoption of a more diffuse security tax that does not exclusively target elites. That a similar outcome took place in El Salvador, a country with considerably higher levels of violent crime than Costa Rica,

---

[1] President Sánchez Cerén's justification of the security tax, addressing legislators' concerns about the incidence of the tax.

suggests that the linkages are responsible for the diffused security tax rather than the levels of violent crime.

EL SALVADOR'S HIGH LEVELS OF VIOLENCE

Between 1979 and 1992, El Salvador experienced a devastating civil war. An armed coup in October 1979 marked the start of the conflict between the military junta and a collection of left-wing guerrilla forces that came together under the umbrella organization Farabundo Martí National Liberation Front (FMLN). The conflict was protracted and bloody: According to UN reports, more than 75,000 people died in the confrontations (United Nations 1993).

In the aftermath of the Civil War, violent crime was extremely high throughout the 1990s, reaching a peak in 1995 of 142 homicides per 100,000 people. As Figure 6.1 shows, violent crime declined somewhat since that peak, and throughout the 2000s, homicide rates fluctuated between 50 and 70 per 100,000 people. Between 2000 and 2011, when the first security tax attempted unraveled, El Salvador experienced a 42 percent increase in the homicide rate, from a trough of 49 homicides per 100,000 people in 2002. After a brief dip in 2012 and 2013 to rates of 41 and 40, respectively – the lowest rate since the end of the Civil War – violence spiked again and the homicide rate more than doubled to reach 105 in 2015.

Violent crime has affected all sectors of the population, including El Salvador's economic elites. Not only do they face the risk of kidnappings but also firms of all sizes are victims of extortion by organized crime, especially gangs such as MS-13. According to the World Bank (2011, 6), the costs of violence to the economy exceeded 9 percent of GDP in 2011. In addition to the personal safety risk, some industries are reported to pay between 10 and 25 percent of their monthly revenue to meet extortion demands (Gagne 2015).

El Salvador's business elites are concentrated in the capital, San Salvador, which is not only the most affluent part of the country but also the area with the highest violent crime rates. As Figure 6.2 suggests, the highest levels of violent crime are mainly concentrated in the metropolitan areas of San Salvador, Santa Ana, and San Miguel, the country's three largest cities (Carcach 2008, 34). However, the metropolitan area of San Salvador – including the municipalities of Antiguo Cuscatlán, Apopa, Ayutuxtepeque, Ciudad Delgado, Cuscatancingo, Ilopango, Mejicanos, Nejapa, San Marcos, San Martín, San Salvador,

FIGURE 6.1 El Salvador's homicide rate (per 100,000 people).
Source: World Bank (2020).

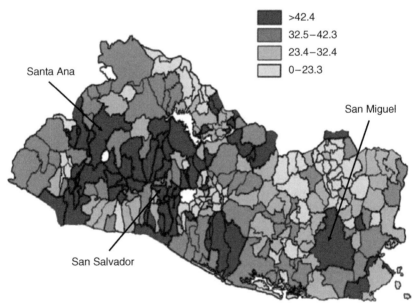

FIGURE 6.2 El Salvador's homicide rate (per 100,000 people) by municipality, 2002–2007.
Source: Adapted from Carcach (2008, 35).

Santa Tecla, Soyapango, and Tonacatepeque – concentrates the highest levels of violent crime. In 2011, when the first security tax was first attempted, 29 percent of all homicides took place in the Department of San Salvador (Ministerio de Justicia y Seguridad Pública 2014).

EL SALVADOR'S FISCAL SITUATION

As with most Latin American countries, El Salvador's fiscal position has been far from comfortable. In the years leading to the first attempt to adopt an elite tax on public safety in 2011, the country's fiscal balance had deteriorated as a consequence of the 2008–2009 global recession, which decreased remittances by 9.5 percent and exports by 16.7 percent, resulting in an economic contraction of 3.1 percent of GDP (Pérez Trejo 2014, 8). In line with worldwide efforts to soften the impact of the crisis through countercyclical measures, the government increased spending in subsidies for public transportation, electricity, and gas, but especially in public employees' salaries.

As a result, the government's fiscal situation has deteriorated since the crisis. While the government's public deficit had remained under – 3 percent of GDP between 2005 and 2008 (see the left panel of Figure 6.3), the deficit reached – 5.7 percent in 2009 (Pérez Trejo 2014, 9). As the right panel of Figure 6.3 shows, the country's levels of public debt also reflected this situation. El Salvador's debt as a share of GDP had remained below 40 percent of GDP between 2005 and 2008, but deteriorated to 50 percent in 2009. In the aftermath of the crisis, the gap between the government's revenue and expenditures became wider and the country's public debt continued to escalate (Pérez Trejo 2014, 9).

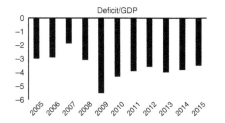
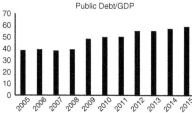

FIGURE 6.3 El Salvador's fiscal position.
Note: The left panel corresponds to El Salvador's General Government Fiscal Balance as a share of GDP. The right panel corresponds to the General Government Public Debt as a share of GDP. Both are expressed in percentage terms.
Source: Rojas Rodríguez (2017).

BUSINESS ELITES' MISTRUST OF EL SALVADOR'S
LEFTIST ADMINISTRATIONS

The government's ideology played an important role in determining the types of linkages with the business sectors and whether these in turn would reduce mistrust of government. As in the Costa Rican case, where left-of-center presidents had only moderate ties to the business community, presidents Mauricio Funes (2009–2014) and Salvador Sánchez Cerén (2014–2019) had leftist reputations to overcome in the eyes of business elites. Contrary to several former presidents of ARENA that hailed from the business sectors themselves, including Alfredo Cristiani (1989–1994), Armando Calderón Sol (1994–1999), and Elías Antonio Saca (2004–2009), Funes and Sánchez Cerén were members of the Farabundo Martí National Liberation Front (FMLN) – the party that emerged out of the left-wing guerrilla from the Salvadorean Civil War. Elías Antonio Saca, the last ARENA president, had a business background in the telecommunications industry and served as president of the Asociacion Salvadoreña de Radiodifusores. Saca's cabinet also included members of the business sectors, including his Minister of Finance William Handal, who had been president of the Salvadorean airline TACA. Saca appointed Ricardo Esmahan, who was the head of Cámara Agropecuaria y Agroindustrial de El Salvador (CAMAGRO), as Ministry of the Economy. ARENA presidents beginning with Cristiani drew on cadres from FUSADES – a think tank founded by the business sectors in the 1980s – and this business sectors' think tank would provide the intellectual foundation for the government's Plan de Desarrollo Económico y Social based on structural adjustment and liberalizing economic policies (Villacorta 2011, 410).

Conversely, the leftist credentials of Saca's successors became an impediment to the establishment of linkages between the government and the business sector, which undermined the FMLN governments' ability to assuage elites' concerns about voice and accountability. A journalist who ran as an outsider but under the FMLN, Mauricio Funes was the first leftist president in the country since President Arturo Araujo was overthrown in a military coup in 1931. Although independent civil society members and even members of other parties were appointed to the main economic posts in his cabinet, Funes filled many social policy and security cabinet positions with members of the FMLN (Ramos et al. 2015, 13).

While the FMLN had moderated its platform since the Salvadorean Civil War, its economic project continued to differ considerably from that of the country's economic elites. The main opposition party since

1994 – the first election in which it participated following the 1992 Chapultepec Peace Accords – the FMLN abandoned communism to embrace socialism within a capitalist system but continued to favor pro-poor policies, redistribution, and rural development. These economic policies contrasted with the business sector's preferred pro-growth and decidedly free-market policies (Sprenkels 2019, 545).[2]

When Funes became president, the FMNL sought to cleanse the state bureaucracy of the ARENA cadres and bureaucrats from previous governments serving the interests of the business elites. This often represented removing personnel with ties to the business sectors in order to reward the FMNL cadre with positions in government (Sprenkels 2019, 548). The replacement of cadres was not well received by the business sectors whose affiliates had provided direct access to policymaking. Although the party further moderated some of its positions during Funes' presidency – for example, it dropped its opposition to both the country's adoption of the US dollar as legal tender and the free trade agreement with the United States (Young 2015) – the business sectors' mistrust continued.

Business elites also feared the leftist credentials of Funes' successor, Sánchez Cerén, who was the second FMLN president but the first former guerrilla combatant to reach power. He had been a member of the General Command (Comandancia General) – the FMLN's highest directive body – and one of the signatories of the Peace Accords (Ramos et al. 2015, 13). From the beginning of his administration, his government accused ARENA and its allies in the business associations of seeking to destabilize the government and even staging a coup (Escobar 2015). For their part, economic elites considered Sánchez Cerén's administration "more of the same" with respect to Funes' hostile attitude toward business groups (Reyes and Alas 2014).[3]

BUSINESS–GOVERNMENT LINKAGES

As in Costa Rica, linkages between government and economic elites meant to bridge political divides were not particularly robust in El Salvador. Although Funes sought to leverage several coordination mechanisms

---

[2] In 1994, moderate sectors of the FMLN – belonging to the original (Ejército Revolucionario del Pueblo (ERP) and Resistencia Nacional (RN) guerrilla organizations under the FMLN umbrella – left the party because of differences over the party's platform.

[3] In the words of Luis Cardenal, president of El Salvador's Chamber of Commerce, Sánchez Cerén's cabinet is "even more political and more FMLN" (Reyes and Alas 2014).

early in his administration, they were characterized by impasse, mutual recrimination, and even breakdown. Some were formal, such as the Economic and Social Council (Consejo Económico y Social – CES), and others ad hoc, including the Dialogue for Productivity and Social Peace, which Funes envisioned as a "mechanism for a frequent and sustained dialogue not just with business leaders, but with all business people" (*La Información* 2012). In both types of mechanisms, however, reciprocal suspicion and misunderstandings became important obstacles toward the adoption of mutually acceptable policies and, at times, the government's ability to move forward its agenda.

These linkages were short-lived and therefore did not contribute to overcoming mistrust toward Funes' left-of-center administration. Instead, some of Funes' policies reinforced this mistrust, such as the FMNL's approval of legislation in Congress allowing the government to directly appoint individuals who would represent business interests before the boards of autonomous institutions (Instituciones Oficiales Autónomas), such as the Social Fund for Housing (Fondo Social para la Vivienda – FSV).[4] Business sectors resented the government's measure and decried Funes' actions as undermining investors' confidence (Fundación Salvadoreña para el Desarrollo Económico y Social 2014, 58). Business elites considered these types of linkages a simulation, which was not conducive toward achieving cooperation between the government and business.

The business sectors also bemoaned that their discussions with the government in the consultation mechanisms rarely led to solutions that took their proposals into account. Instead, the government continued to express sympathy for policies perceived by the business elites as radical, including the nationalization of private industry.

Toward the second half of Funes' administration, linkages between his government and the private sector's peak organizations – the Asociación Nacional de la Empresa Privada (ANEP), the Asociación Salvadoreña de Industriales, and the Cámara de Comercio e Industria de El Salvador – deteriorated to the point where communication was virtually shutdown. Thus, the Economic and Social Council (CES), whose objective was to promote economic dialogue and understanding about public policies related to the economic and social agenda, failed at establishing linkages

---

[4] The FMLN spearheaded legislation toward this end in Congress. Although the bill passed, the Supreme Court reverted the legislation since it was found to contradict ILO agreements.

with the private sector. The coup de grace was when ANEP (Asociación Nacional de la Empresa Privada) left the CES, leaving it without any private-sector representation (Fundación Salvadoreña para el Desarrollo Económico y Social 2014, 55–56).

The constant deterioration in linkages between the government and business sectors was coupled by mutual accusations that became prevalent in the public eye. In 2014, for example, Funes formally accused FECEPE (Fideicomiso Especial para la Creación de Empleos en Sectores Productivos) – an escrow to promote employment in strategic sectors, such as manufacturing, automobile, and textile industries – administrators and several firms that benefited from the funds of embezzlement and misuse (Fundación Salvadoreña para el Desarrollo Económico y Social 2014, 58–59).

In response, the Asociación Salvadoreña de Industriales (ASI) launched a media campaign accusing Funes of undermining the country's investment climate and trying to silence those with opposing political views. ASI's president, Javier Simán, stated that the president was "to blame for the country's lack of investment due to his constant and unnecessary confrontation with business sectors and his lack of respect for institutions and the rule of law, which are indispensable for any foreign firm interested in our country as a destination for investing" and clarified that the peak association did not defend government bureaucrats but rather the companies that invested in the country (Alexander Torres 2014).[5]

A report by FUSADES describes business–government relations during the Funes administrations as confrontational. It suggests that Funes fostered polarization during his five years in office and failed to "create room for dialogue and instead shutdown attempts by business organizations" to establish communication channels (Fundación Salvadoreña para el Desarrollo Económico y Social 2019, 28). Instead, he was deemed to be aggressive, distant, and accusatory toward business groups.

In short, as in the Costa Rican case, the relationship between the government and the business sectors was characterized by confrontation and the lack of strong linkages that would allow for a closer understanding of divergent positions and contribute to the necessary goodwill to find common ground. Without much representation of the business elites inside the government, the formal mechanisms for dialogue often became

---

[5] On numerous occasions, Funes attempted to reestablish dialogue with the business sectors, exhorting them to return to the CES, but the dialogue would always be short lived.

forums where governments and elites exchanged accusations rather than avenues for productive discussion.

The government's conflictual relationship with economic elites had consequences for the prospect of elite taxes. When President Funes attempted to adopt a security tax on elites in 2011, the business sectors expressed that they were tired of round tables and exchanges and wanted government actions instead. Business elites did not believe that the government had a real public-safety plan and opposed the adoption of additional taxes in the absence of a pledge to reduce expenditures and government waste. Even though public safety was their number one concern, business elites had very little trust in the government to be a good steward of additional tax revenue.

The government's wealth tax proposal included different rates assigned to different thresholds starting at $500,000 (Belloso 2011). Marginal tax rates would increase at different thresholds: 0.5 percent between $0.5 million and $1 million; $1 percent (plus a surcharge of $2,500) between $1 million and $5 million; and 1.5 percent (plus a surcharge of $42,500) over $5 million. The tax would be temporary and would last until 2015. The government estimated that about 400 individuals and 2,000 firms would pay the tax and projected revenue of $120 million per year (about 3.3 percent of total government revenue and 0.5 of GDP) or $360 million over three years (Carías 2011). The government expected to add 4,000 officers to the 22,000-strong Policía Nacional Civil (*The Economist* 2011).

When Funes presented the security tax proposal to business elites, they stated two conditions: transparency in how the additional fiscal revenue would be spent and a public-safety plan with new strategies to address the security situation (*La Prensa Gráfica* 2012). In the eyes of business elites, the government was unable to address their concerns. They considered their participation in the oversight of the tax unsatisfactory and the government's security plan as old wine in new bottles. Ultimately, this mistrust in the government's ability to protect their interests became an insurmountable obstacle to the adoption of a security tax on elites.

Before the initiative failed, President Funes and his security cabinet – including the Minister of Justice and Public Safety, David Munguía Payés, and the director of the Policía Nacional Civil, Francisco Salinas – had a series of meetings with business leaders in June and July 2011.[6] The president justified his push to adopt taxes on the wealthiest taxpayers as responding to the need to revise the high investment in private security in El Salvador, where the armed forces had 19,000 personnel and the police 22,000, while private security companies had 25,000 personnel. In his words, "this drains resources that could go to the State, so that the State can provide public safety, not private firms that often do not have the right regulations" (*El Economista* 2011).

The government initiative to introduce the wealth tax elicited strong opposition from business sectors and elites more generally. The main concern was that the tax would "generate a stampede of domestic and foreign investors, contract economic activity and employment, and worst of all, it will deplete the country's capital" (Choto 2011).

In public, the business organizations' position was that the tax would only hurt the average Salvadoran through price hikes and layoffs. In reality, however, they were deeply suspicious of the leftist government's use of the tax revenue. For example, they were concerned that the office of the president's expenditures had more than doubled under Funes from $60 million to $130 million and that public-sector employment had grown by 20,000 personnel in two years (Quintanilla 2011).

They also lamented that in their meetings with government officials, they did not learn about a well-thought-out plan to address public safety. Rather, the government presented them with a wish list from individual ministers regarding the needs of each agency.[7] In a press release, the National Association of Private Enterprises (Asociación Nacional de la Empresa Privada – ANEP) stated that "rather than a strategic plan to

---

[6] The meeting included Jorge Daboub, leader of the National Association of Private Enterprises (Asociación Nacional de la Empresa Privada, ANEP), Luis Cardenal, president of the Chamber of Commerce and Industry (Cámara de Comercio e Industria), Javier Simán, president of the Salvadoran Industrial Association (Asociación Salvadoreña de Industriales – ASI), Agustín Martínez, president of Camagro, Francisco De Sola, president of FUSADES, and Elena de Alfaro and Armando Arias, representing Abansa (*La Prensa Gráfica* 2011a).

[7] Funes also presented crime prevention proposals to the business leaders, seeking to establish a pact to generate education and employment opportunities for youth. In particular, he suggested the creation of a crime prevention program for at-risk population between fourteen- and seventeen-year-olds living in high crime neighborhoods and the creation of "employment parks" to train and employ them. At the meeting, Funes underscored that most sectors agreed that "repression only temporarily contains crime, so it's imperative to go deeper and address the structural roots of the problem, and that's where a crime prevention policy can be effective" (*La Información* 2012).

solve crime, the meeting was about a fiscal problem. The additional funds the government is seeking (about US$500 million), correspond in part to expenditures that are already under way or committed, instead of financing new actions that might generate positive expectations" (Asociación Nacional de la Empresa Privada 2011). For the ANEP, it was essential to see a compelling cost-benefit analysis along with mechanisms to evaluate the effectiveness of the government's measures. As the ANEP (2011) put it, "It is imperative that we first improve trust in the institutions in charge of monitoring the execution of the plans and their respective budgets."

ANEP's executive director, Arnoldo Jiménez, expressed that the business community did not trust that the government would put the tax revenue to good use. For example, he criticized the government's goal to use the tax revenue toward paying police salaries: "If the tax is temporary, and the revenue goes to pay police, what will happen when the tax expires? The money would be better spent by investing it in intelligence, technology, and strengthening the investigative police, and the judiciary" (Carías 2011). Federico Hernández, head of the Chamber of Commerce and Industry (Cámara de Comercio e Industria), objected to the government's characterization of the tax revenue as if it "could flip a switch" and immediately translate revenue into more police and better public safety (Carías 2011).

In the absence of effective mechanisms to build trust between government and economic elites, some members of the elite proceeded to take measures to protect their wealth against the government's proposed tax. The Funes administration detected what Carlos Cáceres, the Minister of Finance, called "unusual transactions" meant to shield assets in the anticipation of the adoption of the tax. The government declined to reveal how many taxpayers had engaged in such transactions, but it had identified 400 individuals who would pay the wealth tax, in addition to about 2,000 corporations (Red de Justicia Fiscal de América Latina y el Caribe 2011).

The FMLN supported the tax and highlighted its progressivity. As Benito Lara, the congressperson leading the FMLN's efforts in the legislature's public-safety committee underscored: The tax makes a lot of sense as a way to address the country's high levels of violence while protecting small and medium firms (Carías 2011).

However, the FMLN lacked a majority in Congress and needed the support of other parties to adopt the tax. Of the eighty-four seats in the National Assembly, the FMLN had thirty-five and fell eight seats short of adopting the measure without support from other parties. Although the recently formed GANA party had shown disposition to support the wealth tax, in the end, the Funes government was unable to muster enough votes for the legislature to adopt the measure.

IMPROVED LINKAGES AND THE 2015 TAX

Funes' successor, President Salvador Sánchez Cerén (2014–2019), also pushed for the adoption of a security tax during his administration. The tax gained urgency after the Constitutional Tribunal (Sala de lo Constitucional de la Corte Suprema de Justicia) blocked the government's attempt to issue bonds to raise $900 million for public-safety expenditures, which had been the preferred policy course of the business sectors and their representatives in Congress through ARENA (Avelar 2015).

Consistent with the experience in Colombia, Costa Rica, and the rest of the region, El Salvador's business sectors continued to be adamantly opposed to increases in their tax burden. This opposition seeking to block the government's efforts to adopt taxes on the wealthy was very visible in 2015 once again. In particular, ANEP, ASI, and the Chamber of Commerce and Industry expressed their disapproval of government efforts to increase taxes. As in 2011, their main response was a demand that the government first reduce waste and expenditures before discussing additional taxes.

As with the 2011 attempt, the country's pro-business think tank, FUSADES, expressed again strong disapproval of the security tax, arguing that the government would be sending the wrong signal to foreign investment (Velásquez et al. 2015). As part of its efforts to oppose the 2015 tax, Fusades generated a document warning that the tax would affect the bulk of the population and challenging the legality of the tax (Fundación Salvadoreña para el Desarrollo Económico y Social 2015). The document also stated that public safety was already the responsibility of the government and that therefore it needed to provide this public good with existing tax revenue from the general tax pool.

Business–government linkages during Sánchez Cerén's administration were never robust, but they were somewhat less antagonistic than those under Funes. Even before his inauguration as president, Sánchez Cerén made a point to seek better linkages with El Salvador's business sectors. During his time as president-elect, Sánchez Cerén's team held meetings with representatives of ANEP and FMLN leaders with the aim of "strengthening the country's economic growth and development" (*El Economista* 2014). At the meetings, the business sectors identified public safety as their number one concern and encouraged the government to reduce waste and unnecessary spending to improve the country's fiscal situation (*La Prensa Gráfica* 2014).

In contrast with the animosity of the relationship during the Funes administration, these efforts were immediately well received by the business sectors. ANEP's president, Jorge Daboub, praised the change in approach and underscored the importance of maintaining an "honest and transparent" dialogue. He also expressed that establishing the right coordination mechanisms was of utmost importance in order to address the country's main challenges, including public safety and fiscal issues (*El Economista* 2014).

In spite of the auspicious start, business–government linkages throughout Sánchez Cerén's presidency never reached the strength seen in countries with right-of-center governments, such as Colombia. Although Sánchez Cerén's forums (mesas de diálogo) to establish a direct and continuous interaction with the business associations constituted progress compared to Funes, business elites nonetheless complained about Sánchez Cerén's lack of will to follow through on their negotiations (Fundación Salvadoreña para el Desarrollo Económico y Social 2019, 28).

After negotiations with the business sectors to adopt the government's preferred wealth tax broke down, the Sánchez Cerén government proposed the adoption of taxes that affected broader sectors of the population, rather than targeting the business elite. Although representing the leftist FMLN, Sánchez Cerén relied on an alliance with an important segment of right-of-center parties – including the Gran Alianza por la Unidad Nacional (GANA), Partido Concertación Nacional (PCN), and the Partido Demócrata Cristiano (PDC) – in order to implement important parts of his government agenda. This alliance took hold both in the legislature – lending support for the adoption of bills – and the electoral arena – participating in coalitions with common tickets. In particular, Sánchez Cerén relied on the right-of-center GANA, which was created in 2012 by former members of the right-of-center ARENA, first to beat ARENA candidate Norman Quijano and then to govern.[8]

These political alliances with the right contributed to the government's ability to assuage business sectors' concerns about increased tax

---

[8] Examples include changes to the Asset Recovery Law, changes to electoral rules, and even modifications to the abortion law (Soriano 2017).

revenue, but the government was forced to look for different types of taxes. Rather than adopting a wealth tax, as Funes first attempted, the government proposed a 10 percent tax on telecommunications services. However, the right-of-center party GANA conditioned its support to the adoption of a 5 percent tax rate on corporations with revenues greater than $500,000 (Velásquez 2015a). GANA legislative leader, Guillermo Gallegos, first introduced the proposal expecting to collect between $80 and $100 million in additional tax revenue and pointing to the need to create an oversight committee formed by representatives of the government, the business sectors, and religious leaders (González 2015) – an important mechanism contributing to assuaging economic elites' mistrust. The tax was adopted with the support of the FMLN-GANA coalition, along with some votes of the PCN and the PDC (Velásquez 2015b).[9]

The business sectors represented in Congress were divided in their support, which allowed the government to adopt a much less ambitious tax than it had intended. Whereas GANA supported the government's initiative, ARENA strongly opposed the tax, arguing that the poor would be most affected by it, that the government was sending the wrong signal to foreign investment, and that the government should reduce waste and public spending. ARENA also proposed instead a voluntary bond program and estimated that this and reducing waste would have represented 246 million in additional revenue, compared to the estimated 100 million in tax revenue (Velásquez 2015a).

Comparable to what the right-of-center opposition in Costa Rica argued in rejecting the adoption of security taxes, ARENA's president, Jorge Velado, requested that the government first reduce spending by at least 43 million before they would be willing to discuss additional taxes.[10] Similarly, the Salvadorean Telecommunications Chamber (Cámara Salvadoreña de Telecomunicaciones – CASATEL) – formed by the four main operators of mobile and fixed-line telephone companies in the country – objected that the 2015 tax did not distinguish between

[9] Opponents across parties argued that the 13 percent of VAT plus a 10 percent tax on communications would amount to 23 percent tax and that this would be too high. ARENA representative René Portillo Cuadra opposed the tax on the grounds that it was "double taxation:" "I have no doubt that the constitutional review court would declare the tax unconstitutional if approved" (Velásquez 2015b).

[10] In addition to cutting public spending by $43 million, ARENA also called for a 3 percent reduction in the budget of the three branches of government, as well as the Corte de Cuentas de la República and the Ministerio Público.

socioeconomic classes and purchasing power. It noted that best practices internationally were aimed at reducing the cost of telecommunications, not increasing it, in order to foster innovation and technology education.

Regarding the destination of the tax, Johanna Hill, Casatel's executive director, lamented that the government did not consult that business association and that "when it comes to public safety we are willing to contribute but this law should have been the result of a broader and more open dialogue for all parties in order to reach appropriate measures to reduce the impact on Salvadoreans pockets" (Velásquez et al. 2015). Representatives of the business sectors also bemoaned that these tax measures would only scare away investment and that their adoption showed that economic growth was a secondary matter to the government.

For its part, the government justified the tax as both affecting and benefiting broad sectors of society. For example, Carlos Cáceres, the Minister of Finance, told legislators when introducing the proposal that: "the tax on telecomm will certainly affect people, but those same people will benefit from the improved security environment that will result from the tax" (Pacheco 2018). President Sánchez Cerén justified the broad incidence of the measure in terms of the need to pay for public safety for everyone, stating that the public-safety plan Safe El Salvador required additional funds to pay for equipment and salaries of the National Civilian Police.[11] He added that the tax would affect rich and poor, but that it was necessary: "It's a contribution in which all Salvadoreans will participate. I know that it will affect the majority of the population, telephone users. I wish I had a magic wand not to affect anybody. Police and soldiers are dying and sacrificing for the population and it is fair that everybody contribute against crime" (García 2015).

In addition to better equipping the police, the president's plan also aimed to reincorporate gang members into society, recover public spaces, keep children and teenagers off the streets, provide financial support to teenagers that do not study or work, and regain control of correctional facilities. In particular, the president pledged to channel funds toward a yearly bonus for the Policía Nacional Civil's (PNC) 22,000 personnel and about 7,000 soldiers conducting public-safety missions. The remaining funds would be channeled toward violence prevention programs and scholarships for youth (*AFP* 2015).

---

[11] Two other taxes that were proposed but not debated: 15 percent on casinos and 15 percent on income of government officials making more than $2,300 per month.

Unlike Funes' 2011 tax proposal, the 2015 measure mustered a majority in Congress. There were two parts to the security tax. The first was a corporate 5 percent tax on profits exceeding US$500,000, which affected El Salvador's largest firms (El Salvador's Legislative Assembly 2015). The second was a tax on telecommunications services (El Salvador's Legislative Assembly 2015). The legislature adopted with forty-eight votes the security taxes (Ley de la Contribución Especial para la Seguridad Ciudadana y Convivencia and Ley de la Contribución Especial a los Grandes Contribuyentes para el Plan de Seguridad Ciudadana) which came into force on November 29, 2015. The parties that approved the taxes in the assembly (FMLN with GANA, PCN, PDC) defended the vote by stating that FMLN wanted a 10 percent tax on corporations, but that they had moderated the proposal to achieve the public-safety goals while protecting people's pockets. ARENA was the only party that voted against the proposal: Diputado Mauricio Vargas criticized the tax as a disguised VAT (Velásquez et al. 2015).

The legislature required the government to report the destination of the tax revenue to the National Council for Citizen Security (Consejo Nacional de Seguridad Ciudadana y Convivencia). The Council has since generated reports outlining how the tax revenue has been spent – one of the business elites' key demands during negotiations. This body agreed in 2015 that 75 percent of the public-safety tax revenue would go to the prevention of violence and 25 percent to punitive aspects of law enforcement, the actual expenditures have not always followed this distribution (Barrera 2018; López 2016).[12]

During the first year, the tax revenue helped fund the government's Plan El Salvador Seguro, among other types of public-safety expenditures. In subsequent years, the tax revenue has been channeled toward strengthening recruiting and training at the National Civilian Police, as well as purchasing equipment and technology (Policía Nacional Civil 2017). The distribution that year was as follows: About 37 percent of the tax revenue was assigned to strengthening the police and judiciary, 13.5 percent went to the armed forces involved in public safety, 9.5 percent went to the Attorney General's Office, 15.5 percent to education, and the rest to a number of agencies, including those in charge of public health and the protection of human rights (*La Prensa Gráfica* 2017b).

---

[12] In 2016, for example, only 63 percent of the revenue was assigned to violence prevention programs.

The tax revenue earmarked for public safety has amounted to an additional 0.5 percent of GDP each year (Ministerio de Hacienda de El Salvador 2020). To put things in perspective, income taxes represent 7.1 percent of GDP and the VAT 8.1 percent of GDP (Ministerio de Hacienda de El Salvador 2019). The additional revenue has been significant enough for state coffers that, at the time of writing, the legislature was debating the renewal of the security tax beyond the original five-year period.

Alternative Explanations

Alternative explanations are less helpful in accounting for the adoption of the security taxes in El Salvador. A nontax revenue perspective would expect elite taxes to be more difficult to adopt in countries dependent on resource rents and easier to adopt in places where resource wealth is absent. However, governments in El Salvador faced significant opposition to elite taxation in spite of the country's very low levels of natural resource rents and foreign aid (World Bank 2020). Further, although El Salvador's comparatively lower levels of inequality would be expected to reduce opposition to elite taxes, Salvadorean business leaders publicly lamented the narrow tax base and openly voiced their perceived unfairness of being targeted to contribute additional resources without cuts to government spending. This was no different from the experiences in other countries, regardless of levels of inequality. Finally, an ideology-based perspective would expect left-of-center governments to adopt greater tax burdens compared to right-of-center administrations. In El Salvador, the leftist ideology of FMLN presidents Funes and Sánchez Cerén guided their administration's preference for increased taxation to address the country's fiscal gap, rather than cutting government expenditures as ARENA proposed. This behavior is consistent with that of leftist presidents in Costa Rica, who also had much less consideration for the nontax alternatives proposed by the opposition to help address the country's fiscal gap.

However, presidents Funes' and Sánchez Cerén's left-of-center ideology was an important obstacle to overcoming mistrust among business elites. Although Funes was an outsider that was nominated by the FMLN, his relations with the business community were paradoxically more conflictual than those of Sánchez Cerén, who was a guerrilla commander himself but made a point to build more durable bridges with the business community than his predecessor. While ideology remained constant across the two administrations, Sánchez Cerén's stronger business–government linkages contributed to overcome business elites' mistrust in spite of the government's leftist orientation.

CONCLUSION

The Salvadorean case illustrates that high violent crime contexts are not a sufficient condition to convince elites to bear a greater tax burden, that business–government linkages can be crucial to reduce elites concerns about the destination of the additional tax revenue, and that design features can play an important role toward the adoption of elite taxes. First, neither high levels nor a recent increase in violent crime generated favorable views among the business community toward tax increases. There was no heightened sense of patriotism or social-mindedness originating from the national crisis facing El Salvador, even when violence-affected elites themselves directly. Instead, elites resorted to the same behavior observed in the rest of our cases: They discredited the government's plans by generating fear about the loss of economic competitiveness and the prospect of capital flight, suggested that the less affluent sectors would be most affected by the additional taxes, and argued that the government was already responsible for providing public safety with existing resources.

Second, elites' concerns about left-of-center administrations did not recede in light of the country's spiral of violent crime. Regardless of this context, which might have prompted economic elites to set aside mistrust about the government's priorities or intentions, deep suspicion toward leftist governments' redistributive priorities remained, as well as concerns about the lack of accountability and oversight. High levels of violence did not seem to make a difference to make elites more sympathetic to what they perceived as a collection of different ministries' wish lists and the absence of a coherent strategy to address crime.

Third, as with the rest of the cases adopting an elite tax, the Salvadoran case underscores the importance of design features that contribute to ameliorating relevant stakeholders' concerns that the additional tax burden would be wasted, embezzled, or put to a different use. Although the government was unable to overcome elites' resistance in 2011, earmarking the tax for public safety, establishing a five-year limit, and appointing an oversight committee were important features that generated the political conditions that made possible, if not the targeted elite tax originally envisioned by Funes, the more diffuse corporate and telecommunications taxes eventually adopted by Sánchez Cerén in 2015.

Finally, although the tax was not as ambitious as originally intended, the increase in revenue from the tax has made a difference to improve the state's capacity to provide public safety. The additional yearly half percentage point in tax revenue as a share of GDP has made a difference for the National Civilian Police, which has relied on the resources to improve both salaries and capacity building in the police academy. Similarly, resources have allowed the government to invest in technology and equipment expenditures, including police cars, helicopters, and surveillance devices. Funds have also been assigned toward improving the judiciary along with preventive measures, such as building schools in at-risk areas. Although the quality of public-safety provision is still lacking, the additional resources increase the human and material resources the state can muster to address crime compared to the pretax baseline.

7

Mexico's Uneven Taxation

Those who leave Monterrey are cowards. We must retake our great city!
[...] Stay here to defend what your ancestors built with so much effort.
Fight, demand, act. [...] If you take the first opportunity to flee, we don't
need you.

Lorenzo Zambrano, CEO of Mexican cement multinational
CEMEX, shaming fellow economic elites for moving
to the US due to violent crime.[1]

The absence of a security tax on economic elites in Mexico is puzzling.
Mexico is a case in which violent crime has skyrocketed in the last decade,
but where elite taxes for public safety have not been adopted. The steep
increase in violent crime with homicide rates more than doubling from
9 per 100,000 people in 2007 to 24 per 100,000 people in 2011 – and
surpassing this level again in 2017 – has resulted in the worst security
crisis in the country's modern history. As this chapter will show, however, although Mexico presents both a window of opportunity from the
security crisis and has many of the ingredients required to overcome mistrust in government – including right-of-center governments and strong
linkages between government and economic elites – other factors have
contributed to the absence of a security tax.

Two factors stand out. First, the spatial distribution of crime has shielded
important sectors of the economic elite from exposure to violent crime. This
is not only mainly because of the geographic concentration of violent crime

---

[1] Zambrano's exhortation was made in a series of tweets on August 29, 2010 (*Milenio Digital* 2014).

outside of Mexico City but also because elites in Mexico's northern states have been able to migrate to the United States to circumvent violence to some extent – many of them while still managing their business in Mexico (Ríos 2014; Internal Displacement Monitoring Center 2010).

Second, although Mexico's tax revenue has remained low and relatively stagnant for decades at about 11–13 percent of GDP, the country's fiscal pressure in terms of government expenditures is relatively low as well compared to other countries in the region (Tello and Hernández 2010). Had fiscal considerations been more pressing for the federal government, security likely would have been higher on the government's agenda (author's interview with Rodrigo Barros Reyes-Retana, the head of the tax unit at the Ministry of Finance, 2015).

These factors help explain why, rather than elite taxes for public safety at the national level in Mexico, comparable taxes have been adopted at the state level in parts of the country facing sharp increases in violent crime. Generally consistent with expectations, state governments have adopted their versions of security taxes in such states as Chihuahua, Nuevo León, and Tamaulipas, where violence has been especially high and government–elite linkages are strong. At the same time, other states with high levels of violence but lacking the same linkages – such as Guerrero and Michoacán – have not adopted security taxes.

In the following sections, I first discuss the security crisis, followed by the factors that would predict the adoption of elite taxation. Next, I address how national elites' relatively low exposure to violence has translated into the absence of taxes at the national level, but local elites' high exposure in some states has followed a pattern consistent with expectations. Finally, I consider the extent to which alternative explanations might account for the absence of security taxes on elites in Mexico.

MEXICO'S SECURITY CRISIS

Beginning in 2007, Mexico experienced a severe deterioration of public safety. Whereas violent crime had been steadily declining since the 1990s, several indicators of the rule of law began to worsen, including rates of homicides, kidnapping, and extortion. As Figure 7.1 shows, Mexico's downward trending homicide rate characteristic of the 1990s and early 2000s was sharply reversed shortly after 2006.

Although the rate of violent crime was at historical lows in 2007, the government militarized public-safety operations. Beginning on December 11, 2006, President Felipe Calderón (2006–2012) drastically intensified militarization by assigning the armed forces the lead role in a protracted

FIGURE 7.1 Mexico's homicide rate (per 100,000 people).
Source: Secretariado del Sistema Nacional de Seguridad Pública, Tasa de Homicido Doloso por Entidad Federativa.

effort across the national territory. Calderón deployed tens of thousands of troops in ongoing formal military operations in several states, including Michoacán in 2006; Baja California and Guerrero in 2007; Chihuahua, Durango, Nuevo León, Sinaloa, and Tamaulipas in 2008; and Veracruz in 2011 (Merino 2011).

In these highly visible operations, rather than the military playing a supporting role for civilian law enforcement, the roles inverted with a military commander in charge of joint operations and the civilian police supporting the armed forces. For example, in Operation Michoacán, the ratio of military to police was close to 4 to 1: 5,254 armed forces were assisted by 1,400 civilian police (*La Crónica* 2006). In Sinaloa, the ratio was 2 to 1: 1,933 military personnel were assisted by 740 civilian police (*El Sol de Sinaloa* 2008). Although the government does not report how many troops have been engaged in antidrug trafficking operations, newspaper reports estimate that more than 45,000 troops are deployed across the country and tasked with preserving public order in more than 1,500 daily operations (*El Universal* 2015).

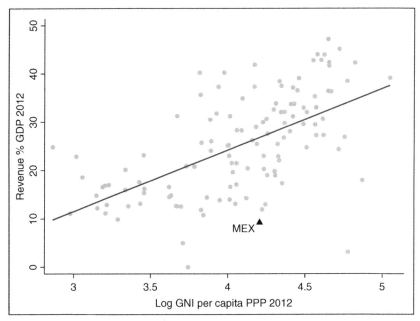

FIGURE 7.2 Tax-to-GDP ratio by GDP per capita, ca. 2012.
Source: IMF Government Finance Statistics and World Bank World Development Indicators Online.

In each of these operations, the armed forces deployed dozens of antidrug aircraft and vessels and hundreds of amphibious vehicles, conducted aerial and ground patrols, set checkpoints on main roads and within cities and towns, and established semipermanent military bases throughout these states' territories (*La Crónica* 2006). In addition to Humvees patrolling the streets and the armed forces' clashes with organized crime, the operations also gained visibility because the government went to great lengths to advertise them nationwide. Adding to this visibility, Calderón himself took to wearing military fatigues in public appearances, surrounded by the armed forces' military commanders – which was extremely unusual for a civilian Mexican president (Daly et al. 2012).

At the same time that the government was increasing its security-related expenditures – doubling them in real terms since 2007 – the country's fiscal revenue remained stagnant. As Carlos Elizondo Mayer-Serra (2014) points out, fiscal reforms in Mexico have not yielded much increase in tax revenue since the mid-twentieth century. In fact, Mexico's tax burden has historically been among the lowest in the region, and it is much lower than expected for its level of development. As Figure 7.2

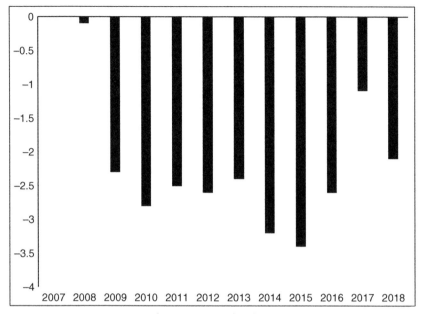

FIGURE 7.3 Mexico's central government fiscal balance (percentage of GDP). *Source:* Secretaria de Hacienda y Crédito Público. Note: Fiscal balance for 2007 was zero.

shows, there is a considerable gap of about 7 percentage points of GDP between what Mexico collects and what would be expected (solid line). With fiscal revenue of about 11 percent of GDP, Mexico collects about a third of what Argentina, Brazil, or Uruguay collect (Ondetti 2019, 2021).

As with most countries at the time, Mexico's government budget became strained in the aftermath of the global financial crisis in 2008. Whereas the central government's fiscal balance in 2007 was zero and in 2008 it was negative but close to zero, the federal deficit quickly jumped to more than 2 percent in 2009 and grew past 3 percent of GDP in 2014 and 2015, as shown in Figure 7.3.

RIGHT-OF-CENTER PRESIDENTS

In addition to the drastic deterioration of violent crime and a tightening fiscal situation, Mexico appeared to have all of the ingredients that would make the adoption of security taxes likely, including pro-business, right-of-center presidents, and strong government–elite linkages. In particular, the two presidents in office since the escalation of violence came from the National Action Party (PAN) – Felipe Calderón (2006–2012) militarized antidrug efforts and presided over a steady escalation of violence unprecedented in Mexico's recent history – and the Party of the Institutionalized Revolution (PRI) – Enrique Peña Nieto (2012–2018), whose administration maintained his predecessor's militarization policy and was unable to reduce violent crime. Although the PAN is decidedly right-of-center and the PRI is closer to the center of the political spectrum, both parties followed very similar orthodox economic policies and enjoyed strong linkages with economic elites – even sharing cabinet members across administrations.[2]

The PAN's pro-business ideology has brought it close to the country's economic elites since its creation early in the twentieth century (Loaeza 1999; Mizrahi 2003). When it was founded, eleven of twenty-nine members of the first National Committee were bankers or businessmen (Story 1987, 265). After the nationalization of the banking industry in 1982, many business elites also migrated to the PAN, which was led, among others, by Manuel Clouthier, who was the head of Mexico' two main peak business associations – the Confederación Patronal de la República Mexicana (COPARMEX) and the Consejo Cordinador Empresarial (CCE) – between 1977 and 1983 (Hernández Rodríguez 2011, 74).

Throughout the 1990s and 2000s, the business sectors increased their control of the PAN, or what was euphemistically called the "Neo-panismo." The PAN's electoral success in the northern states and the Bajío areas was due to the resources and cadres coming from business groups, including Grupo Monterrey,[3] as well as business groups in Chihuahua, Guanajuato, and Sonora. The first seven state governments that the PAN won were possible because it nominated business leaders rather than rank-and-file politicians, as in Baja California (1989), Chihuahua (1992), Jalisco (1995), Guanajuato (1991), Nuevo León (1997), Querétaro (1997), and Aguascalientes (1998) (Hernández Rodríguez 2011, 74).

Although some business leaders were reluctant to openly express affinity with the PAN before democratization, this changed during the process

---

[2] A prominent example is finance minister José Antonio Meade, who served as minister in both the Calderón and Peña Nieto administrations.
[3] A group of the main business leaders in Mexico's second largest city, Monterrey, with considerable national influence. Among the main members are industry leaders Grupo Alfa (steel) and Cemex (cement).

of political opening in the 1990s.[4] Since, the PAN became widely seen as a champion of business interests and market-oriented orthodoxy. The proximity between the PAN and the business sectors was such that it is no coincidence that the first time the PRI governments recognized electoral defeats at the gubernatorial level was to a PAN candidate in the state of Baja California in 1989. Ernesto Ruffo was a businessperson in the fishing industry, who had also served as the president of the national fisheries association (Asociación Nacional Pesquera) and head of the Consejo Coordinador Empresarial – one of Mexico's peak business associations – in the city of Ensenada.

It is also no coincidence that the first president from an opposition party was also from the PAN, which was deemed a "safe" alternative by the business sectors, concerned about the redistributive policies of the left-of-center opposition led by the PRD at the time. Vicente Fox (2000–2006) was a business executive at the Coca-Cola Company, becoming the CEO for operations in Mexico. President Fox famously promised to run the government like a corporation and appointed businesspeople, rather than politicians or technocrats, to more than half of his cabinet positions (BBC World Service 2000). For this reason, he was characterized as Mexico's "first businessman president" (Fazio 2000).

Although President Calderón's presidency pulled back from the hyper-entrepreneurial spirit of Vicente Fox, it continued to have very strong ties to the business sectors. Coming from a prominent PANista family,[5] Calderón was a career politician who served as the PAN's Secretary-General in 1993 and President in 1999, and as state and federal legislator.

President Calderón's political group within the PAN also enjoyed important ties to the business community. In particular, the party's most conservative sectors – such as El Yunque, Muro, DHIAC, and Ancifem – were permeated by members of the business community (Alemán 2005). During Caldéron's presidency (2006–2012), several PAN legislators belonged to business associations, mainly from COPARMEX – another of Mexico's peak business associations (Delgado 2008). Further, Caldéron maintained a pro-business technocratic profile among the main cabinet positions related to economic policy, many of whom had been serving under the PRI administrations.

---

[4] Leading the charge were businesspeople such as Francisco Barrio, Ernesto Ruffo, and Fernando Canales Clariond (Alemán 2005).
[5] Calderón's father, Luis Calderón Vega, was a leader and cofounder of the party.

For example, he appointed Agustín Carstens, who had served in the International Monetary Fund, as Minister of Finance and later governor of Mexico's Central Bank. Georgina Kessel became the Energy Minister, and Luis Téllez became the Minister of Communications and Transportation. Both Kessel and Téllez belonged to a technocratic elite from the PRI administrations of Carlos Salinas (1988–1994) and Ernesto Zedillo (1994–2000). This technocratic elite was very pro-economic orthodoxy and had served in the private sector (Hernández Rodríguez 2011, 92).[6]

Although representing the nominally more centrist PRI, the Peña Nieto administration continued with the same pro-business economic policies of his predecessors from the PAN and the PRI administrations that governed since the debt crisis in the early 1980s. Although there were business sectors that became increasingly disenchanted with the PRI governments during the 1970s and 1980s, the pro-market technocratic branch of the party dominated positions in the party and the government since Miguel de la Madrid's presidency (1982–1988). De la Madrid elevated bureaucrats from the ministries of finance and the Central Bank, where he himself had gained administrative experience, to key posts in his administration (Camp 2002). Those sectors of the PRI who were not in line with pro-business market orthodoxy were marginalized toward the 1988 election, and many of them formed a dissident wing, the Corriente Democrática, which broke away from the party to form the National Democratic Front (FDN) in 1987 and later became the left-of-center Party of the Democratic Revolution (PRD). The PRI presidents before democratization in 2000, Carlos Salinas (1988–1994) and Ernesto Zedillo (1994–2000), hailed from the pro-business wing, which has dominated the party since the split.

Peña Nieto's government was a product of the pro-business PRI. Although he did not emerge out of the financial technocratic elite himself, he went to great lengths to preserve the economic model and push through important structural reforms (Flores-Macías 2013, 2016).[7] Most prominently, he opened up the energy sector to private investment, including the oil industry, which was a major pro-business concession since the industry had remained state owned since 1938. During his administration, business enjoyed important representation in Congress through

---

[6] Téllez, for example, was an adviser to the Carlyle Group.
[7] Before becoming president, Peña Nieto was the governor of Mexico State (2005–2011) and a state legislator (2003–2005).

the PRI, including several legislators clearly identified as representatives of business groups.[8]

GOVERNMENT–ELITE LINKAGES

Another ingredient conducive to the adoption of security taxes is the strong linkages between the government and elites. Mexico's business sectors are among the best organized in Latin America (Schneider 2004, 16) and have enjoyed strong connections with the PAN and PRI governments since the 1990s.[9] Business elites are organized into two main associations. The first is the Mexican Businessmen Council (Consejo Mexicano de Hombres de Negocios – CMHN), an exclusive club created in the 1960s and formed by about forty capitalists with interests in all major sectors of the economy. The second is the Business Coordination Council (CCE), "an economy-wide peak association established by 7 member associations that formally represented nearly a million firms from all sectors of the economy" (Schneider 2004, 8).

As Ben Ross Schneider (2004, 32) has pointed out, both the CMHN and the CCE enjoy privileged access to the president and key ministers on a regular basis through monthly luncheons and dinners. These peak, economy-wide organizations are fairly organized in representing the interests of the business community. The close relations between the business organizations and the government have been due to the exchange of government access for political support and resources.

Given the high concentration of Mexican business, the main business associations are highly cohesive. In addition to meetings with top government officials, the CMHN meets regularly to coordinate policy and build consensus across the rest of the business organizations. For example, the CMHN serves as a bridge across industries and parts of the country and reaches decisions by consensus (Schneider 2004, 78). Since the CMHN has been a central actor in fostering other business associations, including the CCE and COPARMEX, there has been little room for centrifugal forces or outright dissidence (Schneider 2004, 80). The meetings are

---

[8] These included Enrique Dávila Flores, who was the head of the Confederación Nacional de Cámaras de Comercio (CANACO) and headed the Economic Commission in the lower chamber. Nine PRI legislators were closely linked to the two main media groups in Mexico, Televisa, and TV Azteca (*Emeequis* 2012).

[9] Their organization finds its roots in the great mistrust of government due to important threats the business sectors faced in the 1920s, 1930s, 1950s, 1970s, and 1980s (Schneider 2004, 16).

an effective mechanism to "managing the affairs of the bourgeoisie as a whole and communicating to government the concerns of Mexico's largest business groups" (Schneider 2004, 80).[10]

The Puzzle of No Security Taxes

If Mexico has had high levels of violent crime, right-of-center presidents, and fairly cohesive and organized business sectors, why have governments not adopted security taxes in this context? Levels of violent crime are certainly higher than those in Costa Rica, where public safety was deemed a major problem worth addressing through this measure. Although Mexico's fiscal situation was not dire during the period of increasing violent crime, the government did pursue other changes in the tax system, including a tax reform adopted in 2013 (Romero 2015; Unda Gutiérrez and Moreno Jaimes 2015; Ondetti 2021). Why did the federal government not resort to security taxes as a means to strengthen both fiscal coffers and public safety?

Geographic Concentration of Violence

The situation of Mexican business elites differs from that of their counterparts in other countries experiencing high levels of violent crime. In Colombia, business elites faced a dire situation where their personal safety was very much at risk in the capital, Bogotá, as well as the rest of the country's main cities, such as Medellín and Cali. In Central America, the areas where violent crime is most prevalent are the main centers of economic activity where elites are concentrated. For example, in Guatemala, violent crime is concentrated in Guatemala City and Petén. In Honduras, it is concentrated in Tegucigalpa, the Atlantic Coast, and the border region with Guatemala (World Bank 2011, 4). In El Salvador, the metropolitan area of San Salvador both concentrates economic elites and records the highest levels of violent crime.

---

[10] The influence of business is such that President Miguel de la Madrid even asked the CMHN to interview the six PRI candidates to the presidency in 1988 (Schneider 2004, 78). During the negotiations for NAFTA in the 1990s, the CCE served as the main channel of communication for a tight partnership between business and government for the negotiations (Alba Vega 1997; Schneider 2004, 88). The CMHN also works to build support for government policies and build investor confidence, announcing their projected levels of investment for a given year and their support for government bonds (Schneider 2002, 77). The CCE has the Centro de Estudios Económicos del Sector Privado (CEESP), a think tank that influences policy through research.

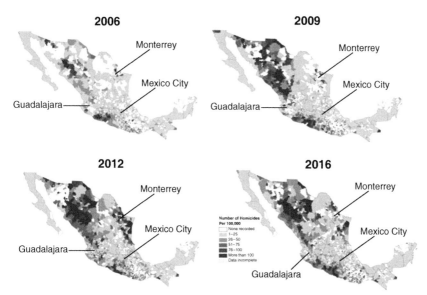

FIGURE 7.4 Spatial distribution of the homicide rate over time.
Source: Labels added to maps from Heinle, Molzahn, and Shirk (2015, 2017).

In contrast, Mexico's business elites have only partially faced similar levels of violence. Whereas, in Colombia, it became extremely dangerous to travel by car between most major cities and no major metropolitan area was exempt from the violence, in Mexico similarly high levels of violence have been fairly concentrated in certain parts of the territory, but not in Mexico City, the economic heart of the country.[11]

Although the spatial distribution of violent crime has evolved over time – with increasingly larger parts of the territory experiencing violent crime – extreme violence has remained fairly concentrated in certain municipalities. In 2011, Mexico's most violent year in the first wave of violent crime, for example, about 37 percent of municipalities recorded no homicides, whereas 22 percent had a homicide rate higher than the national mean of 24 per 100,000 people. In 2016, 42 percent of Mexico's homicides took place in 2 percent of the country's municipalities (about 49 out of 2,446 people) (Heinle, Molzahn, and Shirk 2015, 2017). In particular, the main municipalities affected by violence have been concentrated along the northern border states and the coasts, as shown in Figure 7.4.

[11] This does not mean that violence does not affect economic elites, but rather, that elites in Mexico City are not affected by it in extreme ways as in other parts of the country.

The resort city of Acapulco on the Pacific coast, for example, has become one of the country's most dangerous municipalities, along with northern cities such as Culiacán, Cd. Juárez, Chihuahua, and Tijuana.

Conversely, the economic heart of the country – Mexico City – has not experienced high levels of violent crime for sustained periods of time. Compared to the national mean, levels of violent crime have remained generally low in Mexico City, which concentrates 8.5 percent of the country's population and 18 percent of the country's GDP, and where many of the country's largest firms have their headquarters. Indeed, the head of the tax unit at the Ministry of Finance (Jefe de la Unidad de Impuestos de la Secretaría de Hacienda) confided that, to his knowledge, the Peña Nieto administration did not have any conversations with the business sectors regarding security taxes (interview with Barros Reyes-Retana 2015).

While the threat faced by economic elites in Mexico City may not have prompted a national tax, regional elites did experience considerable increases in the levels of violent crime. They faced extortion – often in the form of having to pay "derecho de piso" or the right to do business – and kidnapping. The business associations were instrumental in channeling these concerns to the local authorities. For example, in the northern city of Tijuana, Baja California, the local offices of the CCE and COPARMEX refused to attend any meetings with the government until the government showed it was taking seriously their demands for public safety (Meza 2015). Once the government showed signs of progress that were deemed satisfactory by the business elites, the business sectors, led by the COPARMEX, would meet with public-safety authorities periodically to coordinate the security strategy.

In particular, regional economic elites in the parts of the country facing high violent crime resorted to three main strategies: (1) relocate across the border to the United States, (2) make one-time donations to fund spending in public safety, and (3) agree to pay taxes earmarked for statewide public-safety expenditures.

(1) Move across the Border to the United States

In the states along the border with the United States, where much of the violence has taken place, many business elites have enjoyed an exit option often not available elsewhere. For example, it has been documented that fear of and dissatisfaction with violent crime have compelled sectors of the population to relocate their businesses across the border (Ríos 2014). One estimate calculates that 10,000 businesses were forced to close in the border city of Cd. Juárez, Chihuahua, between 2007 and 2011 because of violent crime. Although the flow of elites is difficult to quantify, one study has estimated that migration from Mexico into the United States resulting from drug violence reached 115,000 people between 2006 and 2010 (Internal Displacement Monitoring Center 2010). Many of these elites relocated their families to the US side in border cities such as El Paso, McAllen, San Diego, or Laredo, but continued to run their business operations in Mexico. Another estimate puts the migration of Mexicans escaping violence to El Paso alone at 30,000 between 2008 and 2009 (Morales et al. 2013). The migration from upper-middle and upper sectors to the United States from the border states became so visible that the CEO of CEMEX, a Mexican multinational in the cement industry, Lorenzo Zambrano, denounced in public the exodus of fellow business elites and exhorted them to stay in Mexico and find solutions to the public-safety problem (*Notimex* 2013).

(2) Make One-Time Donations to Fund Spending in Public Safety

In addition to the exit option, elites in some states also resorted to one-time donations as a strategy to help address crime. Since violent crime was not affecting elites in Mexico City, regional elites resorted to partnerships with state governments to finance security expenditures on an ad hoc basis. This meant making voluntary contributions through the main business associations toward financing the police and the armed forces.

For example, in the northern state of Coahuila, the private sector contributed to financing the construction of barracks for a brigade of the army's Military Police in San Pedro de las Colonias, Coahuila. The barracks would serve the 11th military region in the states of Coahuila, Chihuahua, and Durango and cost 500 million pesos (US$26.3 million), shared between government and private sectors of La Laguna (Aranda 2016).[12] A similar mechanism was employed to fund infantry barracks in Frontera, Coahuila, and a cavalry regiment in Piedras Negras, Coahuila, each with a cost of 300 million pesos (US$15.7 million).Although these facilities are military infrastructure, they were built with a public-safety objective in mind (Aranda 2016).

Other efforts were considerably less ambitious and more ad hoc, as in the state of Tamaulipas, where businesspeople donated six police vehicles to the state police (Sosa 2017). In Ciudad Juárez, Chihuahua, business

---

[12] The barracks could house up to 3,000 personnel.

owners donated gasoline, communications equipment, and auto repairs to the state's police (Policía Estatal Única). The donations were made through vouchers granted through the local office of the National Chamber of Commerce (CANACO) and the CCE (*Cultura Colectiva* 2017).[13]

(3) Pay a Local Tax Earmarked for Public-Safety Expenditures

The third strategy has contributed to more sustained investment in public-safety efforts. In several states, security taxes were adopted to address the increase in violent crime. These taxes followed a pattern consistent with the cases at the national level in other parts of Latin America discussed earlier in the book. They took place when violence had increased sharply and strong government–elite linkages existed – mainly in the context of a right-of-center administration that could assuage elites' concerns that the tax revenue would be diverted or wasted. States with high levels of violence but lacking government–elite linkages did not adopt security taxes.

Although there were no dire financial crises in Mexico, all states experienced a decrease in federal transfers for public safety after the global financial crisis in 2008.[14] Because of states' limited ability to raise taxes, the federal government's fund for the States' Public Safety (Fondo de Aportaciones para la Seguridad Pública de los Estados – FASP) represents a lifeline for state government's security expenditures. The gray line in Figure 7.5 shows the steady decline after the crisis – 6 percent between 2009 and 2015 – and a sharper drop after 2015 – 24 percent between 2014 and 2018.[15]

At the same time that federal transfers were decreasing, the pressure to increase public-safety expenditures mounted because of rising violent crime, as the black line in Figure 7.6 shows. For example, public-safety expenditures in Chihuahua increased by 31 percent between 2008 and 2014. In Nuevo León, public-safety expenditures increased by 84 percent during the same period (Ramírez Verdugo and Ruiz González 2016).

---

[13] The donations were made to the state police but not the city police because the business sectors did not trust that the resources would be used appropriately (Cultura Colectiva 2017).

[14] The transfers from the Fondo de Aportaciones para la Seguridad Pública de los Estados y del Distrito Federal (FASP) follows the regulations established in the Fiscal Coordination Law (Ley de Coordinación Fiscal).

[15] Whereas all states experienced the decrease, some high-crime states experienced a sharper drop in federal transfers, as in Guerrero, which saw its transfers more than halved in 2016.

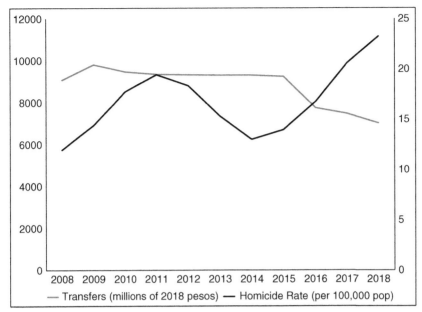

FIGURE 7.5 Federal transfers to states for public safety and homicide rate.
Note: Total federal transfers for public safety to states correspond to the left axis (in millions of 2018 pesos). The country's total homicide rate corresponds to the right axis (per 100,000 people).
Source: Made by the author with data from the Secretariado Ejecutivo del Sistema Nacional de Seguridad Pública's reports on the Fondo de Aportaciones para la Seguridad Pública de los Estados (FASP).

Mexican states are highly dependent on the federal government for resources, however.[16] On average, about 92 percent of states' revenue comes from the federal government and the remaining 8 percent comes from local taxes and fees (Ramírez Verdugo and Ruiz González 2016). Additionally, state governments are limited in their ability to generate revenue through taxes. The main types of taxes that are legally available to state governments include taxes on payrolls, vehicle ownership and transactions, real estate transactions, hospitality, and lotteries. Of these, the one that generates the most revenue is the payroll tax. These considerations make payroll taxes one of the few available avenues whenever state governments seek to extract more revenue from society.

In order to address the public-safety concerns with the limited resources at hand, several states increased payroll taxes: Chihuahua in 2013, Nuevo

[16] For an excellent account of the centralization of fiscal powers in Mexico, see Díaz-Cayeros (2006).

León in 2013, Tamaulipas in 2016, Sinaloa in 2017, Guanajuato in 2018, and Aguascalientes in 2019. In all of these cases, the security taxes followed a sharp increase in violent crime and the arrival of a right-of-center government to power. In states where taxes were adopted, robust government–elite linkages were instrumental in overcoming strong opposition among the business community to an increase in the payroll tax. The first three cases are discussed in detail in the following paragraphs.

The state government in Nuevo León adopted the Program for the Ordering and Strengthening of Public Finance (Programa de Ordenamiento y Fortalecimiento Integral de las Finanzas Públicas, POFIF) in 2013. This program aimed to reduce non-public-safety-related expenditures, restructure debt, and increase the payroll tax rate from 2 to 3 percent of wages, of which half a percentage point (half of the increase) was earmarked for public safety.[17] With the earmarked funds of the increase in the payroll tax, the government's goal was to finance the expansion of the state police. In particular, the government intended to grow the state police from 3,300 personnel to 7,000 (*Notimex* 2013).

Chihuahua followed a similar path regarding the increase in payroll taxes to finance public-safety expenditures.[18] Following a peak in public debt as a share of nonearmarked resources in 2013 – when the public debt reached 200 percent of discretionary revenue – Chihuahua's state government followed a similar strategy as that of Nuevo León: increasing taxes, restructuring debt, and cutting non-security-related expenditures.

Facing comparable constraints, the government of Tamaulipas followed suit in 2016 with an increase in payroll taxes. The PRI governor leveraged linkages with the state's business sectors to reach an agreement to change the payroll tax rate from 2 to 3 percent. With its first modification in forty years, the tax revenue would finance additional police and investment in technology such as surveillance cameras. Each of these cases is discussed in detail later, followed by two cases – Michoacán and Guerrero – with high violent crime but where no taxes were adopted due to the government's weak linkages with the business elites.

---

[17] Debt restructuring allowed the government to save about $4 billion pesos or about 12 percent of non-earmarked revenue in 2014 (non-earmarked federal transfers plus local taxes), which were in turn assigned to public safety (Ramírez Verdugo and Ruiz González 2016).

[18] In addition to the security-related pressures on the state budget, after 2010, the state government faced ballooning expenditures associated with public education and the state pensions system (Ramírez Verdugo and Ruiz González 2016).

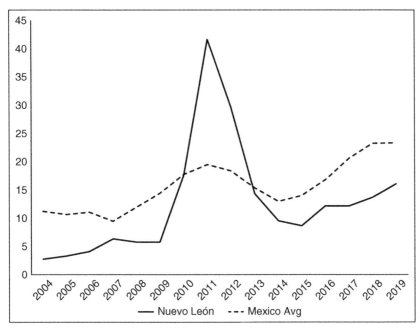

FIGURE 7.6 Nuevo León's homicide rate (per 100,000 people).
Source: Secretariado del Sistema Nacional de Seguridad Pública, Tasa de Homicido Doloso por Entidad Federativa (2004–2019).

Nuevo León's Security Taxes

After Mexico City, the city of Monterrey, the state of Nuevo León's capital, concentrates the most wealth in the country. Although the homicide rate in Nuevo León had historically been lower than the national average, between 2010 and 2013, it experienced a sharp increase with a peak of 42 per 100,000 people in 2011 (Figure 7.6).

During this period, there were several prominent violent events that dominated the public's attention, including the arson at Casino Royale – in which gunmen locked up staff and patrons as the place burned down. Presumed to have been revenge by the Zetas Cartel against its former partner, the Gulf Cartel, fifty-two people died and dozens were wounded at the casino. Other events include the murders of students from two local universities, Tecnológico de Estudios Superiores de Monterrey and the Universidad Autónoma de Nuevo León.

To address the rise in violent crime in the context of the decrease in federal transfers, the state government resorted to an increase in the payroll tax – the main source of tax revenue for states in Mexico – from 2 to

3 percent of wages. Half a percentage point (i.e., half of the increase) was earmarked for public-safety expenditures.[19]

As has been the norm elsewhere in Latin America where security taxes have been adopted, the increase in tax rates prompted public reactions against the measure among the business sectors, complaining that the government had to spend the money more effectively and efficiently before extracting more resources from society (Notimex 2013). However, the government–elite linkages proved instrumental in overcoming this opposition. For example, the PRI governor, Rodrigo Medina de la Cruz (2009–2015), negotiated this arrangement with the business sectors, whom he had incorporated into prominent positions in his own cabinet. Medina de la Cruz had been a federal legislator representing the 2nd district in Nuevo León,[20] which comprises part of the Metropolitan Area of Monterrey – especially the city of Apodaca, which is home to an important concentration of the state's industrial parks, including the steel and aluminum sectors. He also served as an interior minister (Secretario General de Gobierno) under his predecessor's administration between 2007 and 2009. In this capacity, he forged strong ties to the business sectors, with whom he maintained direct communication throughout his administration. Further, his Chief of Staff (Jefe de la Oficina Ejecutiva del Gobernador) was Jorge Domene Zambrano, who began his managerial career with Grupo Alfa – a Mexican multinational conglomerate – and spent between 1979 and 2003 working in different managerial positions in the private sector, including as vice president and president of different companies (Gobierno del Estado de Nuevo León 2017).

This background was instrumental in establishing strong linkages with the business sectors. In particular, the government and economic elites established a partnership, dubbed the *Alliance for Public Safety*. The Alliance established a joint crime-monitoring system to keep track of crime and generate statistics to inform public policy decisions, created a network to facilitate the reporting of crime – the Center for Citizen Integration (Centro de Integración Ciudadana) – and provided funds for the development of a new, more modern state police: Fuerza Civil. This private-sector involvement was a means to ameliorating mistrust toward the police and providing direct avenues for the business community to shape public safety.

---

[19] Although Nuevo León adopted a payroll tax when states were first allowed in 1980, it wasn't until 2005 that all states adopted a payroll tax (Hinojosa and Rivas 2015).

[20] Medina de la Cruz headed the public-safety commission in the LX Congress (2006–2007).

Originally, the Alliance was created as a vehicle for the private sector to put pressure on the government to address the deterioration of public safety. It first emerged out of a series of informal meetings among different levels of government and business elites in October 2010. In these meetings, the business sectors painted a dire picture of the public-safety landscape for businesses. In this sense, the Alliance first became a forum for the business sectors to voice their concerns and demand solutions from the government, and for the government to communicate the fiscal situation they were facing (Mendoza and Montero 2015, 116).

The Alliance was formalized in February 2011, involving a coordinated effort between the state government and the ten largest companies in Nuevo León, or what became known as Grupo Monterrey (Nuncio 2012).[21] The partnership also involved local universities, including Universidad Autónoma de Nuevo León, Universidad Regiomontana (UERRE), Universidad de Monterrey, and Universidad Metropolitana de Monterrey. The formal objectives of the partnership included creating a single chain of command for the different police corporations in the state, purging the police forces of corrupt personnel, providing better salaries and equipment to dignify the profession, strengthening the antikidnapping unit, and increasing the number of places where citizens could file police reports, among others (Mendoza and Montero 2015, 117).

The business elites and the state government reached a series of agreements in which the private sector would become involved in performing a thorough diagnosis of the public-safety problem, elaborating proposals, recruiting personnel, certifying police, and equipping them (Salazar 2013, 60). They agreed on two main strategies, focusing on policing, on the one hand, and preemptive measures – including social programs – on the other hand. An estimated $653.6 million pesos (US$34.2 million) was channeled for policing and $140 million pesos (US$7.33 million) for prevention (*La Jornada* 2010).

The business sectors committed to assisting with evaluations – along the lines of lie detector and drug tests (controles de confianza) – to improve the quality of the police force. They also assisted in the recruiting process statewide in order to address the personnel deficit and modernize the

---

[21] The group first included companies such as Alfa, Vitro, Visa, Cydsa, Cemex, Gamesa, Imsa, Banorte-Gruma, Pulsar y Conductores Monterrey. Down the road, they would be joined by Xignux, Proeza, Soriana, Lamosa, Axtel, and Senda (Nuncio 2012).

state's Police Academy (*La Jornada* 2010). State police were given a 25 percent raise and provided with life insurance (*La Jornada* 2010).[22]

Although hopes were initially high for the success of the program, it has faced important obstacles along the way. After the initial recruitment effort, business elites grew increasingly frustrated with the government's lack of results. For example, the department store chain Soriana became directly involved in the recruitment process, which led the private sector to experience firsthand the difficulty in creating a competent police force. According to Salazar (2013, 64), of every 100 interested people, about 30 would apply, 2 would be selected, and none would end up starting the process.

These linkages were helpful for the business sectors to understand the challenges facing the government and for the government to benefit from the proposals and resources of the business community. Although considerable opposition remained, many influential business elites became less reluctant to shoulder a greater tax burden to address public safety as a result of these linkages. In December 2012, the state legislature approved an increase in payroll tax from 2 to 3 percent, with thirty-seven votes in favor of the measure and two votes against (Carrizales 2012).[23]

The tax revenue has contributed to expanding the state police in Nuevo León. As of June 2019, the tax had financed the hiring of 4,800 Fuerza Civil personnel (Maldonado Rodríguez 2019). According to the National Institute of Statistics and Geography (INEGI)'s National Survey of Urban Public Safety, Fuerza Civil was the state police with the highest favorability ratings in the country in 2018 (*ABC* 2018).

Chihuahua's Security Taxes

In 2008, the homicide rate in the state of Chihuahua climbed considerably. Although it had remained relatively high but stable at around 20 homicides per 100,000 people between the mid-1990s and 2008,

---

[22] With the aim of dignifying the law enforcement profession, investigative police (policías ministeriales, agentes del ministerio público y peritos) were given a 25 percent raise and public-safety officers (policía de seguridad pública) were given a 20 percent raise. Life insurance between $275,000 and $775,000 pesos was also provided, as well as scholarships. A program that would help police become homeowners was also started (*La Jornada* 2010).

[23] The PAN representatives, who had expressed their opposition early in the process, sided with the measure in exchange for additional public-safety funds channeled to the municipalities governed by the PAN (Carrizales 2012).

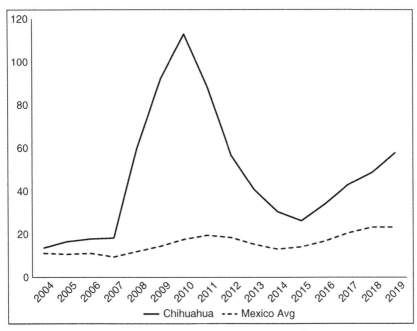

FIGURE 7.7 Chihuahua's homicide rate (per 100,000 people).
Source: Secretariado del Sistema Nacional de Seguridad Pública, Tasa de Homicido Doloso por Entidad Federativa (2004–2019).

in that year, the homicide rate began a sudden increase. By 2010, it had reached 111 per 100,000 people, more than six times the national mean of eighteen (Figure 7.7).

In order to address the deterioration in public safety amid the decline in federal funding for public safety, the state government adopted the Program for the Reordering of the Public Purse (Programa de Reordenamiento de la Hacienda Pública Estatal, PROREHP) in 2013, including the increase of the state payroll tax from 2 to 3 percent. As in Nuevo León, half of the increase (0.5 percent) was earmarked for security taxes. The earmarked tax was transferred to a trust (fideicomiso) overseen by members of civil society (Ramírez Verdugo and Ruiz González 2016).

As has been the constant in the region, there was a lot of public opposition to the tax among business elites. The business sectors complained that the government needed to spend the money it had more effectively and efficiently before considering extracting more resources from the population (Notimex 2013). For example, Eduardo Ramírez, head of CANACO Chihuahua, expressed that "the tax increase shows that the state government wants to kill the goose that lays the golden eggs by extracting more from us, who invest and generate employment in Chihuahua" (*Segundo a Segundo* 2013).The head of CANACINTRA Chihuahua, Francisco Santini, complained that the government had not made it clear what it would do with the tax revenue, and the leader of COPARMEX Chihuahua, Ignacio Manjarrez Ayub, lamented that "If [the administration] charges us for generating jobs, the least it could do is to channel those funds back to supporting businesses, and generating the right conditions to attract investment, to improve the business climate in the state, and we do not see that happening" (*Segundo a Segundo* 2013). Others argued that, in addition to the existing tax burden, they already paid for private security to protect their families. In addition to armored vehicles and five or six bodyguards, many paid for GPS location devices for vehicles and people, and CCTV systems.[24]

However, the creation of strong linkages between government and elites was important to overcome the business sectors' opposition. The governor from the PRI, César Duarte Jáquez (2010–2016), had a business background and maintained strong ties with the business sectors. He had been the commercial director for the electricity company Alta Tensión S.A. de C.V. in the 1980s and a member of the boards of CANACO and COPARMEX in the 1990s (*Código Delicias* 2010a).

Members of his cabinet also came from the private sector or had a background in business associations, including the state's comptroller, José Luis García Mayagoitia (a businessman in the forestry and agricultural industries and member of the board of several commercial banks), the Minister of the Economy, Alberto Chretin Castillo (who was the executive advisor of Prudential Real Estate Investors), chief executive officer at the money wire services company Intermex, Chihuahua, and executive director at Parques Industriales de Chihuahua, S.A. de C.V. He was also part of the leadership of a number of business associations, including the executive director of the Mexican Association at Industrial Parks (AMPIP), president of the Association of Maquiladoras in Chihuahua, president of the Union of Mexican Entrepreneurs, vice president of CANACINTRA, vice president of COPARMEX), and the Minister of Communications and Public Works, Javier Garfio Pacheco (who had been the president of the Mexican Chamber of Construction Industry [Cámara Mexicana de la Industria de la Construcción] and

---

[24] Many hired their bodyguards from Grupo 13, an elite private security group created by the business groups themselves (Coria Rivas 2013).

manager of the construction company Grupo Constructor Montaña Blanca) (*Código Delicias* 2010b).

Against this background, and as many businesspeople were leaving the country, the private sector and the government began to look for ways to collaborate in the search for solutions to the rise in violent crime. According to José Antonio Enríquez Tamez, who was the main liaison between the state government and the private sector for matters of public safety,[25] the governor, members of the state legislature, and business leaders organized a joint "fact finding mission" to Colombia in 2009 to investigate how they had dealt with violent crime. The delegation included César Duarte, who would become the governor and was the president of the state legislature at the time, and business leaders such as Luis Lara Armendáriz – the owner of American Industries, an industrial real estate developer – who made a point to meet not just with the Colombian National Police but also with the Bogota Chamber of Commerce.

There were several lessons that the business elites drew from the trip to Colombia. Most importantly, that business sectors could help turn around the situation. According to Luis Lara, the businesspeople who decided to stay in the country were encouraged by the Colombian experience and were willing to collaborate with the government to improve public safety (Coria Rivas 2013). They began to look for successful experiences elsewhere and brought in consultants from Colombia to conduct a diagnosis of crime in the cities of Ciudad Juárez and Chihuahua and propose solutions.

Another lesson was that improving public safety required investing resources, and staying involved in the process to oversee those resources, as the Colombian business sectors had done. For example, they realized they needed to invest in dignifying the police profession. As Luis Alonso Valles Benítez, a businessman who was kidnapped when he was the head of COPARMEX in Parral, stated, "We need to dignify the police. They receive a salary, but we can do much more than that. We can provide training (capacitación) and bonuses, and make it so that the police officer is a respected member in society" (Rodríguez 2017b).[26]

The joint visit was the first in a series of linkages that government officials and business representatives developed. In 2010, the state government

---

[25] He directed the Observatorio Ciudadano in 2013 and became the secretary for FICOSEC (discussed later).

[26] Valles Benítez became the President of Ficosec's technical committee for a two-year period in February 2017, replacing Luis Lara (Rodríguez 2017b).

created the State Council for Public Safety (Consejo Estatal de Seguridad Pública) and incorporated six members of civil society as members, along with six government representatives. In 2011, the Council proposed the creation of a trust (fideicomiso) in order to foster citizens' participation to improve public safety.

The government and the private sector agreed to the adoption of a temporary emergency 5 percent surcharge on the existing 2 percent payroll tax for three years to fund the trust. Earmarked revenue amounted to about US$8 million per year statewide (FICOSEC 2017). With these funds, the Trust for Competitiveness and Citizen Security (Fideicomiso para la Competitividad y Seguridad Ciudadana, FICOSEC) was created in 2012 with the main goal of "concentrating and administering resources for the realization of programs, actions, plans, and projects that contribute toward public safety and law enforcement, fostering social participation in the competitiveness and citizen security of the state."[27] According to the decree that gave it birth, it would emphasize four courses of action, including the design of public policies with an emphasis on citizen security, strengthening and creation of institutional capacity, intervention for the prevention of violence, and promotion of the rule of law and culture of legality.[28]

FICOSEC's organizational structure further fostered linkages between the state government and economic elites. It was directed by a Technical Committee formed by seventeen members. These included the six civil society members from the State Public Safety Council (Consejo Estatal de Seguridad Pública), along with ten additional members chosen by the citizen side of the Council and proposed by the business sectors and the state's finance minister. A president is elected from among the seventeen committee members.

In 2013, the state government negotiated with the business sectors to expand the funds available for FICOSEC. Because of the close collaboration between the government and the private sector and in particular the involvement of the private sector in the design of solutions and oversight of public-safety expenditures, an increase in payroll tax

---

[27] FICOSEC was created by Decree 842/2012 VI P.E., published in the state's Official Gazette on September 22, 2012.

[28] Along with FICOSEC, two other organizations were created. The Observatorio Ciudadano de Prevención, Seguridad y Justicia de Chihuahua and the Consejo Ciudadano de Seguridad y Justicia de Chihuahua. They were created as auxiliary to the Sistema Estatal de Seguridad Publica, in order to increase the extent of citizen involvement in the generation of information for crime-related decision-making.

from 2 to 3 percent was adopted in December 2013. Half of the increase was earmarked for public safety. The tax passed with twenty-four votes in favor and five against (Mayorga 2013). In 2015, the state legislature approved the renewal of the increase in the payroll tax, which is scheduled to remain in place until 2022.

The additional revenue has funded a number of public-safety projects on several fronts. It has been invested in the evaluation of police to make sure that they meet standards. As a result, the municipal police in Cd. Juárez touts becoming the first police force in Latin America to be certified by citizens (Chávez 2016). Further, in an attempt to dignify the police profession, the funds helped to create the Center for Comprehensive Police Development (Centro de Desarrollo Integral Policial – CEDIPOL), in the city of Chihuahua. The Center is a recreational sports center for police and firefighters and their families. At the Center, the logos of many businesses that contributed funds for its creation are displayed. Additionally, FICOSEC has funded the *2232 telephone number, a hotline to get counseling on how to file a formal report with the police (denuncia formal), and for victims of crime to get counseling. On the prevention side, FICOSEC has funded school dropout prevention programs.

Tamaulipas' Security Taxes

Tamaulipas is another border state where violent crime has been rampant. As Figure 7.8 shows, the homicide rate was 9 per 100,000 people in 2009 before violence skyrocketed. Four years later, the rate had reached 30.

In December 2016, Tamaulipas raised its payroll tax from 2 to 3 percent, as Nuevo León and Chihuahua had done earlier. The government hoped to collect an additional $800 million pesos (US$42.8 million), to reach a total of $2,680 million pesos (US$143.9 million) from the payroll tax. According to Carlos Alberto González García, president of the finance committee in the state legislature, all of the revenue from the 2 percent payroll tax went to service the state's debt, so the government would use the additional revenue for public safety. In defense of the increase, he argued that in Chihuahua and Nuevo León, payroll taxes had already been raised to 3 percent, without the dire consequences that the business sectors had predicted. The reform was approved with twenty-five votes in favor, mostly PAN legislators, and ten votes against (García 2016). The increase in the state's payroll tax was a significant change because it was the first time it had been modified in forty years (*El Gráfico Tamaulipas* 2016).

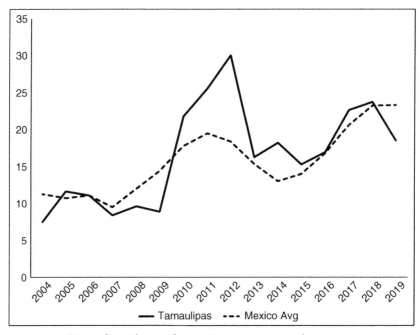

FIGURE 7.8 Tamaulipas' homicide rate (per 100,000 people).
Source: Secretariado del Sistema Nacional de Seguridad Pública, Tasa de Homicido Doloso por Entidad Federativa (2004–2019).

As in Chihuahua and Nuevo León, there was strong opposition among economic elites to the idea of paying more in taxes. The president of CANACO in Ciudad Victoria, Marco Antonio González Salum, expressed that the state's commercial sector was undergoing considerable hardship and would not be able to contribute to the fund, even if they considered it a worthy idea. He stressed that the business sectors were already incurring considerable security-related expenses – including video surveillance systems, alarm systems, and hiring private security guards for their businesses – which increased their operating costs. In his words, "the business sectors in Ciudad Victoria unfortunately do not have the economic capacity to finance public safety. It's not about lack of will, but about not having the funds for it. Of course, we would like to; we would like to become an even more active partner in finding solutions to the public-safety problem, but it would be an illusion to think we have the means to contribute a meaningful amount to fix it." He added that, given market conditions, low sales, and an onerous tax burden, the commercial sector has been forced to adjust the number of employees in order to survive (*El Planeta* 2015).

In spite of this opposition, however, the governor's right-of-center orientation and linkages between government and elites played a role in the adoption of the tax. The tax was adopted as one of the first initiatives of Tamaulipas' governor Francisco Javier García, a member of the right-of-center PAN. García had a background in business as well, being the founder of the confectionery products company Productos Chamoyada, S.A. de C.V., as well as construction companies Maquinados Industriales de Reynosa S.A. de C.V and Desarrolladora Cava S.A. de C.V.

On December 12, 2016, shortly after becoming governor, García convened the state's representatives from industries including hospitality, transportation, commerce, construction, and restaurant, among others, in Ciudad Victoria, the state capital, to discuss the fiscal situation he inherited. In that meeting, he informed them that all of the revenue from the 2 percent payroll tax was mortgaged for thirty years and was assigned to an escrow account to pay a $6 billion pesos debt the state government incurred in 2009 by then-governor Eugenio Hernández Flores – who was arrested on corruption and money laundering charges – of which only 6 percent had been paid by 2016.[29] The payroll tax accounts for about 40 percent of the state's revenue, excluding federal transfers (*El Universal* 2016).

After the meeting, the business leaders were stunned to find this out and reported they had no idea how the government spent the tax revenue. Instead, they thought that the payroll tax was the main source of funding for the state's public-safety expenditures. In the words of Ramón García Garza, president of the National Chamber for Freight Transportation (Cámara Nacional de Autotransporte de Carga – CANACAR) in the city of Reynosa, "This is a surprise to us, we had no idea that previous governments were doing that. How is it possible that they would rob us in this way? Because this is robbery, 2% of payroll, they left this government bankrupt" (*El Universal* 2016).

The meeting was also attended by the governor's Chief of Staff (Jefe de la Oficina del Gobernador), Víctor Manuel Sáenz Martínez, and by the state comptroller, Mario Soria Landeros, who had an extensive background in the private sector, including being the president of COPARMEX Reynosa and a board member on the national board of COPARMEX. Among the business representatives at the meeting were Ramón García

---

[29] The payroll tax revenue was mortgaged to pay for the debt under an escrow (Fideicomiso Irrevocable de Administración y Pago), at 1.15 percent over the interbank interest rate (Tasa de Interés Interbancaria de Equilibrio, TIIE). The monthly cost of servicing the debt was about 40 million pesos (US$2.2 million).

Garza, president of CANACAR Reynosa; Federico Alanís, Consejero Nacional de CANACINTRA; José Alfredo Andrade Castillo, President of CANIRAC Tamaulipas; Julio César Almanza Armas, President of FECANACO; Nohemí Alemán Hernández, President of Colegio de Arquitectos de Reynosa; Roberto Salinas Ferrer, President of CMIC Reynosa and Alfonso Gerardo de León Fuentes, President of CANIRAC Reynosa (Gobierno del Estado de Tamaulipas 2016).

Governor García Cabeza de Vaca made the case to the business leaders that in order to fulfill his public-safety promises he would need additional funds. The state's yearly public-safety expenditures amount to $2,580 million pesos, but the governor sought additional resources for training, purchasing equipment and technology, and increasing the size of the police force. The additional percentage point in payroll tax would bring in an extra $880 million pesos, which the state government aimed to spend in reducing violence and investing in the structural causes of crime.

The business leaders came around to agreeing to pay the governor's proposed increase in the payroll tax from 2 to 3 percent but demanded that an oversight committee be formed in order to supervise the government's spending of the additional tax revenue. Federico Alanís, a member of the national board for the Cámara Nacional de la Industria de la Transformación, stated that "public safety is priceless, it's a priority, it's priceless and so is living in a peaceful environment. That is why we support and give the governor a vote of confidence" (Gobierno del Estado de Tamaulipas 2016).

The additional payroll tax revenue enabled the government to invest in technology to support public-safety tasks, including the purchase of cameras with facial recognition capabilities, as well as new communications systems (Hernández 2018).

The Absence of Public-Safety Taxes in Other States with High Violent Crime Rates

These measures have been absent in other parts of the country where violence has been particularly high, but in which government–elite linkages have been weak. In the southern states of Michoacán and Guerrero, levels of violence more than doubled in a matter of a decade. Although both states had experienced high levels of violence during the 1990s, during the early 2000s homicide rates had been steadily declining. As Figure 7.9 shows, this trend was drastically reversed to reach a rate of

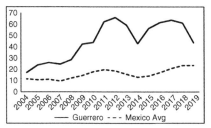 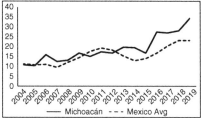

FIGURE 7.9 Homicide rates (per 100,000 people) in Guerrero and Michoacán.
Source: Secretariado del Sistema Nacional de Seguridad Pública, Tasa de Homicido Doloso por Entidad Federativa (2004–2019).

66 homicides per 100,000 people in Guerrero in 2013 and more than twenty-eight in Michoacán since 2016.

In both states, left-of-center administrations have had different relations with the business sectors compared to the experiences in Chihuahua, Nuevo León, and Tamaulipas. In Michoacán, for example, two politicians with strong leftist credentials governed the state during the period of highest violence. The first was Lázaro Cárdenas Batel (2002–2008), the son of Cuauhtémoc Cárdenas, the main founder and three times presidential candidate of the PRD. His grandfather, Lázaro Cárdenas del Río, was the Mexican president (1936–1940) who nationalized the oil industry and adopted a series of highly redistributive measures including land reform. Lázaro Cárdenas Batel's successor in the governor's mansion was Leonel Godoy (2008–2012), a prominent member and founder of the leftist PRD. Godoy had been the president of the PRD and senator from Michoacán. Although the PRD is considered a moderate left by most accounts, the party emerged as a splinter of the PRI out of dissatisfaction with the PRI's embrace of orthodox economic policies and has been much more pro-labor than pro-business since.

The PRD also governed the state of Guerrero throughout most of the period of high violent crime. Between 2005 and 2011, Zeferino Torreblanca presided over the state government. Torreblanca had been a state legislator (1994–1996) and the mayor of Acapulco (1999–2002). Although he came from the private sector (his family-owned department stores in Acapulco), his term as governor was characterized by poor relations with the business community because of his inability to rein in rampant violent crime during his tenure as mayor (Acapulco concentrated about 40 percent of violent crime in the state) and his reluctance to listen to the city's business community.

Torreblanca's dismissiveness of the private sector in Acapulco earned him an antibusiness reputation while governor. For example, after thirty-two business organizations sent him a letter requesting a meeting to discuss the steep increase in violence in Guerrero, he refused to meet with the business sectors (González 2006).[30] Alejandro Martínez Sidney, president of the Federation of Chambers of Commerce of Guerrero state (Federación de Cámaras de Comercio de Guerrero), lamented how the Torreblanca government was unfriendly toward business, showing no regard for the difficulties that the business sectors faced during his tenure (Guerrero 2017).

Torreblanca's successor was Angel Heladio Aguirre Rivero (2011–2014), also from the left-of-center PRD. Aguirre had made a career as a politician with the PRI, but then switched to the PRD after he was passed over for the PRI's nomination to the state government race in 2010.

Lacking the government–elite linkages observed in Chihuahua, Nuevo León, and Tamaulipas, leftist administrations in Michoacán and Guerrero did not adopt elite taxes for security. Rather than contributing additional taxes in these high violence states, some sectors of the business community staged "tax protests" in which they refused to pay taxes until the state government could guarantee a minimum of public safety so that their businesses could operate.

In Guerrero, for example, the representatives of the tortilla industry called for this act of civil disobedience in 2013 to pressure the government to address homicides, kidnappings, and extortion affecting business owners (Miranda 2013). In Michoacán, business leaders from the CANACO Apatzingan stated in 2014 that they would not pay any taxes until a minimum level of public safety was guaranteed for them to operate (*Diario ABC de Morelia* 2014). Although these acts were more symbolic than having any meaningful consequences on state coffers, they are suggestive of the different relations that the business sectors have with left- and right-wing governors, based on the perception of government waste and likelihood of being tough on crime: Leftist governments are perceived as more prone to government waste and being soft on crime.

In short, although Mexico had not adopted national-level elite taxation for public safety at the time of writing, several states plagued by violence adopted increased taxes for public safety. In particular, states

---

[30] Torreblanca's poor relations with the business community include that with his own father, Luis Torreblanca, who sued Zeferino for allegedly forging Luis' signature to sack him as president of the board of the family's grocery stores, La Negrita (Tenorio 2016).

adopted these taxes where violence most affected some of the wealthiest elites outside of Mexico City, as in Nuevo León. This responds to both the existence of wealth in those places and the strong pressure by business elites to address the problem.

But violence is not a sufficient condition for the adoption of these taxes. Right-of-center governments with ties to the business community contributed to making these taxes happen. This does not mean that all right-of-center governments in highly violent states followed this route. Rather, given generalized opposition to increased taxation, right-of-center governments contributed to assuaging some of the elites' concerns regarding how the government would spend the resources in places where business elites were highly threatened by violence and where governments were facing severe fiscal constraints.

Alternative Explanations

Alternative explanations regarding nontax revenue and inequality are worth discussing in the Mexican case. First, one of the most common explanations for Mexico's inability to raise tax revenue is the government's dependence on natural resource rents – oil in particular (Elizondo-Mayer 2014). Mexico's national oil company, Petróleos Mexicanos (PEMEX), contributes close to 40 percent of the government's total fiscal revenue. As Morrison (2014) has pointed out, nontax revenue displaces or crowds out efforts to tax citizens. Mexico is no exception. Additionally, oil wealth generates the perception that the country is wealthy, and therefore, there is no justification for additional taxation.[31] As Elizondo Mayer-Serra (2014) and Romero (2015) have suggested, in Mexico oil has spared economic elites from heavy taxation that might result in redistribution of wealth.

However, while this perception certainly influences citizen's willingness to pay taxes in general and elites' disposition in particular, Gabriel Ondetti (2015, 2019, 2021) notes that Mexico's tax revenue as a share of GDP has remained roughly constant before and after the country's major oil discoveries. In other words, the ebb and flow of Mexico's oil exporting fortunes have not resulted in variation in the country's extraction of tax revenue over time.

Although Mexico's oil dependence might not affect general levels of taxation over time, however, there is some evidence that both the country's

---

[31] For the development of the perceptions argument in a hyper petro-regime such as Venezuela, see Coronil (1997).

economic slowdown resulting from the 2008 global financial crisis and the drop in the price of oil affected states' federal transfers, putting additional pressure on state governments to increase taxes. The federal government redistributes a share of oil revenue (Fondo de Extracción de Hidrocarburos) among states. If hydrocarbons' revenue is affected though lower prices or production, this also impacts state governments' finances.

However, in the case of Nuevo León and Chihuahua, the increases in state taxes took place in 2013 and 2014, respectively, before the collapse of oil prices in the second half of 2014 would take place. This suggests that the general economic slowdown, with Mexico's GDP contracting by 5 percent in 2009, played more of a role than fluctuations in the price of hydrocarbons.

Instead, a consideration that appears to be more related to the state governments' adoption of security taxes is a change in the rules determining the federal government's distribution of transfers to states. In 2008, the criterion for distributing nonearmarked funds for states' discretionary spending changed from redistributive to performance rewarding, such that states with greater GDP growth and greater generation of their own revenue would get larger funds from the federal government (*Diario Oficial de la Federación* 2007). This institutional incentive seems to have encouraged states to increase their own tax revenue and made the option of increasing payroll taxes for security taxes purposes somewhat more appealing.

A second alternative explanation is Mexico's inequality, which has been historically high but in line with Latin American standards. According to Elizondo Mayer-Serra (2014), the wealthiest 10 percent pay about 40 percent of total revenue from the VAT, whereas the poorest 10 percent pay 1.1 percent of VAT revenue. For the personal income tax, the wealthiest decile pays 58 percent of PIT revenue, while the poorest decile contribution is negative (−0.2 percent) due to government subsidies. Not surprisingly, the general arguments business elites give in opposition to government's attempts to raise taxes often point to the business sectors being "captive" sources of revenue for the government. Inequality is one of their main arguments to oppose the payroll tax because the tax burden falls on the formal sector and leaves out a sizable share of informal workers – about 50 percent of the working age population in Mexico (Instituto Nacional de Estadística, Geografía e Informática 2019). This is why broadening the tax base is often one of their main demands.

These figures do not take into account economic elites' tax evasion and avoidance, although this is likely less a consequence of inequality and more a consequence of the Mexican government's weak oversight capacity and unwillingness to enforce compliance. Elites' evasion and avoidance take place both because of the difficulty to monitor nonwage revenue such as consulting fees, dividends, capital gains, interest, rents, etc., but also because the concentration of revenue gives business elites disproportionate power with respect to the government as well – what Fairfield (2015) has dubbed structural and instrumental power. For example, the way that Mexican elites lobbied the finance minister to gut the tax reforms of 1964 and 1972 is well documented (Elizondo Mayer-Serra 1994). Although democratization in the 1990s opened up policymaking – along with lobbying opportunities for economic elites – to the lobbying industry, legislators' conflicts of interest have been poorly regulated and business groups have clearly identified legislators who will serve their interests unconditionally (Elizondo Mayer-Serra 2014, 16). Consequently, business groups have powerful ways to shape tax legislation, as it occurred in the 2007 fiscal reform that introduced the IETU (Impuesto Empresarial a Tasa Única) – a business flat tax (Elizondo Mayer-Serra 2014, 16).

Although inequality does not appear to be a determinant factor, it might influence the type of tax adopted by the Mexican states to bring in additional revenue for public safety. It is possible that high-income inequality between business elites and the rest of society contributes to business elites' ability to influence government policy and fend off more threatening forms of taxation, such as property taxes.[32] While this may be the case, the Mexican case does not allow us to fully evaluate this consideration because state governments do not have many options in their taxation toolbox. Property taxes (impuesto predial) are reserved for municipal governments and represent their only meaningful source of tax revenue (Unda Gutiérrez and Moreno Jaimes 2015). State governments rely mainly on payroll taxes for their tax revenue – other, less important taxes include those on vehicle ownership (tenencia) since 2012, and hospitality taxes on hotels and restaurants (Chapa Cantú et al. 2016, 15–16).

CONCLUSION

In spite of seemingly having the necessary ingredients for the adoption of elite taxation for security purposes, Mexico has not adopted security taxes at the national level. This is mainly due to the country's main economic elites' relative ability to escape violent crime and the federal government's generally good fiscal health, in spite of low levels of tax

---

[32] This asymmetry gives economic elites disproportionate power to shape government policy (Atria 2015; Bogliaccini and Luna 2016; Fairfield 2015).

collection. Whereas in other countries violent crime affected the business elite directly in the principal economic center of the country, mainly the capital, in Mexico the violence has been much more regionally concentrated and business elites in Mexico City have therefore not been as directly exposed to it, at least not for long periods.

The result is the partial replication at the subnational level of what other countries have experienced at the national level. In the Mexican case, an increase in state payroll taxes has become a tolerable solution for elites and an expedient way for state governments to channel additional funds toward public safety. While some elites have moved to the United States and others have made one-time donations to strengthen law enforcement institutions – which in Mexico include the armed forces – in the states of Chihuahua, Nuevo León, and Tamaulipas elites and governments have opted for increasing the tax burden.

Although the revenue from increased payroll taxes is not particularly significant as a share of the country's total because the federal government collects the vast majority of tax revenue, it is consequential for states' public-safety budgets. Development agencies, such as the Inter-American Development Bank, have suggested for years that subnational taxation has a lot of potential in contributing toward economic development in Mexico (e.g., Castañeda and Pardinas 2012). Although incentives have been absent for subnational governments, the change in the federal government's criterion to allocate transfers adopted in 2008 might encourage more subnational taxation. The need to increase public-safety expenditures might be an avenue through which this desired outcome takes place.

Because of Mexico's federal system and the way its fiscal federal arrangement (pacto fiscal federal) is structured, payroll taxes were the only real option for state governments. Since the federal government collects income taxes and VAT and municipal governments collect property taxes, state governments are left with payroll taxes and taxes on vehicle ownership as their main options, but the majority of tax revenue comes from payroll taxes.

Although neither payroll taxes nor vehicle ownership affects the poorest sectors of society, the burden of payroll taxes is perceived – by both the government and elites – to fall more directly on the wealthy because it is seen as a tax on corporations.[33] Although in reality both employers and salaried workers share the burden through wage adjustments (Chapa Cantú et al. 2016; Gruber 1995; Melguizo and

---

[33] A tax on vehicle ownership affects the echelons of society that can afford to own a vehicle, including the lower middle class.

González-Páramo 2013),[34] states are left with little option other than relying on payroll taxes whenever they seek to increase the tax burden, both because of its importance for revenue and the perception that it is a tax that affects the wealthy.

Other explanations commonly found in the literature are less helpful in explaining Mexico's difficulty to adopt taxes. In particular, oil did not seem to play a major role in the adoption of state taxes, which in some cases preceded the collapse in international oil prices. Although fluctuations in the price of oil could generate fiscal problems for the government in the future, Mexico's tax collection as a share of GDP has remained remarkably stable over time, and security taxes have been adopted even in times of oil windfalls.

A final consideration has to do with the mechanisms that have assuaged elites' concerns that taxpayers' resources will be embezzled or wasted. As in other parts of the region, security taxes in Mexico were not only earmarked, but often included civil society oversight mechanisms and sunset provisions as well. In Chihuahua, Nuevo León, and Tamaulipas, these provisions contributed to the adoption of the taxes.

The experiences in these states suggest that high levels of violence make economic elites' willing to pay additional taxes, even when previous administrations have embezzled the state's tax revenue. Remarkably, for instance, elites in Tamaulipas were willing to go along with increases in payroll taxes even after the notification that previous administrations had mortgaged the payroll tax revenue for unknown purposes. Even when the two previous governors and several members of their administrations were wanted on corruption and money laundering charges and remained at large, economic elites were still willing to contribute additional resources and take a chance that the same outcome would take place. Although elites did demand increased oversight over the tax revenue, this suggests how desperate elites can be for improved public safety and how important earmarking for public safety can be to increase taxation.

---

[34] According to the recent empirical studies, about two-thirds of the payroll tax is borne by employees themselves. Only about one-third of the payroll tax burden reduces the companies' after-tax profits (Melguizo and González-Páramo 2013). In the Latin American context, there is evidence that the incidence of payroll taxes lies fully on wages, with little effect on employment (Gruber 1995). This suggests that firms' ability to higher additional workers as a result of the tax is much less affected than business elites claim, but the downward adjustment of wages is of course not possible when firms have a minimum wage floor. In the Mexican case, Chapa Cantú et al. (2016) reach the same conclusion, showing that employees' wages absorb most of the tax. However, while economists might increasingly agree on the real incidence of payroll taxes, perceptions among Mexican business elites are that the payroll tax squarely affects their bottom line.

8

Conclusion

The subjects of every state ought to contribute towards the support of the government, as nearly as possible, in proportion to their respective abilities; that is, in proportion to the revenue which they respectively enjoy under the protection of the state.

Adam Smith[1]

In contrast with the region's early state formation period, contemporary state building in Latin America has the benefit of having an existing institutional foundation to build on along every dimension, including fiscal extraction, public-safety provision, justice administration, and public education and health services provision, to name a few. Rather than starting from scratch and making strides toward a new order, contemporary state building is about improving the existing capacities of the state.

This is no easy or trivial task, even in Latin America, where countries have what can be considered "middle of the road" states: They are not at risk of collapsing but still have serious institutional weaknesses (Soifer 2015, 1). In these countries, state institutions do not have to be created, yet they often woefully underperform. Tax systems and an infrastructural capacity to tax exist, but governments have serious difficulty reaching broad sectors of the population and their wealth (Bergman 2019; Cárdenas 2010). Law enforcement agencies exist, but they struggle to prevent violent crime in vast parts of the national territory and are often

---

[1] In *An Inquiry into the Nature and Causes* of *The Wealth of Nations*, Book V: On the Revenue of the Sovereign or Commonwealth (1976).

overrun by organized crime (Corporación Andina de Fomento 2014; Durán-Martínez 2017; Moncada 2016; Snyder and Durán-Martínez 2009; Trejo and Ley 2020; Yashar 2018).

Whereas the nature of state building might have changed considerably in the contemporary context, the behavior of economic elites has not. Today's economic elites behave in similar ways as their early state formation counterparts. They continue to be self-interested and become involved in the state-building enterprise only when facing severe crises (Bull 2014, 117). Even then, however, their participation is not guaranteed. As recent tax haven scandals – dubbed the Panama Papers and Paradise Papers – have shown, elites will go to great lengths to shield their wealth from governments, even when confronting national emergencies. Not even facing simultaneous crises – public safety and fiscal – will ensure their involvement.

One reading can be that economic elites are more self-interested, even more greedy, than the rest of the population and that their disdain or lack of regard for societal considerations is to blame for their lack of responsiveness. However, another interpretation is that historically corrupt Latin American governments have given elites good reason to be skeptical (Castañeda, Doyle, and Schwartz 2020). Widespread corruption across the bureaucracy persists today in many countries – although with notable variation in the region (Transparency International 2021). It is not unreasonable for any taxpayer to doubt that their tax resources will be put to good use, regardless of their wealth.

This mistrust of government is not unfounded. In Colombia, for example, Óscar Iván Zuluaga, President Uribe's Finance Minister during his second presidency (2007–2010) and one of the main interlocutors with the business sectors during security tax negotiations, was forced to abandon his 2018 presidential run (in which he was one of the frontrunners) because of corruption allegations involving the Brazilian infrastructure company Odebrecht (*El Tiempo* 2017).

Even in Costa Rica, which is among the least three corrupt countries in Latin America according to Transparency International's Corruption Perceptions Index (2021), the Solís administration was rocked by corruption scandals, as well. For instance, an investigation into a dubious loan that the state-owned Bank of Costa Rica awarded to a businessperson in the cement industry reached the highest levels, including President Solís himself, and some of his cabinet members, including his chief of staff (ministro de la Presidencia), Melvin Jiménez, and the former Minister of the Economy, Welmer Ramos (*EFE* 2017).

In Mexico, which is often found among the worst-performing Latin American countries in the Corruption Perceptions Index, corruption was very much in elites' minds during the negotiations for subnational security taxes. The governor of Chihuahua (César Duarte, 2010–2016) was charged with embezzlement and remained at large until July 2020 when he was captured in Miami, and several of his cabinet members – including the Minister of Education and the Minister for Public Works – and government officials in the Finance Ministry have been arrested or are currently facing legal processes (Fagenson and Oré 2020; Fierro 2017; Mendoza 2015).[2] In Nuevo León, former Governor Rodrigo Medina (2009–2015) and several officials in his administration face embezzlement charges as well (*Milenio Digital* 2017; *Expansión* 2019).[3] In Tamaulipas, the previous four governors before the security tax was adopted have face corruption charges – Egidio Cantú (2010–2016), Eugenio Hernández (2005–2010), Tomás Yarrington (1999–2005), and Manuel Cabazos (1993–1999) – and three of those four have faced money laundering charges.

The governors of Chihuahua and Nuevo León plunged their states into debt, at the same time that they were raising taxes and asking the business sectors to contribute more. In Tamaulipas, the news that previous governors had mortgaged payroll taxes toward unknown purposes was communicated to economic elites to make the case for the need to contribute additional taxes. Although most of these legal processes have to run their course, it is highly likely that the very people asking elites for money were embezzling part of these funds for personal gain. Given these experiences, it is remarkable that elites would continue to pay additional taxes knowing there is a good chance they will be embezzled again.

In line with prominent research on state building in Latin America that highlights the importance of politics in earlier periods (Kurtz 2013; Sánchez-Talanquer 2017; Saylor 2014; Soifer 2015), this book found that political factors played a central role in assuaging elites' mistrust of government in the contemporary context. Counter to the notion that left-wing governments are more likely to increase the tax burden on the wealthy than their right-of-center counterparts, a right-of-center

---

[2] These include Gerardo Villegas Madriles, administrator of the Finance Ministry (Administrador de la Secretaría de Hacienda del Gobierno de Chihuahua); Javier Garfio Pacheco, Minister of Public Works; Ricardo Yáñez Herrera, Minister of Education; and Jaime Ramón Herrera Corral.

[3] Including Rolando Zubirán Robert (Minister for Economic Development), Rodolfo Gómez Acosta (Treasurer), Celina Villarreal Cárdenas (Minister for Foreign Investment and International Trade).

government facilitated taxes on elites whenever rising violent crime affected economic elites directly. Although the left is regarded as supporting larger states and progressive taxes, and associated with raising the tax burden to fund expansive government services (Stein and Caro 2013; Santos de Souza 2013; Profeta and Scabroseti 2010),[4] this link did not play out in the context of security taxes on elites. Instead, whenever left-wing governments sought to adopt these taxes, the business sectors did not find the government's commitments credible. Only when the right was involved in the negotiations, whether through a right-of-center president – as in Colombia and Honduras – or as a partner in the governing coalition – as in El Salvador – did economic elites find that their concerns were taken into account and their interests protected.

Leaders' right-wing ideology was important because it was conducive to the creation and cultivation of meaningful linkages between governments and economic elites. Whenever economic elites were incorporated into the bureaucracy to participate in the decision-making process, they better understood the government's revenue needs and were more trusting of the government's stewardship of their resources. Both of these factors made elites less reluctant to shoulder a greater tax burden. Conversely, in the absence of strong government–elite linkages, where governments adopted security taxes without much inclusion of elites as partners in the negotiations, the taxes were much weaker or diffuse. The cases of Costa Rica, where the different leftist administrations adopted security taxes that lacked real teeth, and El Salvador, where Funes' attempt to adopt a security tax failed amid fragile linkages with the business sectors, illustrate this point. Further, due to the lack of incorporation mechanisms to assuage elites' concerns, taxes on elites become more vulnerable to litigation.

These linkages were far from a magic formula. Even in the cases of strong linkages between the government and the business sectors, the process of adopting elite taxes to finance public-safety expenditures was complex and messy. Although a consensus often existed on the need to spend more on public safety to address violent crime – though not always, as the Costa Rican example suggests – disagreement over who should shoulder the bulk of the burden became the norm. Even when business elites considered many in top positions of government as being "one of them," as in Colombia or Mexico's northern states of Chihuahua, Nuevo

---

[4] However, Fairfield and Garay (2017) find that the right may be more inclined to adopt the pro-poor policies associated with the left in contexts of high electoral competition.

León, and Tamaulipas, elites' opposition to paying more in taxes was vigorous. Different perspectives led to disagreement and friction, often in public, regarding the best course of action.

Across countries, governments were certainly frustrated by the lack of resources and business sectors' reluctance to contribute more,[5] while economic elites shared the feeling that they were already paying the bulk of tax revenue and that they were being milked by the government. The process of figuring out the right balance was often fraught with mutual accusation and mistrust. In one case, Colombia's first security tax, the fiscal crisis was so severe and a government shutdown so imminent, that the government could not afford a lengthy negotiation and adopted instead a security tax by decree. This shows that ideological affinity and strong linkages have their limits and do not automatically lead to smooth adoption of elite taxation. However, compared to their leftist counterparts, right-of-center governments had better chances of overcoming these frictions and ameliorating elites' mistrust. The expediency in collecting wealth taxes on elites – compared to other forms of taxation that are gradually collected over the course of the year – and the lack of political opposition among the general population were important reasons governments resorted to elite taxes instead of other forms of extraction presenting their own challenges.

In addition to the notion that right-of-center governments would better protect elites' financial interests, their ability to get elites to shoulder a greater tax burden also relied on the perception that right-wing governments were more committed to addressing public-safety concerns. In particular, right-of-center governments have been more prone to adopting so-called tough-on-crime or "mano dura" approaches to law enforcement, including the militarization of law enforcement – as in Colombia, Honduras, and Mexico – or the adoption of harsher sentences – as in Guatemala and Honduras. Regardless of whether these approaches have proven to be effective – in fact, several studies suggest they have counterproductive consequences[6] – the adoption of public safety as a central concern for right-wing governments has contributed to gain elites' support for these policies.

This support is due to the importance that elites place on public safety, compared to other public goods, as a function of elites' ability to find

---

[5] Most Latin American countries pay less in taxes than expected for their level of development (Flores-Macías 2019).

[6] For example, on the consequences of militarizing antidrug efforts in Mexico, see Merino (2011), Flores-Macías (2018), and Flores-Macías and Zarkin (2019, 2021).

substitutes in the private market. This does not mean that addressing violent crime is not important across social sectors. To be sure, violent crime represents an important burden regardless of socioeconomic level, the most obvious of which are the physical and emotional costs for the victims, be they rich or poor (World Bank 2011, 4).[7] However, whereas economic elites can replace deficient public schools or public hospitals through private alternatives with relative ease, this is much more difficult to accomplish in the case of public safety. The importance of public safety in the hierarchy of public goods for elites was constantly invoked as a major factor contributing to ameliorating their reluctance to pay more in taxes.

Even so, taxation was elites' last recourse to contribute funds to address violent crime. They preferred other, less intrusive forms of financing security-related government expenditures that were less uncertain – as with the defined, one-time donations to build military barracks in Mexico – or less expropriatory – as with Colombia's peace bonds in which bondholders would receive interest on their principal. The more recurrent financing of public-safety expenditures through taxes increased uncertainty for elites and was, therefore, least preferred by them.

Although there is a clear tension between the need to address violent crime and elites' reluctance to pay more in taxes, the book's findings suggest that, given the right political conditions, elites can prioritize public safety over taxes. However, this does not mean that they will renounce attempts to shape the terms of taxation. They can accept additional taxes as a necessary evil, while pushing hard for the inclusion of a series of mechanisms or institutional features that would ameliorate the uncertainty generated from not knowing *what* the government will do with the money, *whether* the government will actually spend the money as intended, and *when* the additional tax burden will end, if ever – that is, not wanting to give a blank check for the government to tax them without out sight.

Although the adoption of these mechanisms was possible because of the interactions that resulted from government–elite linkages, the different

---

[7] Other direct costs for both individuals and corporations include private security, the need to change residence, facilities, or employment (move), as well as the costs to the government to increase the number of police and the cost of judicial processes. There are also downstream consequences associated with crime as well, including the reduction in productivity, the erosion of public trust in the judicial system, and the increase of support for strong hand approaches and vigilantism (World Bank 2011, 4).

experiences with security taxes suggest that institutional design – the creation of "rules and incentives [...] to achieve substantive goals" (Olsen 1997; Weimer 1985, 8) – was important in its own right. Consistent with the field of behavioral economics, which has pointed to the importance of choice architecture – or how the way choices are presented can influence people's decisions (Thaler and Sunstein 2009) – design features generated incentives to elicit elites' support for security taxes.[8]

In spite of the weakness of institutions that characterizes the region (Brinks, Levitksy, and Murillo 2020), design features associated with earmarks, civil society oversight, and sunset provisions ameliorated uncertainty about the fiscal exchange in three ways that reduced the significant animosity that taxation tends to elicit. First, they reduced government officials' discretion in the policymaking process, which threatened elites' future benefits in exchange for today's taxes.[9] Although governments tend to have oversight mechanisms – auditors, legislative committees, and comptrollers, among others – to monitor the performance and financial probity of other agencies, in developing countries these efforts are often considered insufficient and in need of complementary citizens' action to oversee government activity (Goetz and Jenkins 2001, 364). In the countries studied in this book, civil society oversight proved to be effective, including the involvement of business leaders and university presidents to monitor how the additional tax revenue was spent.

Second, design features reduced the threat to benefits in the form of corruption or waste, with government officials embezzling taxpayers' resources or wasting them on extravagant, unnecessary goods. Restricting governments by earmarking the funds for public-safety expenditures contributed to reducing uncertainty about governments' potentially shifting priorities. In order to prevent that future changes in leadership, ideology, or priorities would alter agreements reached today (Bahiigwa et al. 2004; Rodrik and Zechhauser 1988), earmarks generated the perception that governments' hands were tied. Whether in practice governments were,

---

[8] Other scholars have found design features to generate desirable incentives in the areas of corruption (Rose-Ackerman 1978), the political control of administrative agencies (McCubbins et al. 1989), the economic consequences of the independence of central banks (Persson and Tabellini 1993) and revenue collection agencies (von Haldenwang et al. 2014), and the effects of budgetary rules on deficits (Hallerberg et al. 2004).

[9] On the role of these provisions for public policy more generally, see Goetz and Jenkins (2001, 364), Elster (1989), Organization for Economic Cooperation and Development (2008, 32), Prichard (2010), and Scholz and Lubell (1998).

indeed, constrained was less relevant for the adoption of the tax than whether the perception of constraint was generated.[10]

Third, sunset provisions reduced the uncertainty of the duration of the period in which elites would shoulder an increased tax burden. Although not without detractors who blame sunset provisions for biasing policy-making toward the status quo at the expense of meaningful change (Rhee Baum and Bawn 2011; Viswanathan 2007, 672), these provisions force legislatures to reevaluate the consequences of their actions after a period of time and allow for the possibility of adjustment (Deran 1965). In this sense, relatively short-lived taxes provided hope that the additional burden would be brief if elites were dissatisfied with results.

It is worth emphasizing that these design features were central to reducing elites' opposition to taxation regardless of their effectiveness at constraining actual government behavior. Earmarking was expressly forbidden in the constitutions of both Colombia and Honduras. Yet, the experience in both countries suggests that de facto earmarking can be just as effective in convincing elites to pay more in taxes as if the taxes had been legally and formally earmarked.

Further, elite taxes for public safety seem to be fairly sticky, in spite of sunset provisions. In Colombia, Costa Rica, and Honduras, the taxes have been renewed at least once since their inception.[11] Even in cases where violent crime has decreased considerably, as, in Colombia, elite taxes that were originally earmarked for public safety have continued without further earmarking.

However, these design features had limitations in their ability to persuade elites. To be sure, they were not sufficient conditions to elicit support, as the Salvadorean experience suggests: The first attempt to adopt a security tax with President Funes failed in spite of the earmarking, which was not enough to overcome economic elites' mistrust of the leftist

[10] Although earmarks can be circumvented in practice because of the fungibility of public funds, people might still perceive them as addressing the principal-agent problem by tying the government's hands. Just as research has found that earmarking state lottery funds for a particular public good increases participation (Stivender et al. 2016) even if total expenditures on that good do not increase (Jones 2013), earmarking could increase support for a particular tax even if the total amount spent in the intended public good remains unchanged – an outcome that is very difficult for the average citizen to assess. Given this fungibility of revenue and that in some cases earmarking for public safety was not allowed by the Constitution – as in Colombia – perceptions mattered more than whether the funds were actually spent on the announced purpose.

[11] In El Salvador, the legislature was debating the renewal of the security tax at the time of writing.

government and their lack of confidence that the tax revenue would be put to its intended use. It took a second attempt with a broader coalition of parties that included the right-of-center party GANA to establish the negotiation mechanisms required to assuage elites' concerns.

This book responded to Kurtz's call for studying state building in "ordinary contexts" rather than the somewhat exceptional European setting (2013, 6). However, rather than studying interstate conflicts that have become rare in the developing world – as Centeno (2002), Lopez-Alves (2000), and Thies (2005, 2006) among others have done – it studied common forms of violence that are an everyday reality for millions of people across Latin America.

By bringing nuance to our understanding of contemporary state building, this book makes several scholarly contributions. First, it contributes to the emerging body of research challenging the determinism that has characterized the state-building literature (Tarrow 2015). The findings shed light on elites' disposition to contribute to state-building efforts in a context of high insecurity and state weakness, which are common across the developing world. It shows that even in contexts of institutional weakness, as in El Salvador and Honduras, political factors are consequential in mediating the extent to which governments are able to extract resources from elites.

Further, the book contributes to our understanding of what constitutes a threat that economic elites might consider worthy of incurring greater state-building costs in the form of increased taxation. Whereas the previous research has pointed to "existential threats" (Slater 2010) or "elemental dangers" (Saylor 2014) as the bar for elite engagement in state-building efforts, the findings in this book suggest that even in cases where violent crime is extremely high investment in state bulding is not guaranteed. Instead, political factors are important in determining whether elites will partner with the government to fund increased public-safety efforts. At the same time, in some cases, elites are willing to accept modest forms of increased taxation even if the levels of violent crime are moderate – that is, not existential – as in Costa Rica.

Whereas Saylor (2014) suggests that good economic times facilitate state-building pressures by economic actors, who push governments to provide new public goods and stronger institutions in the period of early state formation, I find that contemporary state building in the form of greater fiscal extraction and greater investment in public safety originates not from periods of economic bonanza, but from social demands amid public-safety crises and fiscal strain.

This book's finding also challenges widely held notions that linkages between elites and governments could only be conducive to state capture and lower levels of taxation. For example, Fairfield (2015, 3) suggests that the linkages between governments and economic elites increase – by definition – business sectors' instrumental power, which along with structural power will prevent elite taxation from taking place. However, whereas elites certainly benefit from right-of-center governments in some contexts, in others, strong government–elite linkages can be helpful to reach agreements regarding additional tax burdens. I find that while right-of-center governments do seek to protect the interests of elites, they can also generate mechanisms to assuage elites' concerns and improve the chances of adoption and sustainability of tax reforms.

Finally, whereas a growing volume of research has shown that tax extraction is only one dimension of state capacity and that it is important to study other dimensions as well in order to get a complete picture of state strength (Kurtz 2013; Saylor 2014; Soifer 2015; Sánchez-Talanquer 2017), few studies have focused on the *relationship* between these different dimensions, especially in the contemporary period.[12] One of the main contributions of the book is that it advances our understanding of the nexus between public safety and taxation. The book finds that this nexus, which has been taken for granted in the state formation literature, does not seem to be automatic in contemporary state-building settings. Even in the context of extreme violence, elites are generally unwilling to pay more in taxes to address public safety, and political factors become a key aspect to account for contemporary state building involving both taxation and public safety.

THE POLICY CONSEQUENCES OF SECURITY TAXES

In advancing a theory of elite taxation based on both demand and supply factors, the book's findings also provide a blueprint for contemporary state building in places where addressing violent crime has become a serious challenge. Where adopted, security taxes contributed toward building the fiscal state and the security state. First, on the fiscal dimension,

---

[12] For an exception, see Flores-Macías and Sánchez-Talanquer (2020).

resources raised through the different varieties of security taxes were significant enough to make a difference in terms of the material and human resources governments could make available to provide public safety. Some countries have sought for decades to increase tax revenue through a series of reforms, only to find their tax-to-GDP ratios generally stagnant, as has been the case of Guatemala or Mexico. Although there was variation in how much tax revenue was collected as a result of security taxes, increasing the tax-to-GDP ratio by half a percentage point – as in Honduras – or a full percentage point – as in Colombia – is no small feat.

Second, on the security dimension, these resources were much needed to address budgetary constraints facing law enforcement agencies. In the case of Colombia, for example, the role of the security taxes – about 5 percent of total government revenue – in plugging the gap left by the withdrawal of the US assistance program Plan Colombia was notable. Elsewhere in the region, the additional revenues increased public-safety budgets considerably, allowing law enforcement agencies to invest heavily in equipment and – in some cases – personnel. In the Mexican states of Chihuahua, Nuevo León, and Tamaulipas, security taxes represented close to an additional 50 percent of the tax revenue generated by the state governments.

Although evaluating whether these additional resources have translated into improved public-safety outcomes is beyond the scope of this study, the declining trends in violent crime following the adoption of security taxes are suggestive that those resources can make a difference. The clearest example is Colombia, where violent crime interrupted its upward trend after the adoption of the first security tax in 2002. Since, and during the adoption of subsequent security taxes, violent crime has dropped considerably from its 2002 peak of 70 homicides per 100,000 people. By 2016, the homicide rate had declined to twenty-five. In Honduras, after reaching a peak rate of 91 homicides per 100,000 people in 2011, the homicide rate has declined following the adoption of the security tax in that year. After the renewal of the tax in 2014, the homicide rate dropped to 59 per 100,000 people in 2016. Although with a much shorter time series because of the interruption of the tax by the courts, in Costa Rica, there was a reduction in violent crime from 11 homicides per 100,000 people when the first security tax was adopted in 2011, to 8 homicides per 100,000 people by 2013. However, once the tax was interrupted and the government was unable to rely on those resources for public-safety purposes, violent crime rates in Costa Rica increased again. In El Salvador, the tax was only adopted in 2015, and not much can be read into the behavior of its homicide rate since, but the rate declined from 104 that year to 50 homicides per 100,000 people in 2019. In Mexico, homicide rates have remained roughly constant in the states of Chihuahua and Tamaulipas but decreased considerably in Nuevo León, where the security tax was adopted in 2012 and the homicide rate decreased from 30 to 13 per 100,000 people by 2016.[13]

Although the additional tax revenue is central to the improvement of public safety, it is likely not just the additional revenue that makes for improved conditions. There are many other factors at play, including whether the resources are spent effectively on the proper law enforcement strategies. The adoption of security taxes may also be a reflection of government and society's willingness to address the problem more generally, which might explain the decline in rates of violent crime regardless of the security taxes. However, the combination of the influx of resources, civil society oversight, pressure of sunsetting funds, and targeted approach through the earmarking of resources seems to have made a difference in settings where the government had previously struggled to show much progress. The association between increased resources and public-safety improvements should be taken with caution, but there is suggestive evidence that conditions on the ground have improved – at least in the short to medium term – in the aftermath of the fiscal arrangements between the authorities and business elites.

IMPLICATIONS FOR DEMOCRATIC REPRESENTATION, INEQUALITY, AND THE FISCAL STATE

Beyond security taxes' effectiveness at reducing crime, they also brought about important consequences for democratic representation, wealth redistribution, and fiscal ratchet effects. First, regarding democratic representation, elite taxes earmarked for public safety resulted in the wealthy gaining both the ability to channel tax funds to their own priorities and overseeing government spending directly. In other words, economic elites gained power over the type of public good that would receive priority in government spending, as well as over how the money would be spent

---

[13] In Mexico, after crime rates in the state of Nuevo León declined by 70 percent from their peak, ceremonies were held in which the governor and business elites would exchange awards to recognize each other's contribution to addressing violent crime (Gobierno del Estado de Nuevo León 2015). For reference, in the states of Guerrero and Michoacán, where no security taxes were adopted, homicide rates continued to climb.

once earmarked for public safety. This arrangement is most evident in the Colombian case, where the leaders of the business associations paid taxes to fund their preferred public service and were able to inspect how the government spent the security tax revenue and shape expenditures down to which weapons should be purchased and how many soldiers hired in a particular part of the country.

Although the case could be made that the wealthy have earned these rights since they contribute a disproportionate amount of revenue to government coffers, this runs against the principle of democratic oversight through representative institutions, such as Congress. In theory, elites' oversight would take place in addition to traditional legislative oversight channels. In reality, however, existing channels are extremely weak, so elites became *the* oversight mechanism.

The way in which security taxes have been adopted reinforces trends that have become prevalent in Latin America. Economic elites' determining spending priorities and monitoring security taxes have generated "executive committees of the bourgeoisie," in the words of Schneider (2004, 80), or "virtual senates for the wealthy," in the words of Mahon Jr. (2004b, 23). To the extent that economic elites become a de facto upper chamber or senate in charge of government oversight and with an upper hand over how the tax revenue should be spent, this undermines the democratic principle of equal representation and further erodes the region's already deficient quality of democracy.

Second, elite taxes also resulted in distributional consequences. Although there was variation in the types of security taxes adopted, by and large, the taxes targeted the wealthiest sectors of the population. In this sense, the security taxes were largely progressive, especially those that were targeted, as in Colombia, Honduras, and the proposed tax in Guatemala. The taxes with the greatest incidence on elites were wealth taxes, followed by taxes on financial transactions. Other forms of taxes, including taxes on telecommunications services (El Salvador) and taxes on corporations (Costa Rica) and payroll (state governments in Mexico), had a much more diffuse incidence on broader sectors of the population.

This progressivity contributed to the adoption of the taxes by generating political support for them. Although the real incidence of security taxes did not always correspond to perceptions of who would shoulder the burden, the more the burden of a tax was perceived to fall on the wealthy, the more political support it found among the population and representatives in Congress. For example, even though part of the burden of payroll taxes is transferred to employees in the form of lower wages, in

Mexico the perception that payroll taxes would directly affect corporations was generalized. The business sectors opposed them as if they were
bearing the bulk of the burden. In Costa Rica, the tax on corporations
was perceived as a tax on the wealthy, which also contributed to generate support for the tax. This perception has held in spite of the fact that
the tax was very small to make a real dent on corporations' bottom line
or make a difference to address the country's inequality, and in spite
of the fact that part of the tax burden was likely transferred to consumers. In Colombia, the wealth tax with high thresholds faced virtually
no opposition in Congress because it was perceived as a burden on the
ultrawealthy.

Beyond the political utility of perceptions of burden-sharing, the different types of taxes adopted have different forms of incidence and economic consequences. Although critics of wealth taxes point out that they
discourage savings and investment and encourage the accumulation of
wealth outside of formal financial institutions in order to hide it from
the government, they are deemed to have a greater redistributive impact
than other taxes and can be made highly progressive with stratification
of marginal rates (Flores-Macías 2015, 116). Moreover, research has
associated taxes on wealth with increased adherence to the rule of law,
in part because they are more likely to move taxpayers to participate
in government oversight and hold governments accountable (Mahon Jr.
2019). Although wealth taxes can be difficult to adopt because of their
real incidence affecting the most influential sectors of the population,
this book's findings suggest that under certain conditions, their adoption
becomes more likely.

Conversely, in countries that adopted less targeted forms of taxes,
such as corporate taxes, payroll taxes, and taxes on telecommunications
services, the incidence of security taxes was more broadly shared. In spite
of the business sectors' passionate opposition elicited by the sole men-
tion of these taxes, corporate taxes such as the one adopted in Costa
Rica can easily be transferred to consumers. Similarly, a sizable share of
the burden of payroll taxes adopted by state governments in Mexico is
ultimately shared with employees in the form of foregone salaries (Chapa
Cantú et al 2016; Gruber 1995; Melguizo and González-Páramo 2013).
Telecommunication taxes also tend to be shared by providers and consumers (International Telecommunication Union 2013).

Overall, although with variation as to how directly they targeted
elites, security taxes generally spared the lower echelons of society from
a greater tax burden. The experience of elite taxation in general, and

wealth taxes on elites in particular, suggests that there can be room for highly progressive taxation in Latin America.

Third, regarding the fiscal state, an unintended consequence of the different security taxes is their relative permanence over time. Even in the countries where sunset provisions were incorporated into the design of the tax, legislatures continued to renew them before they expired. Colombia's wealth tax has survived since its inception in 2002. Although the renewal in 2016 was not explicitly earmarked for public-safety expenditures, in part because violent crime rates have decreased considerably, taxpayers still associate the tax with this purpose. It is unclear whether the tax will continue indefinitely, but it has become part of the fiscal landscape for Colombians. Even though public-safety conditions have improved considerably, repealing it becomes more difficult with every year that goes by because the government has become increasingly dependent on it to meet its spending obligations. In Honduras, the security tax was first adopted for a five-year period in 2011, but it was then renewed in 2014 for another ten years. In El Salvador, the legislature is currently debating the renewal of the tax after an initial five-year period. In Chihuahua, a temporary tax adopted in 2013 was renewed again in 2015 to remain in place until 2022. Although these taxes were meant to be a temporary measure necessary to respond to public-safety emergencies, they have persisted even when the emergencies have subsided.

In part, governments have justified this stickiness by pointing to unaddressed public-safety concerns in spite of the progress made. Even in places like Colombia, where the homicide rate has decreased dramatically and surveys no longer reflect crime as the main concern among business executives (World Economic Forum 2016), it would be hard to argue that yearly rates of 24 homicides per 100,000 people are acceptable and that governments can turn to other priorities.

Beyond the unaddressed public-safety needs, however, security taxes have become hard for legislators to let sunset because of the explicit earmarking for public safety. Even if violent crime remains unaddressed, legislators risk appearing soft on crime if they let these taxes expire. They also risk coming across as benefiting the wealthy at the expense of the poor if they eliminate this form of taxation. Therefore, once adopted, security taxes are difficult to end because of politicians' reluctance to signal weakness against crime and a favor to the wealthy. This is ironic since the inclusion of a sunset mechanism contributed to generating support for the taxes by ameliorating elites' concerns that they would not become permanent. By combining earmarking for public safety and a sunset provision, governments generated support for the tax but also made the tax burden more permanent than elites anticipated.

Overall, the experience of the countries studied suggests that the additional tax and law enforcement resources seem to remain in the short to medium run. Although it is unclear whether they will generate long-term outcomes, their contributions stand to put countries on a different path of public safety. Although the fiscal resources are moderate and would not by themselves place countries on a different extractive path, the corresponding law enforcement resources can make a difference in changing the trajectories of these countries, from one where crime is rampant to one where governments gradually reduce the prevalence of violent crime.

If state building is, indeed, "a long-term process that likely involves substantial path dependence," as Kurtz (2013, 30) has pointed out, it behooves us to understand the factors that can get countries closer to a path of institutional strength in today's world. Understanding how to do so is crucial to improving the quality of democracy and improving the lives of the millions of people who are affected by violent crime in the region every day.

References

ABC. 2018. "Fuerza Civil, líder en eficiencia: INEGI," October 19.

AFP. 2015. "Los nuevos impuestos a las comunicaciones entran en vigor," November 22.

Agosín, Manuel, Roberto Machado, and Aaron Schneider. 2009. "The Struggle for Tax Reform in Central America," in Diego Sánchez-Ancochea and Iwan Morgan (eds.) *The Political Economy of Budgets in the Americas*. London: Institute for the Study of the Americas.

Alba Vega, Carlos. 1997. "La COECE: Un caso de cooperacion entre los sectors publico y privado en Mexico," *Comercio Exterior* 47, 2: 149–158.

Alemán, Ricardo. 2005. "Avanza el neopanismo," *El Universal*, March 3.

Alexander Torres, Pedro. 2014. "La ASI exige a Funes no utilizar CAPRES para difamar empresas," *El Salvador.com*, March 4.

Alm, James, Jorge Martinez-Vasquez, and Sally Wallace (eds). 2004. *Taxing the Hard-to-Tax: Lessons from Theory and Practice*. Amsterdam: Elsevier.

Alonzo, Fabricio. 2015. "Impuesto a seguridad no es bien visto," *La Tribuna*, January.

Altman, David and Juan Pablo Luna. 2012. "Introducción: el estado latinoamericano en su laberinto," *Revista de Ciencia Política* (Santiago, Chile) 32, 3: 521–543.

Álvarez, Stephanie and Angelika Rettberg. 2008. "Cuantificando los efectos económicos del conflicto," *Colombia Internacional* 67 (January–June): 14–37.

Amsden, Alice H., Alisa DiCaprio, and James A. Robinson (eds.). 2015. *The Role of Elites in Economic Development*. Oxford: Oxford University Press.

Aranda, Jesus. 2016. "Firman convenio para construir sede de la Policia Militar en Coahuila," *La Jornada*, May 13.

Arias, Juan Pablo. 2015. "87.3% de sociedades aun no han pagado el impuesto a las personas juridicas," *Costa Rica Hoy*, January 30.

Arrieta, Carlos. 2017. "Diputados aprueban en primer debate impuesto a las sociedades anónimas," *ElPaís.cr*, January 9.

Asociacion Nacional de la Empresa Privada. 2011. "Comunicado de prensa," July 2.

Atria, Jorge. 2015. "Elites, the Tax System, and Inequality in Chile: Backgrounds and Perspectives," *Desigualdades Working Paper* 82, Berlin.

Avelar, Bryan. 2015. "Preparan nuevo impuesto para financiar seguridad pública," *Diario Digital Contrapunto*, June 18.

Bahiigwa, Godfrey, Frank Ellis, Odd-Helge Fjeldstad, and Vegard Iversen. 2004. "Rural Taxation in Uganda: Implications for Growth, Income Distribution, Local Government Revenue and Poverty Reduction," *EPRC Research* 35 (January). Kampala: Economic Policy Research Centre.

Bailey, John and Lucía Dammert (eds.). 2005. "Public Security and Police Reform in the Americas," in *Public Security and Police Reform in the Americas*. Pittsburgh, PA: University of Pittsburgh Press.

Baker, Andy. 2009. *The Market and the Masses in Latin America: Policy Reform and Consumption in Liberalizing Economies*. New York: Cambridge University Press.

Baker, Dean and Nicole Woo. 2015. *The Incidence of Financial Transaction Taxes*. Washington, DC: Center for Economic Policy and Research.

Barnett, Michael. 1992. *Confronting the Costs of War: Military Power, State, and Society in Egypt and Israel*. Princeton, NJ: Princeton University Press.

Barrera, Ezequiel. 2018. "Cuánto ha recaudado el gobierno en impuesto para la seguridad y cómo lo ha utilizado?" *La Prensa Gráfica*, May 26.

BBC World Service. 2000. "Fox ya tiene gabinete," *BBC Mundo.com*. November 28.

Belloso, Mariana. 2011. "Impuesto para seguridad: de 0.5% a 1.5%," *La Prensa Gráfica*, June 25.

Bensel, Richard. 1991. *Yankee Leviathan: The Origins of Central State Authority in America, 1859–1877*. New York: Cambridge University Press.

Bergman, Marcelo. 2009. *Tax Evasion and the Rule of Law in Latin America: The Political Culture of Cheating and Compliance in Argentina and Chile*. University Park, PA: Penn State University Press.

Bergman, Marcelo. 2019. "Economic Growth and Tax Compliance in Latin America," in Gustavo Flores-Macías (ed.) *The Political Economy of Taxation in Latin America*. New York: Cambridge University Press.

Bergman, Marcelo and Lawrence Whitehead (eds.). 2009. "Introduction: Criminality and Citizen Security in Latin America," in *Criminality, Public Security, and the Challenge to Democracy in Latin America*. Notre Dame, IN: Notre Dame Press.

Bersch, Katherine, Sérgio Praça, and Matthew Taylor. 2017. "Bureaucratic Capacity and Political Autonomy within National States: Mapping the Archipelago of Excellence in Brazil," in Miguel Angel Centeno, Atul Kohli, and Deborah Yashar, with Dinsha Mistree (eds.) *States in the Developing World*. New York: Cambridge University Press.

Best, Michael. 1976. "Political Power and Tax Revenues in Central America," *Journal of Development Economics* 3, 1: 48–82.

Bird, Richard. 1992. "Tax Reform in Latin America: A Review of Some Recent Experiences," *Latin American Research Review* 27, 1: 7–36.

Bird, Richard, Jorge Martinez-Vazquez, and Benno Torgler. 2008. "Tax Effort in Developing Countries and High-Income Countries: The Impact of Corruption, Voice and Accountability," *Economic Analysis and Policy* 38, 1: 55–71.

Bogliaccini, Juan and Juan Pablo Luna. 2016. "Deflecting My Burden, Hindering Redistribution: How Elites Influence Tax Legislation in Latin America," *WIDER Working Paper* 92.

Bonilla, Heraclio. 1978. "The War of the Pacific and the National and Colonial Problem in Peru," *Past and Present* 81: 92–118.

Botero, Jorge Humberto. 2005. Op-ed "Enemigo," *El Tiempo*, July 20.

Brautigam, Debora and Stephen Knack. 2004. "Aid Dependence, Institutions, and Governance in Sub-Saharan Africa," *Economic Development and Cultural Change* 52, 2: 255–285.

Brautigam, Debora, Odd-Helge Fjeldstad, and Mick Moore. 2008. *Taxation and State Building in Developing Countries: Capacity and Consent*. New York: Cambridge University Press.

Bresser Pereira, Luiz Carlos and Peter Spink (eds.). 1999. *Reforming the State: Managerial Public Administration in Latin America*. Boulder, CO: Lynne Rienner.

Brinks, Daniel, Steven Levitksy, and María Victoria Murillo. 2020. "The Political Origins of Institutional Weakness," in Daniel Brinks, Steven Levitksy, and María Victoria Murillo (eds.) *The Politics of Institutional Weakness in Latin America*. New York: Cambridge University Press.

Bull, Benedicte. 2014. "Toward a Political Economy of Weak Institutions and Strong Elites in Central America," *European Review of Latin American and Caribbean Studies* 97 (October): 117–128.

Burke, Edmund. 1790. *Reflections of the Revolution in France, and on the Proceedings in Certain Societies in London Relative to that Event in a Letter Intended to be Sent to a Gentleman in Paris*. London: J. Dodsley.

Casar, María Amparo. 2013. "Los mexicanos contra los impuestos," *Revista Nexos*, November 1.

Castañeda, Néstor. 2017. "Business Coordination and Tax Politics," *Political Studies* 65, 1: 122–143.

Castañeda, Luis César and Juan Pardinas. 2012. "Subnational Revenue Mobilization in Mexico," *IDB Working Paper Series* 354, Inter-American Development Bank.

Castañeda, Néstor, David Doyle, and Cassilde Schwartz. 2020. "Opting Out of the Social Contract: Tax Morale and Evasion," *Comparative Political Studies* 53, 7: 1175–1219.

Camp, Roderic. 2002. *Mexico's Mandarins: Crafting a Power Elite for the 21st Century*. Berkeley, CA: University of California Press.

Caracol Radio Online. 2016. "Colombia va a recibir cero pesos por ingresos del petróleo este año: MinHacienda," June 11.

Carcach, Carlos. 2008. *Mapa de violencia y su referencia histórica*. San Salvador: Open Society Institute and Catholic Relief Services.

Cárdenas, Mauricio. 2010. "State Capacity in Latin America," *Economia* 10, 2 (Spring): 1–45.

Carías, Patricia. 2011. "Los 2,365 contribuyentes más acaudalados pagarían impuesto para la seguridad," *El Faro*, May 23.

Carrizales, David. 2012. "Aprueban alza a impuesto sobre la nómina en Nuevo León," *La Jornada*, December 24.

Casaús Arzú, Marta Elena and Teresa García Giráldez (eds.). 1996. *Elites, empresarios y estado en Centroamérica*. Madrid: Fundacion CEDEAL.

Castañeda, Néstor. 2017. "Business Coordination and Tax Politics," *Political Studies* 65, 1: 122–143.

Castañeda, Néstor, David Doyle, and Cassilde Schwartz. 2020. "Opting Out of the Social Contract: Tax Morale and Evasion," *Comparative Political Studies* 53, 7: 1175–1219.

Castro, Manuel, Jorge Wartenberg, and Andrés Celis. 1999. "El conflicto armado: La estrategia económica de los distintos actores y su incidencia en los costos de la violencia, 1990–1998," *Planeación y Desarrollo* 30, 3: 81–105.

Centro de Investigacion y Docencia Económica. 2012. *Los impuestos en Mexico: ¿quién y cómo los paga?* Mexico, DF: CIDE.

Centeno, Miguel Angel. 1997. "War and Taxation in 19th Century Latin America," *American Journal of Sociology* 102, 6 (May): 1565–1605.

Centeno, Miguel Angel. 2002. *Blood and Debt: War and the Nation State in Latin America*. University Park, PA: Penn State University Press.

Centeno, Miguel Angel and Agustin Ferraro (eds.). 2014. *State and Nation Making in Latin America and Spain*. New York: Cambridge University Press.

Centeno, Miguel Angel, Atul Kohli, and Deborah Yashar. 2017. "Unpacking States in the Developing World: Capacity, Performance, and Politics," in Miguel Angel Centeno, Atul Kohli, and Deborah Yashar, with Dinsha Mistree (eds.) *States in the Developing World*. New York: Cambridge University Press.

CentralAmericaData.com. 2014. "Quo Vadis Costa Rica," August 12.

CentralAmericaData.com. 2016. "Costa Rica: Empresarios se desmarcan de principal gremial," March 8.

Cerdas, Daniela and Aaron Sequeira. 2016. "Gobierno perdería ₡180.000 millones si se perdona impuesto," *La Nación*, July 11.

Chapa Cantú, Joana, Edgardo Ayala, and René Cabral. 2016. *¿Quién paga el impuesto sobre nóminas de los estados de México?: Un Análisis de Incidencia Económica*. Mexico City: Centro de Estudios de las Finanzas Públicas.

Chávez, Francisco. 2016. "Certifican a la Secretaría de Seguridad Pública Municipal," *El Diario de Juárez*, July 13.

Choto, Daniel. 2011. "El impuesto de seguridad descapitalizara al pais," *El Salvador.com*, July 17.

Código Delicias. 2010a. "La biografia de César Duarte Jáquez," January 8.

Código Delicias. 2010b. "Currículum de integrantes del gabinete de Duarte," October 2.

Collier, Paul. 2006. "Is Aid Oil? An Analysis of whether Africa Can Absorb More Aid," *World Development* 34, 9: 1482–1497.

Collier, Ruth Berins and David Collier. 1991. *Shaping the Political Arena: Critical Junctures, the Labor Movement, and Regime Dynamics in Latin America*. Princeton, NJ: Princeton University Press.

Colprensa. 2009. "48 Empresas libres del impuesto al patrimonio," December 11.

Coria Rivas, Carlos. 2013. "Empresarios en Chihuahua pagan observatorio anti-crimen," April 4.

Coronil, Fernando. 1997. *The Magical State: Nature, Money and Modernity in Venezuela*. Chicago: University of Chicago Press.

Corporación Andina de Fomento. 2014. *Toward a Safer Latin America: A New Perspective to Prevent and Control Crime*. Colombia: CAF.

Corrales, Javier. 1997–98. "Do Economic Crises Contribute to Economic Reform? Argentina and Venezuela in the 1990s," *Political Science Quarterly* 112, 4: 617–644.

Corrales, Javier. 2002. *Presidents without Parties: The Politics of Economic Reforms in Argentina and Venezuela*. University Park, PA: Penn State University Press.

Cruz, José Miguel. 2011. "Criminal Violence and Democratization in Central America: The Survival of the Violent State," *Latin American Politics and Society* 53, 4 (Winter): 1–33.

Cummings, Ronald, Jorge Martinez-Vazquez, Michael McKee, and Renno Torgler. 2009. "Tax Morale Affects Tax Compliance: Evidence from Surveys and an Artefactual Field Experiment," *Journal of Economic Behavior and Organization* 70, 3: 447–457.

Cultura Colectiva. 2017. "Empresarios donan gasolina para la policía de Ciudad Juárez," April 21.

Daly, Catherine, Kimberly Heinle, and David Shirk. 2012. *Armed with Impunity: Curbing Military Human Rights Abuses in Mexico*. San Diego, CA: University of San Diego Trans-Border Institute.

Davis, Diane. 2010. "The Political and Economic Origins of Violence and Insecurity in Contemporary Latin America: Past Trajectories and Future Prospects," in Daniel Goldstein and Enrique Desmond Arias (eds.) *Violent Democracies in Latin America*. Durham, NC: Duke University Press.

Delgado, Pamela. 2008. "El grupo parlamentario de Acción Nacional en la LX Legislatura del Congreso de la Unión," *El Cotidiano* 23, 149: 73–81.

Departamento Nacional de Planeación. 2003. *Cifras de Justicia 1996–2002*. Bogotá, Colombia: Documento de la Dirección de Justicia y Seguridad.

Departamento Nacional de Planeación. 2007. *Documento CONPES 3460*, Consejo Nacional de Política Económica y Social, February.

Deran, Elizabeth. 1965. "Earmarking and Expenditures: A Survey and a New Test," *National Tax Journal* 18 (December): 354–361.

De Swan, Abraam. 1998. *In Care of the State: Healthcare, Education, and Welfare in Europe and the USA in the Modern Era*. London: Polity Press.

DIAN. 2014. *Impuesto sobre la renta para las personas naturales*. Power Point Presentation, Bogotá: DIAN.

Diario ABC de Morelia. 2014. "Sigue firme CANACO Apatzingán en no pagar impuestos," January 28.

Diario Oficial. 2002. "Decreto 1837 de 2002, por el cual se declara el estado de conmoción interior," August 11 (Issue 44897).

Diario Oficial. 2003. Issue 45,415, "Ley 863 de 2003, Por la cual se establecen normas tributarias, aduaneras, fiscales y de control para estimular el crecimiento económico y el saneamiento de las finanzas públicas," December 29.

Diario Oficial. 2005. Issue 45,963, "Ley 963 o de Estabilidad Jurídica," July 8.

Diario Oficial de la Federación. 2007. "Decreto por el que se reforman, adicionan, derogan y abrogan diversas disposiciones de la Ley de Coordinación Fiscal, de la Ley del Impuesto sobre Tenencia o Uso de Vehículos y de la Ley del Impuesto Especial sobre Producción y Servicios," December 21.

Díaz-Cayeros, Alberto. 2006. *Federalism, Fiscal Authority, and Centralization in Latin America.* New York: Cambridge University Press.

Dirección de Impuestos y Aduanas Nacionales. 2011. *Ingresos tributarios recaudados por tipo de impuesto administrado por la DIAN, 1970–2011,* Bogotá: DIAN.

Doyle, David. 2011. "The Legitimacy of Political Institutions: Explaining Contemporary Populism in Latin America," *Comparative Political Studies* 44, 11: 1447–1473.

Drazen, Allan and Vittorio Grilli. 1993. "The Benefits of Crises for Economic Reforms," *American Economic Review* 83, 3: 598–607.

Durán-Martínez, Angélica. 2017. *The Politics of Drug Violence: Criminals, Cops, and Politicians in Colombia and Mexico.* New York: Oxford University Press.

Eckstein, Susan. 2004. "Dollarization and Its Discontents: Remittances and the Remaking of Cuba in the Post-Soviet Era," *Comparative Politics* 36, 3: 313–330.

EFE. 2017. "El cementazo, el caso que salpica a tres poderes del Estado en Costa Rica," October 14.

Elisa, Reis. 2011. "Elite Perceptions of Poverty and Inequality in Brazil," in Merike Blofield (ed.) *The Great Gap: Inequality and the Politics of Redistribution in Latin America.* University Park, PA: Penn State University Press.

Elizondo Mayer-Serra, Carlos. 1994. "In Search of Tax Revenue: Tax Reform in Mexico under the Administrations of Echeverría and Salinas," *Journal of Latin American Studies* 26, 1: 159–190.

Elizondo Mayer-Serra, Carlos. 2014. *Progresividad y eficacia del gasto público en México: Precondición para una política recaudatoria efectiva.* Washington, DC: Woodrow Wilson Center.

El Economista. 2011. "Funes busca impuesto para financiar seguridad," May 12.

El Economista. 2014. ANEP y nuevo gobierno inician serie de diálogos. April 9, 2014.

El Gráfico Tamaulipas. 2016. "Suben tasas del ISN a 3% para 2017." December 12.

El Heraldo de Honduras. 2013. "Gobierno saca a Juan Ferrara del FONAC y de la tasa de seguridad," September 26.

El Heraldo de Honduras. 2015a. "Tasón de seguridad tendrá vigencia por 10 años más," June 1.

El Heraldo de Honduras. 2015b. "DEI no logró cumplir la meta de recaudación de ingresos en 2014," January 14.

El Heraldo de Honduras. 2015c. "Tasa de seguridad ya registra deuda de 1,318 millones de lempiras," May 4.

El Heraldo de Honduras. 2019. "El 92% de ingresos de la Tasa de Seguridad son de usuarios bancarios," November 12.

El Periódico de Guatemala. 2015. "Gobernación propondrá impuesto para la seguridad," January 27.

El Planeta. 2015. "Comerciantes no apoyaran al Fideicomiso de Seguridad Pública, no cuentan con recursos por la crisis," June 24.

El Sol de Sinaloa. 2008. "Operativo Culiacán-Navolato," May 14.

El Salvador's Legislative Assembly. 2015. *Legislative Decree 161/2015.* San Salvador: Asamblea Legislativa de la República del Salvador.

El Tiempo. 1999. "Paz sí, pero sin Victor G y sin canje," October 24.

El Tiempo. 2002a. "Cautela por inversión en Bonos," July 23.

El Tiempo. 2002b. "Debate por Bonos de Guerra," July 23.

El Tiempo. 2003a. "No a reforma tributaria," July 24.

El Tiempo. 2003b. "Reforma política o ajuste fiscal," January 12.

El Tiempo. 2003c. "Corte tumbó IVA del 2 por ciento," September 10.

El Tiempo. 2003d. "Malestar de Uribe por lo aprobado de la reforma tributaria en el Congreso," December 11.

El Tiempo. 2003e. "Soplan vientos de más reformas," December 30.

El Tiempo. 2017. "Hay evidencias de que Odebrecht sí asumió costos de campaña de Zuluaga," October 24.

El Universal. 2015. "Hay 45 mil soldados en la calle para seguridad," May 22.

El Universal. 2016. "Denuncian pago secreto de deuda," December 13.

Elster, Jon. 1989. "Social Norms and Economic Theory," *Journal of Economic Perspectives* 3, 4: 99–117.

Emeequis. 2012. "Difunden la lista de integrantes de la #Telebancada del PRI en el próximo Congreso," June 5.

Escobar, Ivan. 2015. "Medardo González: En El Salvador estamos listos para defender al gobierno," *Diario Co Latino*, July 21.

Everest-Phillips, Max. 2010. "State-Building Taxation for Developing Countries: Principles for Reform," *Development Policy Review* 28, 1: 75–96.

Expansión. 2019. "La UIF presenta denuncia ante la FGR contra el exgobernador Rodrigo Medina," December 29.

Fagenson, Zachary and Diego Oré. 2020. "Fugitive Former Mexican Governor Arrested in Miami," *Reuters*, July 8.

Fairfield, Tasha. 2010. "Business Power and Tax Reform: Taxing Income and Profits in Chile and Argentina," *Latin American Politics and Society* 52, 2: 51–71.

Fairfield, Tasha. 2013. "Going Where the Money Is: Strategies for Taxing Elites in Developing Countries," *World Development* 47 (July): 42–57.

Fairfield, Tasha. 2015. *Private Wealth and Public Revenue in Latin America: Business Power and Tax Politics.* New York: Cambridge University Press.

Fairfield, Tasha. 2019. "Taxing Latin America's Economic Elites," in Gustavo Flores-Macías (ed.) *The Political Economy of Taxation in Latin America.* New York: Cambridge University Press.

Fairfield, Tasha and Candelaria Garay. 2017. "Redistribution under the Right in Latin America: Electoral Competition and Organized Actors in Policymaking," *Comparative Political Studies* 50, 14: 1871–1906.

Fairfield, Tasha and Michel Jorratt. 2015. "Top Income Shares, Business Profits, and Effective Tax Rates in Contemporary Chile," *Review of Income and Wealth* 62, S1: 120–144.

Fajnzylber, Pablo, Daniel Lederman, and Norman Loayza. 1998. *Determinants of Crime Rates in Latin America and the World, an Empirical Assessment.* Washington, DC: World Bank.

Fajnzylber, Pablo, Daniel Lederman, and Norman Loayza. 2002. "Inequality and Violent Crime," *Journal of Law and Economics* 45, 1: 1–40.

Fazio, Carlos. 2000. "Fox, el primer presidente empresario," *La Jornada*, August 28.

FICOSEC. 2017. "Historia de FICOSEC." Ficosec's website: http://ficosec.org/fideicomiso/historia/.

Fierro, Luis. 2017. "Encarcelan a exalcalde Javier Garfio por peculado," *El Universal*, March 28.

Fjeldstad, Odd-Helge and Joseph Semboja. 2001. "Why People Pay Taxes: The Case of the Development Levy in Tanzania," *World Development* 29: 2059–2074.

Flores-Macias, Gustavo. 2013. "Mexico's 2012 Elections: The Return of the PRI," *Journal of Democracy* 24, 1: 128–141.

Flores-Macías, Gustavo. 2014. "Financing Security through Elite Taxation: The Case of Colombia's Democratic Security Taxes," *Studies in Comparative International Development* 49, 4 (December): 477–500.

Flores-Macías, Gustavo. 2015. "The Political Economy of Colombia's 2012 and 2014 Fiscal Reforms," in James Mahon Jr., Marcelo Bergman, and Cynthia Arnson (eds.) *Progressive Tax Reform and Equality in Latin America*. Washington, DC: Woodrow Wilson Center.

Flores-Macías, Gustavo. 2016. "Latin America's New Turbulence: Mexico's Stalled Reforms," *Journal of Democracy* 27, 2: 66–78.

Flores-Macías, Gustavo. 2018. "The Consequences of Militarizing Anti-Drug Efforts for State Capacity in Latin America: Evidence from Mexico," *Comparative Politics* 51, 1: 1–20.

Flores-Macías, Gustavo. 2019. "Introduction: The Political Economy of Taxation in Latin America," in Gustavo Flores-Macías (ed.) *The Political Economy of Taxation in Latin America*. Cambridge University Press.

Flores-Macías, Gustavo and Sarah Kreps. 2013. "Political Parties at War: A Study of American War Finance, 1789–2010," *American Political Science Review* 107, 4: 833–848.

Flores-Macías, Gustavo and Sarah Kreps. 2017. "Borrowing Support for War: The Effect of War Finance on Public Attitudes toward Conflict," *Journal of Conflict Resolution* 61, 5: 1997–1020.

Flores-Macías, Gustavo and Mariano Sánchez-Talanquer. 2020. "Building the Modern State in Developing Countries: Understanding the Relationship between Security and Taxes with Evidence from Mexico," *Politics & Society* 48, 3: 423–451.

Flores-Macias, Gustavo and Jessica Zarkin. 2019. "The Militarization of Law Enforcement: Evidence from Latin America," *Perspectives on Politics*, Online First.

Flores-Macías, Gustavo and Jessica Zarkin. 2021. "Militarization and Perceptions of Law Enforcement: Evidence from a Conjoint Experiment in Mexico," *British Journal of Political Science*, Online First.

Flores-Macías, Gustavo and Jessica Zarkin. 2022. "The Consequences of Militarized Policing for Human Rights: Evidence from Mexico," *Working Paper*, Cornell University.

Font, Juan Luis. 2015. "Impuesto para la seguridad," *Revista Contrapoder*, June 1.

Forsythe, Michael. 2017. "Paradise Papers Shine Light on Where the Elite Keep their Money," *New York Times*, November 5.

Fuentes Knight, Juan Alberto. 2012. *Rendicion de cuentas*. Guatemala: F&G Editores.

Fundación Salvadoreña para el Desarrollo Económico y Social. 2014. *Quinto año de gobierno del Presidente Funes: Apreciación General*. Departamento de Estudios Políticos. June, San Salvador: FUSADES.

Fundación Salvadoreña para el Desarrollo Económico y Social. 2015. *Posición Institucional: Estamos frente a una contribución especial para la seguridad ciudadana o un impuesto?* Departamento de Estudios Legales 5, October, San Salvador: FUSADES.

Fundación Salvadoreña para el Desarrollo Económico y Social. 2019. *Año político 5: junio 2018 – mayo 2019*, San Salvador: FUSADES.

Gaceta del Congreso de Colombia. 2003. Issue 572. "Proyecto de Ley 155 de 2003," November 6.

Gaceta Oficial de Costa Rica. 2011. "Decreto 36693, Moratoria a la explotación petrolera," August 19.

Gaceta Oficial de Costa Rica. 2017. "Ley No. 9428, Impuesto a las personas jurídicas," March 21.

Gaceta Oficial de Honduras. 2011. "Ley de Seguridad Poblacional," July 8.

Gagne, David. 2015. "Insecurity Hurting El Salvador's Economy: Banks," *InSight Crime*, June 5.

García, Arnoldo. 2016. "Aprueban incremento del 3% al impuesto sobre la nomina," *La Silla Vacia*, December 15.

García, Jaime. 2015. "Sánchez Cerén justifica impuesto a servicios de telefonía," *ElSalvador.com*, September 21.

Geddes, Barbara. 1996. *Politician's Dilemma: Building State Capacity in Latin America*. Berkeley, CA: University of California Press.

Gibson, Edward. 1996. *Class and Conservative Parties: Argentina in Comparative Perspective*. Baltimore: Johns Hopkins University Press.

Gilbert, Charles. 1970. *American Financing of World War I*. Westport, CT: Greenwood Publishing.

Giraudi, Agustina. 2012. "Conceptualizando la naturaleza del estado: más allá de los estados débiles o fuertes," *Revista de Ciencia Política* (Santiago, Chile) 32, 3: 599–611.

Glaser, Mark and Bartley Hildreth. 1996. "A Profile of Discontinuity between Citizen Demand and Willingness to Pay Taxes: Comprehensive Planning for Park and Recreation Investment," *Public Budgeting and Finance* 16, 4 (December): 96–113.

Gobierno de la Republica de Honduras. 2013. "Gabinete economico analiza presupuesto con empresa privada," Press release, January 2.

Gobierno del Estado de Nuevo Leon. 2015. "Reconoce Gobernador Rodrigo Medina a integrantes de la "Alianza por la Seguridad," Press release, September 23.

Gobierno del Estado de Nuevo Leon. 2017. "Currículo de Jorge Domene Zambrano," Página de la Unidad de Transparencia, last visited on November 30, 2017.

Gobierno del Estado de Tamaulipas. 2016. "Explica el gobernador a empresarios hipoteca heredada del ISN," Press release, December 12.

Goetz, Anne Marie and Rob Jenkins. 2001. "Hybrid Forms of Accountability: Citizen Engagement in Institutions of Public Sector Oversight in India," *Public Management Review* 3, 3: 363–383.

Gonzalez, Carmen. 2006. "No acepto ningún emplazamiento de empresarios para dialogar: Zeferino," *El Sur*, June 1.

González, Douglas. 2015. "GANA propone nuevo impuesto para seguridad a quienes ganen más de medio millón de dólares al año," *El Blog*, September 22.

Grindle, Merilee. 2000. *Audacious Reforms: Institutional Invention and Democracy in Latin America*. Baltimore: Johns Hopkins University Press.

Gruber, Jonathan. 1995. "The Incidence of Payroll Taxation: Evidence from Chile," *NBER Working Paper* 5053, March.

Guerrero, Jesús. 2017. "Matan en Acapulco a 150 empresarios en 18 meses," *Reforma*, July 8.

Gutiérrez, Tatiana. 2016. "Agricultura se aleja de la posición de UCCAEP sobre impuestos," CRHoy.com, March 3.

Haggard, Stephan, Silvia Maxfield, and Ben Ross Schneider. 1997. "Theories of Business and Business-State Relations," in Sylvia Maxfield and Ben Ross Schneider (eds.) *Business and the State in Developing Countries*. Ithaca, NY: Cornell University Press.

Hallerberg, Mark, Rolf Strauch, and Jürgen von Hagen. 2004. "The Design of Fiscal Rules and Forms of Governance in European Union Countries," Working Paper Series 419. Frankfurt: European Central Bank.

Harbers, Imke. 2014. "Taxation and the Unequal Reach of the State: Mapping State Capacity in Ecuador," *Governance* 28, 3: 373–391.

Harding, Luke. 2016. "What Are the Panama Papers? A Guide to History's Biggest Data Leak," *The Guardian*, April 5.

Hart, Austin. 2010. "Death of the Partisan? Globalization and Taxation in South America, 1990–2006," *Comparative Political Studies* 43, 3: 304–328.

Haugaard, Lisa, Adam Isacson, and Jennifer Johnson. 2011. *A Cautionary Tale: Plan Colombia's Lessons for U.S. Policy toward Mexico and Beyond*. Washington, DC: Washington Office on Latin America.

Heinle, Kimberly, Cory Molzahn, and David Shirk. 2015. *Drug Violence in Mexico: Data and Analysis through 2014*, Justice in Mexico Project, Department of Political Science and International Relations, University of San Diego.

Heinle, Kimberly, Cory Molzahn, and David Shirk. 2017. *Drug Violence in Mexico: Data and Analysis through 2016*, Justice in Mexico Project, Department of Political Science and International Relations, University of San Diego.

Herbst, Jeffrey. 1990. "War and the State in Africa," *International Organization* 14, 4: 117–139.

Herbst, Jeffrey. 2000. *States and Power in Africa: Comparative Lessons in Authority and Control*. Princeton, NJ: Princeton University Press.

Hernández, Julián. 2018. "Pide IP resultados en seguridad tras aumento de ISN en Tamaulipas," *Gaceta*. May 7.

Hernández Rodríguez, Rogelio. 2011. ¿Aprende a gobernar la oposición? Los gabinetes presidenciales del PAN, 2000–2010," *Foro Internacional* 51, 1: 68–103.

Hinojosa, Adriana and Eduardo Rivas. 2015. "El impuesto sobre nóminas en Nuevo León: Fundamento para una iniciativa de reforma a traves de su análisis sustantivo," Proceedings of the XX Congreso de Contaduría, Administración e Informática. Mexico City, Mexico.

Hirschman, Albert. 1968. "The Political Economy of Import-Substituting Industrialization in Latin America," *The Quarterly Journal of Economics* 82, 1 (February): 1–32.

Hirschman, Albert. 1981. *Essays in Trespassing: Economics to Politics and Beyond*. New York: Cambridge University Press.

Herrera, Manuel. 2014. "Próximo viernes vence el tiempo para el pago del impuesto a personas jurídicas," January 28.

Holden, Robert. 2004. *Armies without Nations: Public Violence and State Formation in Central America, 1821–1960*. Oxford: Oxford University Press.

Huber, Evelyne and Fred Zolt. 2004. "Successes and Failures of Neoliberalism," *Latin American Research Review* 39, 3 (October): 150–164.

Huber, Evelyne and John Stephens. 2012. *Democracy and the Left: Social Policy and Inequality in Latin America*. Chicago: University of Chicago Press.

Hui, Victoria. 2005. *War and State-formation in Ancient China and Early Modern Europe*. New York: Cambridge University Press.

Hunter, Wendy. 1997. "Continuity or Change? Civil-Military Relations in Democratic Argentina, Chile, and Peru," *Political Science Quarterly* 112, 3 (Fall): 453–475.

Internal Displacement Monitoring Center. 2010. *Briefing Paper by the Norwegian Refugee Council Internal Displacement Monitoring Center on Forced Displacement in Mexico due to Drug Cartel Violence*, December.

Instituto Nacional de Estadística, Geografía e Informática. 2019. *Resultados de la Encuesta Nacional de Ocupación y Empleo* (Press release). August 14.

Instituto Nacional de Estadística y Censos (INEC). 2012. *X Censo de Población y VI de Vivienda 2011*. San José: INEC.

Instituto Nacional de Estadística y Censos (INEC). 1993–2015. *Anuario Estadístico: Seguridad Ciudadana y Justicia*. San José: INEC.

Instituto Mexicano para la Competitividad. 2013. *Perspectivas de una reforma fiscal en México*. Mexico City: IMCO.

International Telecommunication Union. 2013. *Taxing Telecommunication/ICT Services: An Overview*. Switzerland: ITU.

Jones, Daniel. 2013. "Education's Gambling Problem: The Impact of Earmarking Lottery Revenues for Education on Charitable Giving and Government Spending," *Working Paper* 13/307, Centre for Market and Public Organisation, Bristol University.

Joshi, Anuradha, Wilson Prichard, and Christopher Heady. 2014. "Taxing the Informal Economy: The Current State of Knowledge and Agendas for Future Research," *Journal of Development Studies* 50, 10: 1325–1347.

Karl, Terri. 1997. *The Paradox of the Plenty: Oil Booms and Petro-States*. Berkeley, CA: University of California Press.

Kurtz, Marcus. 2009. "The Social Foundations of Institutional Order: Reconsidering War and the 'Resource Curse' in Third World State Building," *Politics and Society* 37, 4: 479–520.

Kurtz, Marcus. 2013. *Latin American State Building in Comparative Perspective Social Foundations of Institutional Order*. New York: Cambridge University Press.

Kurtz, Marcus and Andrew Schrank. 2012. "Capturing State-Strength: Experimental and Econometric Approaches," *Revista de Ciencia Política* (Santiago) 32, 3: 613–621.

La Crónica. 2006. "Anuncia gabinete de seguridad Operativo Conjunto Michoacán," December 12.

La Información. 2012. "Funes inicia diálogo para alcanzar un acuerdo nacional contra la inseguridad," March 5.

La Jornada. 2010. "Presentan en NL el programa Alianza por la Seguridad," September 14.

La Nación. 2016. "Ministro de seguridad renunciará si no se aprueba impuesto a sociedades," October 3.

La Nación. 2017a. "Diputados reviven impuesto hasta de ₡212.000 anuales a las personas jurídicas," January 9.

La Nación. 2017b. "Gobierno cortará en obras y educación para contener gasto," September 2.

La Prensa Gráfica. 2011a. "A debate impuesto a seguridad," July 2.

La Prensa Gráfica. 2011b. "Impuesto a patrimonios superiores a $500 mil," July 1.

La Prensa Grafica. 2012. "Banco Mundial reclama a empresarios colaboración en seguridad," April 20.

La Prensa Gráfica. 2014. "ANEP tiende nuevos puentes para diálogo con el gobierno," September 11.

La Prensa Gráfica. 2015. "Nuevo impuesto o fideicomiso podría financiar plan para seguridad," February 13.

La Prensa Gráfica. 2017a. "El Salvador usará dinero de impuesto seguridad para traer helicópteros regalados, pero viejos," September 13.

La Prensa Gráfica. 2017b. "22% del impuesto para seguridad se destinó a CAPRES," June 9.

La Prensa de Honduras. 2011. "Empresarios y gobierno consensuan tasa de seguridad," June 1.

La Prensa de Honduras. 2013a. "Con fondos de tasón pondrán en operación el Halcón I y el II," December 21.

La Prensa de Honduras. 2013b. "Hoy aprobarán reformas a la ley de Tasa de Seguridad," August 15.

Lamuno, Morielle. 2014. "El 90% de los panamenos gana menos de 900 dólares," *Panama America*, June 10.

Latinobarómetro. 2013. *Informe 2013*. Santiago: Corporación Latinobarómetro.

Leff, Nathaniel. 1982. *Underdevelopment and Development of Brazil*. London: George Allen and Unwin.

Leitón, Patricia. 2013. "A Costa Rica le toma diez años cumplir con meta en educación," *La Nación*, November 25.

Levi, Margaret. 1988. *Of Rule and Revenue*. Berkeley, CA: University of California Press.

Lieberman, Evan. 2003. *Race and Regionalism in the Politics of Taxation in Brazil and South Africa*. New York: Cambridge University Press.

Lipset, Seymour and Stein Rokkan. 1967. *Party Systems and Voter Alignments: Cross National Perspectives*. New York: Free Press.

Loaeza, Soledad. 1999. *El Partido Acción Nacional: la larga marcha, 1939–1994*. Mexico: Fondo de Cultura Económica.

Lofstrom, William. 1970. "Attempted Economic Reforms and Innovation in Bolivia under Antonio Jose de Sucre, 1825–1828," *Hispanic American Historical Review* 50, 2: 279–299.

López, Alberto. 2016. "El Salvador recauda 50.1 millones de dólares con su impuesto de seguridad," *Infodefensa.com*, October 14.

Lopez-Alves, Fernando. 2000. *State Formation and Democracy in Latin America 1810–1900*. Durham, NC: Duke University Press.

López-Alves, Fernando. 2001. "The Transatlantic Bridge: Mirrors, Charles Tilly, and State Formation in the River Plate," in Miguel Angel Centeno and Fernando López-Alves (eds.) *Grand Theory through the Lens of Latin America*. Princeton, NJ: Princeton University Press.

Lopez-Calva, Felipe and Nora Lustig (eds.). 2010. "Explaining the Decline in Inequality in Latin America: Technological Change, Educational Upgrading, and Democracy," in *Declining Inequality in Latin America: A Decade of Progress?* Washington, DC: Brookings Institution Press and United Nations Development Program.

Loría, Max Alberto. 2014. "Perfil de los homicidios en Costa Rica en la última década," Vigesimo Informe Estado de la Nación en Desarrollo Humano Sostenible, San José: Programa Estado de la Nación.

Luna, Juan Pablo and Sergio Toro Maureira. 2014. "State Capacity and Democratic Governance in Latin America: A Survey Data-Based Approach to Measurement and Assessment," Americas Barometer Insights 102.

Mahon, James. Jr. 2004a. "Causes of Tax Reform in Latin America, 1977–95," *Latin American Research Review* 39, 1: 3–30.

Mahon, James. Jr. 2004b. *Mobile Capital and Latin American Development*. Penn State University Press.

Mahon, James. Jr, Marcelo Bergman, and Cynthia Arnson (eds.). 2015. *Progressive Tax Reform and Equality in Latin America*. Washington, DC: Woodrow Wilson Center.

Mahon, James. Jr. 2019. "Weak Liberalism and Weak Property Taxation in Latin America," in Gustavo Flores-Macías (ed.) *The Political Economy of Taxation in Latin America*. New York: Cambridge University Press.

Maldonado Rodríguez, Orlando. 2019. "Reducirán número de policías de en Fuerza Civil en Nuevo León," *Milenio*, June 21.

Mann, Michael. 1984. "The Autonomous Power of the State: Its Origins, Mechanisms, and Results," *European Journal of Sociology* 25, 2: 185–213.

Mares, Isabela and Didac Queralt. 2013. "Taxation and the Development of Fiscal Capacity," *Working Paper* 281, Madrid: Juan March Institute.

Mayorga, Patricia. 2013. "Sube congreso del estado impuesto sobre nómina del 2 al 3 por ciento," *El Diario de Juárez*, December 10.

Mazzuca, Sebastián. 2021. *Latecomer State Formation: Political Geography and Capacity Formation in Latin America*. New Haven, CT: Yale University Press.

McCubbins, Matthew, Roger Noll, and Barry Weingast. 1989. "Structure and Process, Politics, and Policy: Administrative Arrangements and the Political Control of Agencies," *Virginia Law Review* 75, 2: 431–482.

Melguizo, Angel and Jose Manuel González-Páramo. 2013. "Who Bears Labour Taxes and Social Contributions? A Meta-Analysis Approach," *SERIEs* 4, 3: 247–271.

Mendoza, Israel. 2015. "Encubre Duarte maniobras de su secretario de hacienda," *Capital Mexico*, September 8.

Mendoza, Héctor and Juan Carlos Montero. 2015. "Gobernanza para la gobernabilidad: La construcción de Fuerza Civil, la nueva policía de Nuevo León," *Revista Mexicana de Análisis Político y Administración Pública* 4, 2: 103–128.

Merino, José. 2011. "Los operativos conjuntos y la tasa de homicidios: Una medición." *Nexos*, June 1.

Messner, J. J. and Melody Knight. 2011. *Natural Disasters and Their Effect on State Capacity. Failed States Index 2011*. Fund for Peace.

Meza, Mariana. 2015. "El sector privado y la seguridad ciudadana: el caso Tijuana," *Forbes Mexico*, December 7.

Migdal, Joel. 1988. *Strong Societies and Weak States: State-Society Relations and Capabilities in the Third World*. Princeton, NJ: Princeton University Press.

Milenio Digital. 2014. "Es cobarde quien se va de Monterrey: Lorenzo Zambrano," December 5.

Milenio Digital. 2017. "Ex gobernador Medina regresará a los tribunales," May 13.

Ministerio de Defensa Nacional. 2008. "Metodología para el cálculo de gasto en defensa y seguridad," Serie de Prospectiva, Documento #1, Bogotá, Colombia.

Ministerio de Defensa Nacional. 2009. "Gasto en Defensa y Seguridad 1998–2011," Serie de Prospectiva, Estudio #2, Bogotá, Colombia.

Ministerio de Hacienda de Costa Rica. 2015. *Ingresos totales del gobierno central, 1990–2014*. San José: Ministerio de Hacienda.

Ministerio de Hacienda de El Salvador. 2019. *Estadísticas tributarias básicas al 2018*. Dirección de Política Económica y Fiscal, May 7.

Ministerio de Hacienda de El Salvador. 2020. *Estadísticas básicas sobre las finanzas públicasa diciembre de 2019*. Dirección de Política Económica y Fiscal, April 29.

Ministerio de Justicia y Seguridad Pública. 2014. *Consolidado de revisión de homicidios*. San Salvador: Ministerio de Justicia y Seguridad Pública.

Miranda, Flor. 2013. "Empresarios de Guerrero dejarán de pagar impuestos tras asesinatos," *Los Angeles Press*, August 22.

Mizrahi, Yemile. 2003. *From Martyrdom to Power: The Partido Accion Nacional in Mexico*. South Bend: Notre Dame University Press.

Moncada, Eduardo. 2016. *Cities, Business, and the Politics of Urban Violence in Latin America*. Palo Alto: Stanford University Press.

Morales, María Cristina, Óscar Morales, Angelica Menchaca, and Adam Sebastian. 2013. "The Mexican Drug War and the Consequent Population Exodus: Transnational Movement at the US-Mexico Border," *Societies* 3: 80–103.

Morrison, Kevin. 2009. "Oil, Non-Tax Revenue, and the Distributional Foundations of Regime Stability," *International Organization* 63, 1 (January): 107–138.

Morrison, Kevin. 2014. *Non-Taxation and Representation*. New York: Cambridge University Press.

Moody's. 2017. *Moody's Downgrades Costa Rica's Government Bond Rating to Ba2, Continued Negative Outlook*. New York: Moody's Investors Service.

Moore, Mick. 2004. "Revenues, State Formation, and the Quality of Governance in Developing Countries," *International Political Science Review* 25: 297–319.

Muggah, Robert and Ilona Szabó de Carvallo. 2018. "Violent Crime in São Paulo Has Dropped Dramatically. Is This Why?" World Economic Forum, Online Blog, March 7.

Murillo, Maria Victoria. 2001. *Labor Unions, Partisan Coalitions, and Market Reforms in Latin America*. New York: Cambridge University Press.

Navas, Lucia. 2011. "Nicaragua no creará impuesto para la seguridad," *La Prensa*, August 2.

Nelson, Jane. 2000. *The Business of Peace: The Private Sector as a Partner in Conflict Prevention and Resolution*. London: Council on Economic Priorities.

Neumayer, Eric. 2005. "Inequality and Violent Crime: Evidence from Data on Robbery and Violent Theft," *Journal of Peace Research* 42, 1: 101–112.

North, Douglass. 1981. *Structure and Change in Economic History*. New York: Norton.

Noticias de Guatemala. 2010. "Organismo ejecutivo ve como buena alternativa el impuesto de seguridad," November 3.

Notimex. 2013. "Monterrey, ejemplo de transformación en seguridad: The Economist," June 14.

Nuncio, Abraham. 2012. "El grupo de los diez," *La Jornada*, February 4.

OECD. 2015. *OECD Economic Surveys: Colombia*. Paris: OECD.

O'Kane, Rosemary. 2000. "Post-Revolutionary State-Building in Ethiopia, Iran, and Nicaragua," *Political Studies* 48, 5: 970–988.

Olsen, Johan. 1997. "Institutional design in democratic contexts," *Journal of Political Philosophy* 5, 3: 202–229.

Olson, Mancur. 1971. *The Logic of Collective Action*. Cambridge, MA: Harvard University Press.

Ondetti, Gabriel. 2021. *Property Threats and the Politics of Anti-Statism: The Historical Roots of Contemporary Tax Systems in Latin America*. New York: Cambridge University Press.

Ondetti, Gabriel. 2015. "The Power of Preferences: Economic Elites and the Politics of Light Taxation in Mexico," prepared for the meeting of the Latin American Studies Association in San Juan, Puerto Rico.

Ondetti, Gabriel. 2019. "Once Bitten, Twice Shy: Path Dependence, Power Resources and the Magnitude of the Tax Burden in Latin America," in Gustavo Flores-Macías (ed.) *The Political Economy of Taxation in Latin America*. New York: Cambridge University Press.

Oreamuno, José María. 2015. "Declaran inconstitucional el impuesto a las personas jurídicas," *El Financiero de Costa Rica*, January 28.

Organization for Economic Cooperation and Development. 2008. *Governance, Taxation, and Accountability: Issues and Practices*. Paris: OECD Development Assistance Committee.

Organization for Economic Cooperation and Development. 2015. *Revenue Statistics in Latin America and the Caribbean 1990–2013*. Paris: OECD.

Ortiz Mena, Antonio. 1998. *El desarrollo estabilizador: reflexiones sobre una época*. Mexico: Fondo de Cultura Económica.

Pacheco, Melissa. 2018. "ARENA ya pidió eliminar el impuesto a la telefonía," *La Prensa Gráfica*, December 5.

Paige, Jeffrey. 1997. *Coffee and Power: Revolution and the Rise of Democracy in Central America*. New York: Cambridge University Press.

Peacock, Alan and Jack Wiseman. 1961. *The Growth of Public Expenditures in the United Kingdom*. Princeton, NJ: Princeton University Press.

Pérez Trejo, Carlos. 2014. *Equidad tributaria en El Salvador: progresividad e impacto redistributivo del sistema impositivo*. El Salvador: Fundación Nacional para el Desarrollo.

Persson, Torsten and Guido Tabellini. 1993. "Designing Institutions for Monetary Stability," *Carnegie-Rochester Conference Series on Public Policy* 39, 1: 53–84.

Policía Nacional Civil. 2017. "Entregan propuesta de distribución de fondo de Contribución Especial para la Seguridad Pública," Press release, May 24.

Porter, Bruce. 1994. *War and the Rise of the State: The Military Foundations of Modern Politics*. New York: Free Press.

Pribble, Jennifer, Evelyne Huber, and John Stevens. 2009. "Politics, Policies, and Poverty in Latin America," *Comparative Politics* 41, 4: 387–407.

Pricewaterhouse Coopers. 2013. *Mexico: 2014 Tax Reform Law Passed*. December 6.

Prichard, Wilson. 2010. "Taxation and State Building: Towards a Governance Focused Tax Reform Agenda," *IDS Working Paper* 341, Brighton: Institute of Development Studies.

Prillaman, William. 2003. *Crime, Democracy, and Development in Latin America*. Washington, DC: CSIS.

Profeta, Paola and Simona Scabrosetti. 2010. *The Political Economy of Taxation: Lessons from Developing Countries*. Cheltenham, UK: Edward Elgar.

PWC. 2014. *Colombia Oil and Gas Industry 2014*. Online Report.

Quintanilla, Lourdes. 2011. "Pacto fiscal no se decidira al interior del CES," *La Prensa Gráfica*, August 31.

Rasler, Karen and William Thompson. 1985. "War Making and State Making: Governmental Expenditures, Tax Revenues, and Global Wars," *American Political Science Review* 79, 1 (March): 491–507.

Ramos, Carlos, Roberto López, and Aída Quinteros. 2015. *The FMLN and Post-War Politics in El Salvador: From Included to Inclusive Actor?* Inclusive Political Settlements Papers 13, June. Berlin: Berghof Foundation.

Red de Justicia Fiscal de América Latina y el Caribe. 2011. "El Salvador: perseguirán elusión de impuesto a seguridad," June 28.

Restrepo, Luis Alberto. 2006. "Los Arduos dilemas de la democracia en Colombia," in IEPRI (ed.) *Nuestra guerra sin nombre: transformaciones del conflicto en Colombia.* Bogotá: Universidad Nacional de Colombia, IEPRI.

Rettberg, Angelika. 2002. "Administrando la adversidad: Respuestas empresariales al conflicto colombiano," *Colombia Internacional* 55: 37–54.

Rettberg, Angelika. 2004. "Business-Led Peacebuilding in Colombia: Fad or Future of a Country in Crisis?" London School of Economics Crisis Program Working Paper 56 (December).

Rettberg, Angelika. 2005. "Business vs. Business? Grupos and Organized Business in Colombia," *Latin American Politics and Society* 47, 1: 31–54.

Rettberg, Angelika. 2007. "The Private Sector and Peace in El Salvador, Guatemala, and Colombia," *Journal of Latin American Studies* 39, 3: 463–494.

Reuters. 2017. "Fitch Downgrades Costa Rica to BB." January 19.

Revista Diálogo. 2011. "Basan proyecto de impuesto para seguridad en exitoso modelo colombiano," September 26.

Revista Dinero. 2011a. "Impuesto al patrimonio: estrategia de persuasión," June 14.

Revista Dinero. 2011b. "Los reyes del lobby," August 18.

Reyes, Magdalena and Liseth Alas. 2014. "ANEP dice que nuevo gabinete de gobierno es más de lo mismo," *El Salvador.com*, May 22.

Rhee Baum, Jeeyand and Kathleen Bawn. 2011. "Slowing at Sunset: Administrative Procedures and the Pace of Reform in Korea," *Journal of East Asian Studies* 11, 2: 197–221.

Ríos, Viridiana. 2014. "The Role of Drug-Related Violence and Extortion in Promoting Mexican Migration: Unexpected Consequences of a Drug War," *Latin American Research Review* 49, 3: 199–217.

Roberts, Kenneth. 2007. "Latin America's Populist Revival," *SAIS Review* 27, 1: 3–15.

Roberts, Kenneth. 2012. "The Politics of Inequality and Redistribution in Latin America's Post-Adjustment Era," *NU-WIDER Working Paper* 2012/8.

Robinson, James. 2010. "Elites and Institutional Persistence," *UNU-WIDER Working Paper* 85/2010.

Rodrik, Dani and Richard Zeckhauser. 1988. "The Dilemma of Government Responsiveness," *Journal of Policy Analysis and Management* 7, 4: 601–620.

Rodríguez, Andrea. 2013. "Pymes deben registrarse en MEIC antes del 16 de diciembre para evitar pago de impuesto a sociedades," *La Nación*, November 4.

Rodríguez, Andrea. 2014. "Menos del 6% ha cancelado el impuesto a sociedades del 2014," *La Nación*, January 14.

Rodríguez, Andrea. 2017a. "Ministerio de Justicia es impreciso en cómo se utilizó el dinero recaudado por impuesto a sociedades," El Financiero (Costa Rica), April 2.

Rodríguez, Karina. 2017b. "Nombran a Luis Valles Benítez nuevo presidente de FICOSEC," *El Sol de Parral*, February 12.

Rodríguez-Franco, Diana. 2016. "Internal Wars, Taxation, and State Building," *American Sociological Review* 81, 1: 190–213.

Rojas Rodríguez, Juan. 2017. "Impago en El Salvador," *Blog del Centro Regional de Estrategias Económicas Sostenibles*, October 6.

Romero, Mauricio. 2002. "Democratización política y contrarreforma paramilitar en Colombia," *Política y Sociedad* 39, 1: 273–292.

Romero, Vidal. 2015. "The Political Economy of Progressive Tax Reforms in Mexico," in James E. Mahon Jr., Marcelo Bergman, and Cynthia J. Arnson (eds.) *Progressive Tax Reforms and Equity in Latin America*. Washington, DC: Woodrow Wilson Center.

Rose-Ackerman, Susan. 1978. *Corruption: A Study in Political Economy*. New York: Academic Press.

Rosen, Jonathan and Sebastián Cutrona. 2020. "Understanding Support for Mano Dura Strategies: Lessons from Brazil and Colombia," *Trends in Organized Crime*, Online First.

Ross, Michael. 2012. *The Oil Curse: How Petroleum Wealth Shapes the Development of Nations*. Princeton, NJ: Princeton University Press.

Rouquie, Alain. 1987. *The Military and the State in Latin America*. Berkeley, CA: University of California Press.

Rueda, David and Daniel Stegmueller. 2016. "The Externalities of Inequality: Fear of Crime and Preferences for Redistribution in Western Europe," *American Journal of Political Science* 60, 2: 472–489.

Salazar, Horacio. 2013. *Fuerza Civil*. México: Gobierno del Estado de Nuevo León.

Sanchez, Omar. 2006. "Tax System Reform in Latin America: Domestic and International Causes," *Review of International Political Economy* 13, 5: 772–801.

Sanchez, Omar. 2011. *Mobilizing Resources in Latin America: The Political Economy of Tax Reform in Chile and Argentina*. New York: Palgrave Macmillan.

Sánchez-Ancochea, Diego. 2005. "Domestic Capital, Civil Servants and the State: Costa Rica and the Dominican Republic under Globalization," *Journal of Latin American Studies* 37: 693–726.

Sánchez-Ancochea, Diego and Salvador Martí i Puig. 2014. "Introduction: Central America's Triple Transition and the Persistent Power of the Elite," in Diego Sánchez-Ancochea and Salvador Martí i Puig (eds.) *Handbook of Central American Governance*. Abingdon: Routledge.

Sánchez-Talanquer, Mariano. 2017. "States Divided: History, Conflict, and State Formation in Mexico and Colombia," PhD Dissertation, Department of Government, Cornell University.

Santos de Souza, Saulo. 2013. "The Political Economy of Tax Reform in Latin America: A Critical Review," Woodrow Wilson Center Update on the Americas, February.

Sater, William. 1986. *Chile and the War of the Pacific*. Lincoln, NE: University of Nebraska Press.

Saylor, Ryan. 2014. *State Building in Boom Times: Commodities and Coalitions in Latin America and Africa*. New York: Cambridge University Press.

Saylor, Ryan and Nicholas Wheeler. 2017. "Paying for War and Building States: The Coalitional Politics of Debt Servicing and Tax Institutions," *World Politics* 69, 2: 366–408.

Scheve, Kenneth and David Stasavage. 2016. *Taxing the Rich: A History of Fiscal Fairness in the United States and Europe.* Princeton, NJ: Princeton University Press.

Schneider, Aaron. 2012. *State-Building and Tax Regimes in Central America.* New York: Cambridge University Press.

Schneider, Aaron. 2019. "Federalism and Taxation: Periods of Brazilian International Insertion," in Gustavo Flores-Macías (ed.) *The Political Economy of Taxation in Latin America.* New York: Cambridge University Press.

Schneider, Ben Ross. 1991. *Politics within the State: Elite Bureaucrats and Industrial Policy in Authoritarian Brazil.* Pittsburgh, PA: University of Pittsburgh Press.

Schneider, Ben Ross. 2002. "Why Is Mexican Business So Organized?" *Latin American Research Review* 37, 1: 77–118.

Schneider, Ben Ross. 2004. *Business Politics and the State in Twentieth-Century Latin America.* New York: Cambridge University Press.

Schneider, Ben Ross. 2013. *Hierarchical Capitalism in Latin America: Business, Labor, and the Challenges of Equitable Development.* New York: Cambridge University Press.

Scholz, John and Mark Lubell. 1998. "Trust and Taxpaying: Testing the Heuristic Approach to Collective Action," *American Journal of Political Science* 42, 2: 398–417.

Schultze-Kraft, Markus. 2012. "La cuestión militar en Colombia: la fuerza pública y los retos de la construcción de la paz," in Angelika Rettberg (ed.) *La construcción de la paz en Colombia.* Bogotá: Universidad de Los Andes.

Segundo a segundo. 2013. "Analizan la posibilidad de aumentar impuesto sobre nómina," December 4.

Sequeira, Aarón. 2017. "Diputados reviven impuesto hasta de ¢212.000 anuales a las personas jurídicas," *La Nación*, January 9.

Skocpol, Theda. 1985. "Strategies of Analysis in Current Research," in Peter B. Evans, Dietrich Rueschemeyer, and Theda Skocpol (eds.) *Bringing the State Back In.* New York: Cambridge University Press.

Slater, Dan. 2010. *Ordering Power: Contentious Politics and Authoritarian Leviathans in Southeast Asia.* New York: Cambridge University Press.

Smith, Adam. 1976. *An Inquiry into the Causes and Nature of the Wealth of Nations, Book V: On the Revenue of the Sovereign or Commonwealth.* [Edwin Canaan ed.] Chicago: University of Chicago Press.

Snyder, Richard and Angélica Durán-Martínez. 2009. "Does Illegality Breed Violence? Drug Violence and State-Sponsored Protection Rackets," *Crime, Law, and Social Change* 52, 3: 253–273.

Soares, Rodrigo Reis. 2004. "Development, Crime, and Punishment: Accounting for the International Difference in Crime Rates," *Journal of Development Economics* 73, 1: 155–184.

Soifer, Hillel. 2009. "The Sources of Infrastructural Power: Evidence from 19th Century Chilean Education," *Latin American Research Review* 44, 2: 158–180.

Soifer, Hillel. 2012. "Measuring State Capacity in Contemporary Latin America," *Revista de Ciencia Política* (Santiago) 32, 3: 585–598.

Soifer, Hillel. 2015. *State Building in Latin America.* New York: Cambridge University Press.

Soifer, Hillel and Matthias vom Hau. 2008. "Unpacking the Strength of the State: The Utility of State Infrastructural Power," *Studies in Comparative International Development* 43: 219–230.

Solano, Jacqueline. 2016. "Guevara: El impuesto va a joder un montón de empresarios," *Diario Extra*, September 9.

Soriano, Antonio. 2017. "FMLN y GANA llevan su alianza a elecciones," *DiarioEl Mundo* (El Salvador), August 28.

Sosa, Antonio. 2017. "Empresarios donan 6 patrullas a la Policía Estatal," *El Sol de Tampico*, August 4.

Sprenkels, Ralph. 2019. "Ambivalent Moderation: The FMLN Ideological Accommodation to Post-War Politics in El Salvador," *Government and Opposition* 54, 3: 536–558.

Spruyt, Hendrik. 1994. *The Sovereign State and Its Competitors: An Analysis of Systems Change.* Princeton, NJ: Princeton University Press.

Spruyt, Hendrik. 2007. "War, Trade, and State Formation," in Carles Boix and Susan Stokes (eds.) *Oxford Handbook of Comparative Politics.* New York: Oxford University Press.

Stein, Ernesto and Lorena Caro. 2013. *Ideology and Taxation in Latin America. Inter-American Development Bank Working Paper* 407. Washington, DC: IDB.

Steiner, Roberto and Hernán Vallejo. 2010. "Mining and Energy," in Red Hudson (ed.) *Colombia: A Country Study.* Washington, DC: Library of Congress Federal Research Division.

Stepan, Alfred. 2015. *The Military in Politics: Changing Patterns in Brazil.* Princeton, NJ: Princeton University Press.

Stivender, Carol, Paul Gaggl, Louis Amato, and Tonya Farrow-Chestnut. 2016. "The Impact of Education Earmarking on State-Level Lottery Sales," *B.E. Journal of Economic Analysis & Policy* 16, 3: 1473–1500.

Stokes, Susan. 2001. *Mandates and Democracy: Neoliberalism by Surprise in Latin America.* New York: Cambridge University Press.

Story, Dale. 1987. The PAN, the Private Sector, and the Future of the Mexican Opposition," in Judith Gentleman (ed.) *Mexican Politics in Transition.* Boulder, CO: Westview Press.

Stotsky, Janet and Asegedech WoldeMariam. 2002. "Central American Tax Reforms: Trends and Possibilities," *IMF Working Paper* 227, Washington, DC: IMF.

Superintendencia de Administración Tributaria. 2015. *Carga tributaria neta del gobierno central, 1995–2015.* Guatemala City: SAT.

Swedberg, Richard. 1991. *Joseph A. Schumpeter: The Economics and Sociology of Capitalism.* Princeton, NJ: Princeton University Press.

Sweigart, Emilie. 2018. "Reducing Homicide: What Presidents Are Doing," *Americas Quarterly*, July 20.

Tanenbaum, Barbara. 1986. *The Politics of Penury: Debt and Taxes in Mexico, 1821–1856.* Albuquerque, NM: University of New Mexico Press.

Tarrow, Sidney. 2015. *War, States, and Contention: A Comparative Historical Study.* Ithaca, NY: Cornell University Press.

Tello, Carlos. 2010. "Notas sobre el desarrollo estabilizador," *Economía Informa* 364 (July–September): 66–71.

Tello, Carlos and Domingo Hernández. 2010. "Sobre la Reforma Tributaria en México," *Economía (UNAM)* 7, 21: 37–56.

Tenorio, Tomas. 2016. "Luis Torreblanca denuncia a su hijo Zeferino," *El Sur*, February 5.

Thaler, Richard and Cass Sunstein. 2009. *The Nudge.* Penguin Books.

The Economist. 1999. "Few Friends Left for Colombia's Peace Talks," December 14.

The Economist. 2011. "Government Considers New Tax for Crime Fighting," June 2.0.

The Economist. 2014. "Plucking the Geese," February 20.

Thies, Cameron. 2004. "State Building, Inter-State, and Intra-State Rivalry: A Study of Post-Colonial Developing Country Extractive Efforts, 1975–2000," *International Studies Quarterly* 48: 53–72.

Thies, Cameron. 2005. "War, Rivalry, and State Building in Latin America," *American Journal of Political Science* 49, 3: 451–465.

Thies, Cameron. 2006. "State Capacity and Public Violence in Central America," *Comparative Political Studies* 39, 10 (December): 1264–1282.

Tilly, Charles. 1985. "War-Making and State-Making as Organized Crime," in Peter B. Evans, Dietrich Rueschemeyer, and Theda Skocpol (eds.) *Bringing the State Back In.* Cambridge: Cambridge University Press, 169–191.

Tilly, Charles. 1992. *Coercion, Capital, and European States, AD 990–1992.* Cambridge, MA: Blackwell.

Tilly, Charles. 2009. "Foreword," in Isaac William Martin et al. (eds.) *The New Fiscal Sociology: Taxation in Historical and Comparative Perspective.* New York: Cambridge University Press, p. xiii.

Timmons, Jeffrey, 2005. "The Fiscal Contract: States, Taxes, and Public Services," *World Politics* 57, 4: 530–567.

Timmons, Jeffrey. 2010. "Taxation and Credible Commitment: Left, Right, and Partisan Turnover." *Comparative Politics* 42, 2: 207–227.

Torgler, Benno. 2007. *Tax Compliance and Tax Morale: A Theoretical and Empirical Analysis.* Northampton, MA: Edward Elgar.

Transparency International. 2021. *Corruption Perceptions Index*, Transparency International.

Trejo, Guillermo and Sandra Ley. 2020. *Votes, Drugs, and Violence: The Political Logic of Criminal Wars in Mexico.* New York: Cambridge University Press.

Ugarte, César. 1926. *Historia Economica del Peru.* Lima, Peru: Cabieses.

Unda Gutiérrez, Mónica. 2015. "La reforma tributaria de 2013: los problemas de la Hacienda pública y la desigualdad en México," *Espiral: Estudios sobre estado y sociedad* 22, 64: 69–99.

Unda Gutiérrez, Mónica and Carlos Moreno Jaimes. 2015. "La recaudación del impuesto predial en México: un análisis de sus determinantes económicos en el periodo 1969–2010," *Revista Mexicana de Ciencias Politicas y Sociales* 60, 225: 45–77.

Ungar, Mark. 2007. "The Privatization of Citizen Security in Latin America: From Elite Guards to Neighborhood Vigilantes," *Social Justice* 34, 3–4: 20–37.

United Nations. 1993. *Report on the UN Truth Commission on El Salvador*. New York: United Nations.

UN Development Program. 2013. *Informe Regional de Desarrollo Humano 2013–2014*. New York: UNDP.

UN Economic Commission for Latin America and the Caribbean. 2010. *La hora de la igualdad: Brechas por cerrar, caminos por abrir*. Santiago, Chile: UNECLAC.

UN Economic Commission for Latin America and the Caribbean. 2015. *Revenue Statistics in Latin America and the Caribbean 2015*. Santiago: UNECLAC.

UN Office of Drugs and Crime. 2014. *Global Study on Homicides 2013*. Vienna: UNODC.

van de Walle, Nicolas. 2001. *African Economies and the Politics of Permanent Crisis, 1979–1999*. New York: Cambridge University Press.

Vargas, Alejo and Viviana García. 2008. "Seguridad ciudadana y gasto público: reflexiones sobre el caso colombiano," *América Latina Hoy* 50: 37–51.

Velásquez, Eugenia. 2015a. "Gobierno reduce porcentaje en propuesta de impuesto a usuarios de telefonía," *El Salvador.com*, October 28.

Velásquez, Eugenia. 2015b. "Aprueban impuesto del uso de telefonía y a empresas," *El Salvador.com*, October 29.

Velásquez, Eugenia, Pedro Mancía, and Patricia García. 2015. "Las operadoras telefónicas previenen impacto por impuestos." *El Salvador.com*, October 20.

Verdugo, Ramírez and Ruiz González. 2016. "Estrategias de seguridad: Experiencias de los estados de Chihuahua y Nuevo León," *Este País*, February 1.

Villacorta, Carmen. 2011. "El Salvador en la ARENA neoliberal," *Revista Realidad* 29: 405–442.

Villalobos, Joaquín. 2015. "Un millón y medio de muertos," *El Pais*, May 7.

Viswanathan, Manoj. 2007. "Sunset Provisions in the Tax Code: A Critical Evaluation and Prescriptions for the Future," *NYU Law Review* 82, 656–688.

Von Haldenwang, Christian, Armin von Schiller, and Melody Garcia. 2014. "Tax Collection in Developing Countries: New Evidence on Semi-Autonomous Revenue Agencies (SARAs)," *Journal of Development Studies* 30, 4: 541–555.

Wagner Faegri, Christina and Carol Wise. 2011. "Economic and Fiscal Policy in Latin America," *Latin American Research Review* 46, 1: 240–250.

Weber, Max. 1965. *Politics as a Vocation*. Philadelphia, PA: Fortress Press.

Weimer, David. 1985. "Institutional Design: Overview," in David Weimer (ed.) *Institutional Design*. Norwell, MA: Kluwer Academic Press.

Weyland, Kurt. 1996. "Risk-taking in Latin American Economic Restructuring," *International Studies Quarterly* 40, 2: 185–207.

Weyland, Kurt. 1997. "Growth with Equity in Chile's New Democracy?" *Latin American Research Review* 32, 1: 37–67.

Weyland, Kurt. 2009. "The Rise of Latin America's Two Lefts: Insights from Rentier State Theory," *Comparative Politics* 41, 2: 145–164.

Weyland, Kurt. 2013. "The Threat from the Populist Left," *Journal of Democracy* 24, 3: 18–32.

Williamson, John. 1990. "What Washington Means by Policy Reform," in John Williamson (ed.) *Latin American Adjustment: How Much Has Happened?* Washington, DC: Institute for International Economics.

World Bank. 2011. *Crimen y violencia en Centroamérica: Un desafío para el desarrollo.* Washington, DC: World Bank.

World Bank. 2020. *World Development Indicators.* Online Resource.

World Economic Forum. 2016. *The Global Competitiveness Report, 2016–2017.* Switzerland: World Economic Forum.

Yashar, Deborah. 2018. *Homicidal Ecologies: Illicit Economies and Complicit States in Latin America.* New York: Cambridge University Press.

Young, Kevin. 2015. "War by Other Means in El Salvador," *NACLA News*, March 16.

AUTHOR'S INTERVIEWS CITED

2 Anonymous members of Uribe's cabinet. 2011. June.

Barco, Carolina. 2010. Minister of Foreign Affairs and Ambassador to the United States under President Uribe, November.

Barros Reyes-Retana, Rodrigo. 2015. Head of the Tax Unit at Mexico's Ministry of Finance. November.

Borja, Wilson. 2011. Representative Serving in the Economic Committee, Polo Democrático, June.

Buendía, Paola. 2010. Director for Planning and Security at the National Planning Department, March.

Camacho, Edna. 2016. Former Vice-Minister of Finance and Researcher at the Think Tank Academia Centroamericana, June.

Castro, Santiago. 2010. Representative Serving in the Economic Committee, Conservative Party, March.

Gallardo, Roberto. 2016. Former Minister for the Economy and Planning in Laura Chinchilla's Administration, June.

García, Juliana. 2010. Deputy Director for Planning and Security at the National Planning Department, March.

Gaviria, Simón. 2011. Representative Serving in the Economic Committee, Liberal Party, June.

Giha, Yaneth. 2011. Deputy Defense Minister for Foreign Affairs and Former Director of Defense Budgets at the National Planning Department, June.

González, Armando. 2016. Director Editorial del Grupo La Nación de Costa Rica, June.

Guevara Guth, Otto. 2016. Legislator, Presidential Candidate, and Leader of Costa Rica's Libertarian Movement Party, July.

Jaramillo, Sergio. 2010. Former Vice-Minister of Defense and Special Adviser to President Santos, March.

Jiménez, Fernando. 2010. Director General for the Budget, Colombia's Ministry of Finance, March.

Junguito, Roberto. 2012. Former Minister of Finance and Head of Colombia's Insurers Federation, April.

Llorente, María Victoria. 2010. Director of the NGO Fundación Ideas Para la Paz, March.

Marín, Bernardita. 2016. Costa Rica's Vice-Minister for Public Safety, June.

Mejía, Rafael. 2011. Vice-President of the Consejo Gremial and President of the Colombian Agricultural Society, June.

Mesalles, Luis. 2016. General Manager of La Yema Dorada, Vicepresidente of UCCAEP, Vicepresident at the National Aviculture Association, and UCCAEP's Representative for the President's Council for Competitiveness and Innovation, June.

Morales, Pedro. 2016. Economic Adviser, Cámara de la Industria de Costa Rica, July.

Muñoz, Pedro. 2016. President of Costa Rica's Partido de la Unidad Social Cristiana (PUSC) and partner of the law firm Arias y Muñoz, June.

Ortiz, Rutty. 2010. Deputy Director for the Budget, Colombia's Ministry of Finance. March.

Pinzón, Juan Carlos. 2011. Former Deputy Minister of Defense under President Uribe.

Ramírez, José. 2016. Costa Rican Congressman for the Frente Amplio, June.

Ramírez, Martha Lucía. 2010. President Uribe's First Defense Minister, March.

Rodríguez Garro, Fernando. 2016. Vice-Minister for Revenue at Costa Rica's Finance Ministry, June.

Urcuyo, Constantino. 2016. Former PUSC Legislator and Presidential Adviser, July.

Vargas, Mauricio. 2010. Budget Director at Colombia's Ministry of Defense, March.

Vélez, María Zulema. 2011. President of the Colombian Association of Electricity Generators (ACOLGEN), June.

Zúñiga, Guillermo. 2016. Costa Rica's Finance Minister during Óscar Arias Presidency (2006–2010), June.

Index

Printed by Printforce, United Kingdom